# THE
# GOLF
# BOOK
## OF DAYS

# THE
# GOLF
# BOOK
## OF DAYS

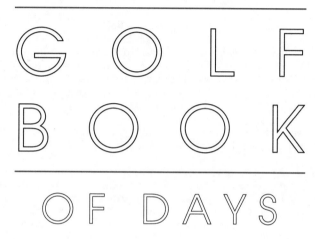

## Fascinating Golf Facts and Stories
## for Every Day of the Year

### ROBERT MCCORD

A Birch Lane Press Book
Published by Carol Publishing Group

A Birch Lane Press Book
Published by Carol Publishing Group
Birch Lane Press is a registered trademark of Carol Communications, Inc.
Editorial Offices: 600 Madison Avenue, New York, N.Y. 10022
Sales and Distribution Offices: 120 Enterprise Avenue, Secaucus, N.J. 07094
In Canada: Canadian Manda Group, One Atlantic Avenue, Suite 105, Toronto,
Ontario M6K 3E7

Queries regarding rights and permissions should be addressed to Carol
Publishing Group, 600 Madison Avenue, New York, N.Y. 10022

Carol Publishing Group books are available at special discounts for bulk
purchases, sales promotion, fund-raising, or educational purposes. Special
editions can be created to specifications. For details, contact: Special Sales
Department, Carol Publishing Group, 120 Enterprise Avenue,
Secaucus, N.J. 07094

MANUFACTURED IN THE UNITED STATES OF AMERICA
10 9 8 7 6 5 4 3 2 1

Library of Congress Cataloging-in-Publication Data

McCord, Robert R.
The golf book of days : fascinating golf facts and stories for
every day of the year / by Robert McCord.
p.   cm.
"A Birch Lane Press book."
ISBN 1–55972–292–4 (cloth)
1. Golf Miscellanea.   I. Title
GV965.M335   1995
796.352 ' 02—dc20          94–44302
CIP

*To Max and Bertha Unger,*
*their charming daughter, Nancy,*
*and*
*David and Marsha Unger, and*
*their beguiling daughter, Marissa*

# Introduction

When I was a kid growing up in South Buffalo, New York, in the shadow of Bethlehem Steel and Republic Steel, now vacant lots, we used to frequent the nine-hole Cazenovia Park Golf Course to play a round or two. There was a simple clubhouse, with a snack bar, and nearby was a putting green. You had to show up early for a tee time and place your bags in a waiting line as millions of people still do at munis all over the world.

The course was not only a source of pleasure, it was a source of revenue. We caddied there for a dollar or two, since there were no motorized carts in those days, the 1950s. We also looked for lost golf balls along the fairways or dived for them in the creek that bordered the third and ninth holes. Balls then cost approximately what they do now, so the used ball market, at twenty-five cents to fifty cents apiece, was a brisk one.

My brother Frank, five years older than myself, first took me golfing. We used my father's hickory-shafted clubs, which he had used to play with his father in his native North East, Pennsylvania. I never learned a proper golf swing in that milieu, and I sometimes would have bad dreams about errant shots and lost bets. A goal was to become good enough to be asked to play with my uncle Robert, an excellent lawyer and competent golfer, who played at the Cherry Hill Golf Club in nearby Canada. Finally he asked me to play. By then, as a young teenager, I had saved enough money to buy a set of used clubs at a local country club pro shop, and I was all keyed up for the rite of passage.

The Dunlop Company was one of my uncle Robert's clients, and every Christmas he received one dozen new golf balls cleverly encased in a hollowed out book. As we stepped to the first tee (which was actually the tenth tee because it was ladies day on the front nine at Cherry Hill), my uncle generously handed me three Dunlop Maxflis to carry me through the round. The custodial responsibilities of this golfer's gold was too much for me. I promptly sliced two tee shots down the country road bordering the right fairway. This was the beginning of a long afternoon punctuated by trees, rough, sand traps, and other hazards not readily found on our burnt-out muni in South Buffalo.

After traveling other roads and playing other sports, I have returned to golf, partly out of respect for knees that can no longer pivot and accelerate like they used to do, but also out of renewed interest and curiosity about this most elegant of games. I find that the antics of golfers are better than the comedy and tragedy that can be found in other theatrical venues. The endless variety of golf courses adds a dimension to golf that no other sport played within delineated boundaries can provide. Golf also has its Olympian heroes like Old Tom Morris, Young Tom Morris, Harry Vardon, Joyce Wethered, Walter Hagen, Bobby Jones, Glenna Collett Vare, Gene Sarazen, Ben Hogan, Sam Snead, Byron Nelson, Babe Zaharias, and more recently, Arnold Palmer, Mickey Wright, Jack Nicklaus, Kathy Whitworth, Lee Trevino, Nancy Lopez, and many others.

Much has been written about golf. It seems that baseball, boxing, fishing, and golf, for some odd reason, have produced the best sports chronicles. It is from the golf treasury of magazine articles, newspaper accounts, media guides, collected essays, yearbooks, instructional manuals, biographies, histories, and other sources that this *Golf Book of Days* has been assembled. Hopefully, in aggregate, it will provide a sense of the richness and history of golf, a subject that seemingly cannot be exhausted.

Robert McCord
New York City
1995

## Acknowledgments

Many thanks to my editor, Kevin McDonough, and publisher, Steven Schragis, who encouraged me to write this book. Special thanks to Nancy Stulack, Karen Bednarski, and the rest of the fine staff at the United States Golf Association in Far Hills, New Jersey, and thanks to Marge Dewey and her colleagues at the Ralph W. Miller Golf Library and Museum in the City of Industry in California. Also, special thanks to George and Susan Lewis at Golfiana in Mamaronack, New York, for their general support and golf wisdom.

A special word of appreciation to my brother, Frank, who first took me golfing, and all the duffers I've duffed with since—especially Bob Baldanzi, Bill Barich, Bill Black, Charlie Fitzgerald, John Fitzgerald, Michael Fitzgerald, Johnnie and Skip Gebhardt, Rhonda Glenn, John Hanley, Robert Hitchcock, John Horner, Pete McGinnis, Dr. Elmer Reed, Richard Saunders, Bob Sheldon, and an assortment of slashers at Colgate University Camp in the Adirondack Mountains.

Any factual errors in this book are my responsibility. Any comments or suggestions you might have are welcome and can be sent to my attention at the publisher's address.

# THE
## GOLF BOOK
### OF DAYS

# January 1

## 1932: The United States Golf Association Standardizes the Golf Ball

It has taken centuries for the golf ball to evolve. Wooden golf balls with a diameter of approximately two inches and weighing about one and one-half ounces have been traced back to the Dutch in the thirteenth century. Later, a leather ball stuffed with wool or feathers coexisted with the wooden balls. As golf began to emerge in Scotland, the featherie ball, a leather ball stuffed with feathers, was the spheroid of choice. In Scotland, featheries could range in size from one and a half to two inches in diameter and weigh from 1.56 to 2.06 ounces; it remained the preferred ball until the 1840s.

Gutta-percha, a rubbery substance derived from the hardened sap of an East Asian tree, was used as packing material to protect shipments from India. Its properties made it adaptable for use in golf balls. The gutta-percha, which could be hit approximately two hundred yards by a capable male golfer, was first noted at a match at Blackheath, near London, England. The long life and relatively low cost of the gutta-percha ball paved the way for the increased popularity of golf.

Next came the Haskell ball, developed by a wealthy businessman from Cleveland, Coburn Haskell, and placed on the market by the B. F. Goodrich Rubber Co. in 1899. Although these balls, nicknamed "bouncing billies," traveled about twenty-five yards farther than the gutta-perchas, they were hard to control. When the Haskell patent expired in 1915, numerous manufacturers competed to develop a better golf ball. As a result, in 1920, the United States Golf Association (USGA) and the Royal and Ancient Golf Club of St. Andrews, Scotland, stepped in to standardize the size of the golf ball and limit its power.

In 1932, the USGA once again standardized the ball; it could weigh no more than 1.62

*Opposite:* Jack Nicklaus

3

ounces and measure not less than 1.68 inches in diameter. Later refinements were made to regulate the velocity of the ball. What became the American ball is now generally used as a worldwide standard. On January 1, 1990, the Royal and Ancient Rules Committee adopted the 1.68-inch ball and an overall distance standard restricting the distance a ball can normally carry.

# January 2

## 1948: Ben Hogan Successfully Defends His Los Angeles Open Title

Ben Hogan teed it up at the Riviera Country Club in Los Angeles to defend the title that he had won the previous year by firing a 280 on the 7,029-yard, par-71 layout. He had also won the event in 1942, when it was held at the Hillcrest Country Club. Hogan, who won ten PGA Tour events and $32,112 in 1948, won the Los Angeles Open for the fourth and last time. He lost in a playoff to Sam Snead in 1950 after suffering a near-fatal automobile accident in February of 1949. Hogan won the Vardon Trophy with a 69.30 scoring average in 1948 and was named PGA Player of the Year, the first time that award was given.

# January 3

### 1993: Mark Brooks Wins Pebble Beach Invitational
### Pro-Am

Mark Brooks fired rounds of 68, 68, and 72 for a 208 to win the Pebble Beach Pro-Am by five strokes over Bob May. Brooks's previous experience on the Monterey Peninsula had been an unpleasant one. He started the final round of the 1992 U.S. Open one shot off the pace, but blew up to an 84 at Pebble Beach. In the Pro-Am, Brooks opened with 68 at Pebble Beach, scored 68 at Poppy Hills, then closed with a 72 at Spyglass to earn the $54,000 winner's check. Brooks, who was a two-time all-American selection at the University of Texas, joined the Tour in 1984. He finished sixty-sixth in earnings in 1993 with $249,696. By late 1994, he had moved up to thirtieth place on the money list.

# January 4

### 1990: Paul Azinger Leads Off With a 66, Goes On to
### Win MONY Tournament of Champions

Paul Azinger fired an opening round 66, then followed with 68, 69, and 69 to total 272 and win the MONY Tournament of Champions by a single stroke over Ian Baker-Finch at the 7,022-yard, par-72 La Costa Country Club. In 1990, Azinger finished ninth on the World Money List (earnings from all events including the PGA Tour) with earnings of $1,106,009 and was rated the sixth-best golfer in the world, according to the final Sony rankings. The top five golfers that year were Greg Norman, Nick Faldo, Jose Maria Olazabal, Ian Woosman, and Payne Stewart.

# January 5

## 1959: Ken Venturi Wins the Los Angeles Open

Ken Venturi won the Los Angeles Open with a 72-hole score of 278 at the Rancho Park Municipal Golf Course, a 6,827-yard, par-71 layout in Los Angeles. Venturi was born in San Francisco in 1931 and played on the 1953 Walker Cup team after graduating from San Jose State. His father was the coprofessional and manager of the golf shop at the Harding Park municipal golf course in San Francisco and encouraged him to play the game. Venturi showed his promise in the Walker Cup, teaming with Sam Urzetta, the 1950 Amateur champion, in beating Joe Carr and Ronald White by 6 and 4 in their alternate-shot match, then trouncing Jim Wilson, a capable Scottish golfer, by 9 and 8 in singles.

Robert Sommers, in his book *The U.S. Open,* describes Venturi's swing: "He had an elegant, compact, rhythmic motion, and when his hands entered the hitting zone, they whipped through with power and control. He was particularly adroit with the long irons."

After finishing second in the Masters in 1956 as an amateur and 1960 as a professional, Venturi injured his back and had to restrict his swing. By 1964, no longer exempt from qualifying for events, he had to plead for sponsors' exemptions. Although he had to modify his swing, he was gaining confidence in his game and himself with the help of Father Murray, a family friend and adviser. Venturi fought dehydration and heat exhaustion to win on the final day of the U.S. Open at Congressional, then a 36-hole marathon. Further ailments forced Venturi to retire early, but he would always cherish his U.S. Open title. He later became one of the best television network commentators on golf.

# January 6

## 1960: Birthday of Paul Azinger, 1993 PGA Championship Winner

The year 1993, Paul Azinger's eleventh on the PGA Tour, was the best of his career. He won the Memorial Tournament, the New England Classic, and his first major, the PGA Championship, and finished second in Tour earnings with $1,458,456 in the bank.

Paul Azinger's gain was Greg Norman's loss in the PGA Championship, held for the second time at the 7,024-yard, par-71 Inverness Club in Toledo, Ohio. Azinger birdied four of the last seven holes to shoot 30 on the back nine and tie Norman at 272, twelve under par. Thirty-one players bettered par in the 72-hole event, and seventy-five players either chipped in or holed out from bunkers, from the fairway, or off the green.

The sudden-death play-off began at the eighteenth hole, and Norman, with a chance to win, spun a birdie putt in and out of the hole. He had missed an earlier birdie putt on the eighteenth that would have given him the win. The players then moved on to the tenth hole, a 365-yard par-4, where Norman's drive caught the edge of the left-hand rough. His approach shot landed twenty feet above the hole and he lag-putted to gain par. Azinger landed a pitching-wedge approach within eight feet of the flagstick and birdied the hole for the win and the $300,000 first-place prize. Norman joined Craig Wood as the only men in history to lose all four major championships in a play-off.

Azinger has played on the Ryder Cup team (1989, 1991, 1993) and the World Cup team (1989). He won the PGA Player of the Year Award in 1987 when he won four tournaments and finished second in Tour earnings with $822,481. He has earned over $6.7 million on the Tour, but treatment for lymphoma in his right shoulder blade sidelined him for most of the 1994 season. He is attempting a comeback.

# January 7

## 1938: Birthday of Lou Graham, Winner of 1975 U.S. Open

Lou Graham won only six Tour events, but one of them was the 1975 U.S. Open. He took everyone by surprise by shooting 74, 72, 68, and 73 for 287 to tie John D. Mahaffey Jr. at Medinah's 7,032-yard, par-71 No. 3 course in Illinois. Graham, thirty-seven, defeated the twenty-seven-year-old Mahaffey 71 to 73 in the 18-hole playoff. Graham took the lead with a birdie on the fourth hole and was never caught.

Graham, noted for his well-disciplined swing and controlled game, had his best PGA Tour years from 1976 through 1978, when he exceeded $100,000 in earnings each year. He was a member of the 1973, 1975, and 1979 Ryder Cup teams and played on the World Cup team in 1975. Graham's Tour earnings exceeded $1.3 million before he joined the Senior Tour in 1988.

# January 8

## 1984: Gene Littler Wins Seiko-Tucson Senior Match Play Championship

Gene Littler's golf swing is considered by most golf purists to be a thing of beauty. The native of San Diego has a steady disposition that is reflected in his approach to every shot, his easy stance, and the smooth pace of his takeaway and downswing. After winning the U.S. Amateur in 1953, Littler was considered the heir apparent to Ben Hogan, then golf's dominant player. When Littler joined the PGA Tour in 1954 after attending San Diego State, he was nicknamed the Machine because of his smooth tempo swinging the golf club. Later Littler decided to balance his family life and his family interests with the grind of the Tour and began to play a limited number of events. He still managed to win twenty-nine Tour tournaments including the 1961 U.S. Open and the 1965 Canadian Open.

Littler contracted cancer of the lymph system and underwent surgery in the spring of 1972. He returned to the Tour in the fall of 1972. He received the Bob Jones and Ben Hogan awards in 1973 for that courageous comeback. Gene Littler played on the U.S. Ryder Cup teams in 1961, 1963, 1965, 1967, 1969, 1971, and 1975. He was among the top sixty money winners on the PGA Tour twenty-five times in twenty-six years, winning a total of $1,578,626.

Littler's win in the Seiko-Tucson Senior Match Play Championship at Randolph Municipal Golf Course in Tucson earned him $100,000, the richest prize on the Senior Tour that year. Gene has won over $2 million on the Senior Tour. Littler's swing, which Al Barkow once described as "a quiet, synchronized thing, poetry in motion, a classic of the genre," has stood him well over the years.

# January 9

## 1948: USGA Announces Plans for Junior Amateur Championship

The USGA's Executive Committee announced plans to inaugurate a Junior Amateur Championship for boys who had not reached their eighteenth birthday. Earlier Junior competitions of note include the Western Junior, established in 1914, and competitions sponsored by the U.S. Junior Chamber of Commerce and the Hearst newspapers in 1946.

The first USGA-sponsored Junior tournament included 128 golfers drawn from 495 entries who qualified at forty-one sites. The event was held at the University of Michigan Golf Course and was won by Dean Lind of Rockford, Illinois, who defeated future U.S. Open champion Ken Venturi of San Francisco, 4 and 2, in the match-play final. Other PGA Tour players who won the Junior Amateur are Gay Brewer (1949), Mason Rudolph (1950), Johnny Miller (1964), and Gary Koch (1970). Eldrick "Tiger" Woods, the first three-time winner of the event (1991, 1992, 1993), is likely to be a major force on the PGA Tour in the near future.

To date, the largest number of entries in the event was 2,349 in 1987. The tournament is difficult to win because of the age limitation and the match-play format that currently requires the winner to take six straight contests in three days after qualifying in 36-hole stroke play at one of approximately fifty-five sites. Exemptions are given to U.S. Junior Amateur champions and semifinalists from the preceding year.

In 1976, the PGA began sponsoring national Junior tournaments for girls as well as for boys.

# January 10

## 1950: Sam Snead Shoots Final Round 66, Later Wins
## Los Angeles Open in a Play-off With Ben Hogan

The 1950 Los Angeles Open marked the return of Ben Hogan to the PGA Tour after suffering a near-fatal car accident in February of 1949. Hogan had won the Los Angeles Open in 1942, 1947, and 1948. Sam Snead dominated the Tour in Hogan's absence, winning the 1949 Masters and PGA championships, the Vardon Trophy, and the PGA money title. Hogan had returned to regain his golf preeminence. Riviera was nicknamed Hogan's Alley because of his past success in the Los Angeles Open as well as his 1948 U.S. Open victory there.

In 1950, Riviera was par 71 and measured 7,029 yards for the Los Angeles Open. Fast greens, well-placed bunkers, as well as a meandering stream and the winding barranca added to the challenge of the golf course. When Hogan completed his final round with a 72-hole total of 280, most observers thought he had won the golf tournament. Snead was still out on the golf course needing improbable birdies on the last two holes to tie. Sam birdied the par-5 seventeenth by sinking a 20-foot putt. He then walked to the tee at the 443-yard, par-4 eighteenth, a gradually ascending dogleg right with a series of bunkers guarding the fairway. Snead's tee shot left him 195 yards to the green, but overhanging eucalyptus trees forced him to cut a 3-iron around the trees in order to bounce the ball in from the front of the slick green. Snead somehow succeeded in getting his approach to within fourteen feet of the pin. Sam then dropped the left-to-right-breaking putt for a 66 and a tie.

The play-off was postponed for a week so the players could compete in the Bing Crosby Pro-Am. After they returned to Riviera, Snead handily won the play-off with a 69 to Hogan's 76. Neither golfer would win the Los Angeles Open again.

# January 11

## 1952: Birthday of Ben Crenshaw, 1984 Masters Winner

As a young golfer, Ben Crenshaw seemed the heir apparent to Jack Nicklaus, a tall order indeed. Crenshaw impressed the golf critics in 1970 when at age eighteen he shot 75, 73, 77, and 76 for a 301 total to tie for low amateur with John D. Mahaffey Jr. at the U.S. Open on the 7,151-yard, par-72 Hazeltine layout. Crenshaw finished tied for thirty-sixth out of a field of 3,605 entries and 150 starters. He then won three consecutive individual NCAA Championships (1971, 1972, 1973) while a member of the University of Texas golf team. The 1972 title was shared with Tom Kite, his teammate and a fellow student of the noted golf guru Harvey Penick. Crenshaw then won his first PGA Tour event, the Texas Open, by two strokes in 1973. His first-year earnings of $76,749 placed him thirty-fourth on the PGA money list.

Crenshaw, who is one of the best putters ever, had an extremely long backswing and a decided sway on the takeaway, which often led to errant shots off the tee. In trying to adjust his game to be more competitive on the intense PGA Tour, he began to lose confidence in his swing and had trouble winning tournaments. He finished second in the British Open in 1978 and 1979. Later tournaments saw double bogeys at critical points in the competitions. Crenshaw dropped to $54,277 in winnings in 1982 and missed the cut for the PGA Championship. He was advised by Harvey Penick to go back to his natural swing and improve his setup, balance, and rhythm.

Crenshaw regained his form, winning his first major when he caught Tom Kite at the turn in the final round at the 1984 Masters by birdieing the second and eighth holes. He then birdied the ninth to go ahead, holed a 60-foot putt for a birdie at ten, then managed his game to ensure a two-shot victory with a final-round 68 and a total of 277.

Crenshaw played on the Ryder Cup team in 1981 and 1983. He has seventeen Tour wins and over $5.5 million in career Tour earnings.

# January 12

### 1869: Birthday of Harold H. Hilton, Winner of the British Open, British Amateur, and U.S. Amateur

Harold Hilton, who was born in West Kirby, a few miles from Hoylake, was an excellent amateur golfer who won two British Opens (1892, 1987), four British Amateurs (1900, 1901, 1911, 1913), and the U.S. Amateur (1911). He learned his golf over the famed Hoylake links of the Royal Liverpool Golf Club.

Hilton's first British Open title, in 1892, was won at Muirfield with a score of 305, the first time the championship was extended from thirty-six to seventy-two holes. His second victory, in 1897, came on his home course at Royal Liverpool where he defeated James Braid 314 to 315. Hilton's victory in the U.S. Amateur at the Apawanis Club in Rye, New York, in 1911, was the first time a foreign national had won that tournament. Hilton had won the British Amateur earlier at Prestwick, marking the first time a golfer had won both the British and U.S. Amateurs in the same year.

Hilton was noted for his intelligent play and an explosively fast, but controlled swing. An excellent putter, he'd roll the ball with topspin up to the hole. Also a master of backspin, he could improvise shots in a variety of situations. Hilton, a noted golf writer, was editor of *Golf Monthly* and was the author of books on golf, most notably *My Golfing Reminiscences*.

# January 13

### 1951: Al Watrous Defeats Jock Hutchison in Play-off to Win PGA Seniors'

Al Watrous and Jock Hutchison tied at 142 after regulation play, forcing an 18-hole play-off at the old PGA National Golf Club located at Dunedin, Florida. Hutchison, then sixty-eight years old, fired a 3-under-par 69 on the second 18-hole round to tie the match. Watrous, fifty-one years old and the defending champion, shot 75 in the play-off round as Hutchison faded to a 37-44 total of 81. The PGA Seniors' Championship became a 54-hole event in 1954 and then adopted its current 72-hole format in 1958.

Al Watrous, a native of Yonkers, New York, turned professional in 1920 after serving in the United States Navy. He became a leading competitor on the professional circuit, winning the Canadian Open in 1922. He was runner-up in the 1926 British Open and played on the first U. S. Ryder Cup team (1927), where he won his foursomes match (with Gene Sarazen) and his singles match for the victorious American side. He also played on the 1929 Ryder Cup team and won three PGA Seniors' Championships (1950, 1951, 1957).

The British golfer and journalist Bernard Darwin wrote of Watrous: "He had no tremendous power, but he had all the American virtues of smoothness and rhythm and he was a very fine putter." On the seventeenth hole on the last day of the 1926 British Open, unfortunately, Watrous's putting deserted him. Paired with Bobby Jones, he was two strokes ahead with five holes to play, but Jones drew even after sixteen. Jones made a spectacular shot from the sand on the seventeenth to pick up two strokes on Watrous, who three-putted. Jones went on to win his first of three British Opens with a 291 to Watrous's 293.

# January 14

### 1945: Byron Nelson Wins Phoenix Open, First of
### Eighteen Record Wins in 1945

Byron Nelson began his PGA Tour string of eighteen victories in one calendar year after having won eight tournaments in 1944. Nelson was awarded the Associated Press Male Athlete of the Year Award in both 1944 and 1945 for his accomplishments. The only other golfers to win this award are Gene Sarazen (1932), Ben Hogan (1953), and Lee Trevino (1971). The closest anyone has come to Nelson's total victories in a calendar year is Ben Hogan, who won thirteen tournaments in 1946. Nelson also holds the record for consecutive tournaments without missing a cut, 113, during the 1940s.

Byron Nelson shot 274 to win $1,333 in the 1945 Phoenix Open. He also won the event, one of the oldest on the Tour, in 1939. Ky Laffoon won the first tournament, held in 1935 at the Phoenix Country Club, with a 72-hole total of 281 over the 6,726-yard, par-71 layout.

# January 15

### 1949: Birthday of Howard Twitty, Journeyman Golfer

Howard Allen Twitty has won only three times since joining the Tour in 1975, but he has managed to win over $2.4 million in purses. His best money year thus far was 1993, when he earned $416,833, thirty-fourth in earnings. Howard, a native of Phoenix, Arizona, was an all-American golfer at Arizona State (1970, 1972) before joining the Tour. A big man at 6 feet 5 inches and 210 pounds, Howard had a 70.70 scoring average in 1993 for thirty-fourth place in the PGA rankings, less than two strokes behind Nick Price's record low of 69.11. A 1972 graduate from Arizona State in business administration, Twitty has collaborated with Roger Maltbie on golf-course redesign.

# January 16

### 1955: Jackie Pung Wins Sea Island Open, Winner's Prize is $700

Jackie Pung, winner of the 1952 U.S. Amateur and runner-up in the U.S. Women's Open in 1953 before she turned professional, won the Sea Island Open with a 36-hole score of 151 to lead off the 1955 LPGA tour. Her first prize was $700 out of a purse of $3,000. The event became a 54-hole contest in 1957, and Mickey Wright won her first of four Sea Island titles that year. She won again in 1958, 1960, and 1963.

# January 17

## 1901: Birthday of Olin Dutra, Winner of 1932 PGA Championship and 1934 U.S. Open

Olin Dutra, who won the 1932 PGA Championship and 1934 U.S. Open and was a member of two Ryder Cup teams (1933, 1935), was born in Monterey, California. As a teenager, Dutra worked in a hardware store; three days a week, he got up before dawn to practice golf. This remained his routine for several years, even after he became a professional. A member of the PGA Tour from 1928 through 1940, Dutra was also known as an excellent golf teacher. He toured with Walter Hagen in 1933 and was chairman of the PGA Tournament Committee in 1935. He was elected to the PGA Hall of Fame in 1962.

Dutra's 1932 PGA Championship was won at the Keller Golf Club in St. Paul, Minnesota, where he won five match-play tournaments in a span of five days and shot 19 under par for the 196 holes that he played. He won the medalist prize in the 36-hole qualifier by shooting 140. Dutra trailed the leaders by eight strokes at the end of the second round of the U.S. Open at the Merion Cricket Club in 1934, but scored 71 and 72 on the last day to pass seventeen golfers to win by one stroke over Gene Sarazen, 293 to 294. In those days, the final thirty-six holes of the Open were played on the same day.

# January 18

## 1942: Eddie Williams Wins First of Three PGA Seniors' Championships

Eddie Williams posted a pair of 69s to win the fifth PGA Seniors' Championship, then a 36-hole contest, by six strokes over Jock Hutchinson at the Fort Myers Golf and Country Club. The tournament was not played in 1943 and 1944 due to World War II, but was resumed in 1945 at the old PGA National site in Dunedin, Florida. That year, Williams birdied the last two holes to overcome a one-stroke advantage by Hutchinson, who finished second with a score of 150. Williams won his third consecutive PGA Seniors' in 1946 when he defeated the luckless Hutchison in a play-off after they tied at 146.

Jock Hutchison, who won the first PGA Seniors' Championship held at Augusta National in 1937, finally broke his jinx in 1947 when he again won the tournament with a 74-71 for 145. Hutchison finished second in the PGA Seniors' in 1940, 1942, 1945, 1946, 1949 (tie), and 1951.

# January 19

## 1950: Tampa Open Begins, First Event in History of LPGA Tour

The newly formed Ladies' Professional Golf Association (LPGA) kicked off its first tour with the Tampa Open. Its predecessor, the Women's Professional Golf Association, was founded by Hope Seignious.

The WPGA conducted the original U.S. Women's Open, which was won by Patty Berg in 1946. The LPGA managed the Open from 1949 until 1952; the USGA took it over in 1953, the year it was won by Betsy Rawls.

Women golfers initially relied heavily on amateurs such as Polly Riley, Peggy Kirk, Bea Barrett, Maureen Orcutt, Ellen Griffin, and others to round out the field in their circuit of events. The last time the WPGA sponsored the Tampa Open, in 1949, only 6 of the 130 entries were professionals—Patty Berg, Babe Zaharias, Louise Suggs, Kathryn Hemphill, Mary Mozel, and Hope Seignious.

In 1950, Polly Riley from Fort Worth, Texas, who played on six Curtis Cup teams, shot a 72-hole score of 295 to win the Tampa Open. The total purse in this first LPGA-conducted tournament was $3,500. There were eleven events on the Tour that year, culminating in the U.S. Women's Open, which had the largest total purse, $5,000. Mrs. Zaharias won that event and four others.

The founding members of the LPGA were Alice Bauer, Patty Berg, Bettye Danoff, Helen Dettweiler, Marlene Hagge, Opal Hill, Betty Jameson, Sally Sessions, Marilyn Smith, Shirley Spurk, Louise Suggs and Babe Zaharias. The major tournaments on the LPGA Tour are now the LPGA Championship, U.S. Women's Open, du Maurier Classic, and Nabisco. The Titleholders and Western Open were majors in the early days of the Tour. Patty Berg, who won one U.S. Women's Open, seven Titleholders and seven Western Opens is the all-time leader in LPGA major victories with fifteen.

# January 20

## 1974: Johnny Miller Wins Third Straight Tournament to Open the 1974 PGA Tour

Johnny Miller shot a 272 to win the Dean Martin–Tucson Open, his third straight win on the 1974 PGA Tour. He had also won the Bing Crosby Pro-Am and the Phoenix Open earlier in the month.

Miller rose to stardom by winning the 1973 U.S. Open by firing a final round 63 at Oakmont, one of the toughest golf courses in the world. He finished in a tie for second in the British Open, losing to Tom Weiskopf by three shots at Troon. Miller finished ninth in PGA Tour earnings in 1973, his best year since turning professional in 1969. He teamed up with Jack Nicklaus, the leading money winner, to win the World Cup in 1973.

In 1974, Miller proved that he was going to be a major force on the professional circuit. He won a PGA Tour–leading eight tournaments, dethroned Nicklaus as the leading money winner ($353,021), and was named PGA Player of the Year. He went on to win twenty-four Tour victories and over $2.7 million in career earnings. Miller won the 1976 British Open and played on the Ryder Cup team in 1975 and 1981.

# January 21

## 1940: Birthday of Jack Nicklaus, Winner of Twenty Major Tournaments

As a boy, Jack Nicklaus—born in Columbus, Ohio, the son of a pharmacist—idolized the great Bobby Jones. Nicklaus took up the game of golf at the age of ten, and by the time he was nineteen, he had won his first U.S. Amateur Championship and was on the Walker Cup team. Two years later, he won the Amateur again, after setting a record 282 for an amateur in the 1960 U.S. Open, finishing second to Arnold Palmer.

Jack Nicklaus has won twenty major championships, finishing in the top three an impressive forty-five times in all those that he has entered. He has won four U.S. Opens (1962, 1967, 1972, 1980), two U.S. Amateurs (1959, 1961), three British Opens (1966, 1970, 1978), six Masters (1963, 1965, 1966, 1972, 1975, 1986) and five PGA Championships (1963, 1971, 1973, 1975, 1980). Jack has won numerous other awards, including the 1961 NCAA Championship, six Australian Opens, membership on six winning World Cup teams (1963, 1964, 1966, 1967, 1971, 1973), membership on six Ryder Cup teams (1969, 1971, 1973, 1975, 1977, 1981) and Ryder Cup team captain in 1983 and 1987. Nicklaus has won a total of seventy PGA Tour events, second only to Sam Snead (81) and ahead of Ben Hogan (63) and Arnold Palmer (60). He won at least one tournament for seventeen straight years (1962–78) and was named PGA Player of the Year in 1967, 1972, 1973, 1975, and 1976. He was named to the World Golf Hall of Fame in 1974.

Among the most memorable of Nicklaus's many duels were those with Arnold Palmer, the "King of Golf" when Nicklaus arrived on the scene at the 1960 U.S. Open as an amateur. Jack served notice on Arnie that day as he finished second with a 282 as Arnie burned up the back nine in 30 at Cherry Hills to finish with a 65 and a 72-hole total of 280. Nicklaus was not a welcome threat to the charismatic Palmer. Many fans disdained Jack's crewcut and burly presence. But Jack lost some weight, improved his mode of dress, and became more relaxed over the years as he gained the admiration and respect of millions of golf fans. He defeated Palmer in a play-off in the 1962 U.S. Open at Oakmont and later had some memorable matches against Tom Watson, most notably in the 1982 U.S. Open at Pebble Beach and the 1977 British Open at Turnberry. Watson birdied the last two holes at Pebble, including his holing of a memorable wedge out of the rough at the seventeenth, to steal a tournament that Nicklaus seemed to have won. Watson again prevailed with a then record 268 (later surpassed by Greg Norman's 267 in 1993) in the 1977 British Open at Turnberry, Scotland. Nicklaus's duels with Lee Trevino were also memorable, especially his one-stroke loss to Lee at Muirfield in 1972 when a British Open win would have given him the third leg of the Grand Slam. Always a contender, Nicklaus finished second in the British Open seven times to such great players as Tony Lema, Roberto de Vicenzo, Gary Player, Lee Trevino, Johnny Miller, Seve Ballesteros, and Watson. Nicklaus has been in a position to win more than any other golfer in history.

When observers try to pinpoint the secret of Nicklaus's success, his tremendous powers of concentration are often cited. So is his tremendous lower-body strength and his ability to hit the ball a long way. The late Jack Grout, originally the pro at Nicklaus's home Scioto Country Club in Ohio, and Nicklaus's instructor until 1989, had a profound influence on his career, as did his father, who had the financial means to provide for Jack's early golf training and encouraged him to pursue the sport. Now Jack is a success on the Senior Tour, but his primary interests are golf-course architecture and other golf-related business activities. He has become an excellent golf-course designer, having crafted Shoal Creek, Alabama (1976), PGA West Golf Club, California (Nicklaus Resort Course, Private Course [1987]), Grand Cypress, Florida (1984, 1985, 1986), Muirfield Village Golf Club, Ohio (with Desmond Muirfield), Glen Abbey Golf Club, Ontario, Canada (1976), and many others in all parts of the world.

A stirring moment in Jack Nicklaus's career came when he walked up the eighteenth fairway in the 1986 Masters, acknowledged the warm reception from the thousands of fans surrounding the green, and two-putted for par from well below the hole to win his record sixth Masters at the age of forty-six. His idol, Bob Jones, who had died in 1971, could not be there to help him put on his green jacket, but he would no doubt have been proud. As Jones once graciously commented about Jack's game, "He plays a kind of golf with which I am not familiar."

# January 22

## 1973: Bruce Crampton Wins Tucson Open, Second Victory in a Row

Bruce Crampton, a native of Sydney, Australia, who turned professional in 1953 and won his first PGA Tour event in 1961, shot a 277 at the 7,305-yard, par-72 Tucson National Course to win the Dean Martin–Tucson Open. Eight days earlier he had won the Phoenix Open by shooting a 72-hole total of 268. The first Tucson Open was held in 1945 at the 6,418-yard, par-70 El Rio Golf and Country Club. The winner of that event was Ray Mangrum, a journeyman professional and the brother of Lloyd Mangrum, winner of the 1946 U.S. Open.

Crampton, noted for his excellent putting stroke, physical-fitness regimen, stamina, and strength of will, became a consistent money winner on the highly competitive PGA Tour. One of his best years was 1973, when he won four tournaments and the Vardon Trophy (70.57 strokes-per-round average), which he won again in 1975 (70.51). He had a total of fifteen PGA Tour victories before joining the Senior Tour in 1985. Crampton has had remarkable success on the Senior Tour with more than twenty tournament wins and career earnings in excess of $3.5 million.

# January 23

### 1977: Tom Watson Wins Crosby Pro-Am, Named PGA Player of the Year

Tom Watson had a breakthrough year in 1977, which began with his win in the Bing Crosby Pro-Am held at the 6,815-yard, par-72 Pebble Beach Golf Links, the 6,506-yard, par-72 Cypress Point Country Club, and the 6,810-yard, par-72 Spyglass Hill Golf Club in Monterey Peninsula, California. Watson shot a 273 to win $40,000, then won the San Diego Open the following week. The first winner of the Bing Crosby Professional-Amateur was Sam Snead, who shot 68 in the rain-abbreviated 18-hole event, first held on the 6,769-yard, par-73 Rancho Santa Fe Country Club Course in San Diego in 1937. The event was moved to the Monterey Peninsula in 1947.

Watson won four tournaments in 1977, won the most Tour money ($310,653), the Vardon Trophy (70.32 strokes-per-round average), and was named PGA Player of the Year. He became the most dominant player in golf as he won three straight Vardon Trophies (1977–79), four straight PGA Player of the Year awards (1977–80) (plus two others, in 1982 and 1984) and four consecutive money-earnings titles (1977–80) (with another in 1984). He defeated Jack Nicklaus in the Masters and the British Open in 1977 and has won a total of eight majors—five British Opens, two Masters, and one U.S. Open. He was a member of the 1977, 1981, 1983, and 1989 Ryder Cup teams and was nonplaying captain of the 1993 team, which defeated the European team, 15 and 13, at The Belfry.

# January 24

## 1984: Arnold Palmer Wins His Second PGA Seniors' Championship

Arnold Palmer shot a record 63 on the 6,520-yard, par-72 Champion course at PGA National and went on to win the PGA Seniors' Championship by two strokes over Don January, the defending champion. Palmer ballooned to a 79 in the third round when stiff winds and 40-degree temperatures made the course much tougher to play. He came back with a 71 to post a 6-under-par 282 and win the $35,000 first prize out of a total purse of $200,000. Palmer won his first Seniors' Championship in 1980 and collected $20,000 after defeating Paul Harney in a play-off on the first extra hole. Palmer's significant wins as a senior include the U.S. Senior Open (1981) and the Senior Tournament Players Championship (1985).

# January 25

## 1982: Lanny Wadkins Wins Phoenix Open

Lanny Wadkins, a native of Richmond, Virginia, won his first tournament of the 1982 PGA Tour season by firing a 21-under-par 263 at the Phoenix Open held at the 6,726-yard, par-71 Phoenix Country Club. Wadkins also won the MONY Tournament of Champions and the Buick Open in 1982 to finish seventh in earnings with $306,827. Since joining the Tour in 1971, he has earned over $6 million. At the end of 1993, he had won twenty-one tournaments, placing him in a tie on the all-time list with Willie Macfarlane, Bill Mehlhorn, Gary Player, and Craig Wood.

Wadkins won the PGA Championship in 1977 and was named PGA Player of the Year in 1985 when he won three tournaments and finished second in money winnings. Lanny Wadkins is considered a great competitor by his peers. He has been a member of eight Ryder Cup teams (1977, 1979, 1983, 1985, 1987, 1989, 1991, 1993), three World Cup teams (1977, 1984, 1985) and two Walker Cup teams (1969, 1971).

# January 26

## 1907: Birthday of Henry Cotton, Winner of Three British Opens

Henry Cotton, born in Cheshire, England, was the only Briton to win the Open more than once between 1914 and 1989. He was the predominant figure in British golf as player, teacher, writer, course architect, and encourager of youth from 1930 until his death in 1987. He was elected to an honorary membership in the Royal and Ancient Club in 1968 and was the first to receive a knighthood for service to golf.

Cotton won his first British Open at Royal St. George's in Sandwich, England, in 1934, defeating Sidney Brews, 283 to 288. His victory put an end to ten years of American domination of his country's national championship. After shooting opening rounds of 67 and 65, Cotton stood ten strokes ahead of the field after a third round of 72. In 1937, Cotton fired a 71 on a rain-soaked final day at Carnoustie, Scotland, to win by two strokes with a 72-hole total of 290. He shot a record 66 on the course at Muirfield, Scotland, in 1948 and finished with a 284 to win his third Open by five strokes over Fred Daly.

Not a naturally gifted golfer, Cotton developed his game through incessant practice. He won several European tournaments including the Belgian Open (1930, 1934, 1938), the German Open (1937, 1938, 1939), and the French Open (1946, 1947). He won the Vardon Trophy, for best stroke average, in 1938 and was a member of the Britain and Ireland Ryder Cup teams in 1929, 1937, and 1947. He was playing captain in 1947 and nonplaying captain in 1953.

After retiring from championship play, Cotton devoted his time to writing articles on golf, several books, support for the Golf Foundation, and the development of his own golf course in Portugal where he lived in his later years.

# January 27

### 1977: Julius Boros Opens With a 71, Goes On to Win
### His Second PGA Seniors' Championship

Facing icy rain, numbing cold, and rising winds at the 1977 PGA Seniors' Championship at the Walt Disney World Resort in Orlando, Florida, Julius Boros opened with a 1-under-par 71. Boros then fired 69, 71, and 72 for a 5-under-par 283 to edge former champion Fred Haas Jr. by a single stroke. Haas three-putted the seventy-first hole to finish with 284. A total of 180 started in this event and Boros was awarded $7,500 for his first-place finish. Boros had also won the event in 1971, when it was held at the old PGA National Golf Club, now known as Ballenisles Country Club of JDM in Palm Beach Gardens.

# January 28

### 1973: Sam Snead Wins His Record Sixth PGA Seniors'
### Championship by Fifteen Strokes

Sam Snead, then sixty years old, shot a 20-under-par 268 with rounds of 66, 66, 67, and 69 to win the 1973 PGA Seniors' Championship by fifteen strokes. Julius Boros, winner in 1971 of the same title on the same course (known as Ballenisles) with a score of 285, finished second with a respectable 283. The total purse for this event was $40,000 and the winner's share was $4,000. Snead also won the event in 1972, 1970, 1967, 1965, and 1964. Snead was too late to thrive on the Senior Tour, although he did play from 1981, when he was sixty-nine, through 1992, winning no tournaments but netting $106,574.

# January 29

### 1923: Birthday of Jack Burke Jr., Winner of 1956 Masters

Jack Burke Jr., a great American golfer out of Fort Worth, Texas, won fifteen PGA events in his career, but 1956 was by far his best year. Burke won the 1956 Masters with rounds of 72, 71, 75, and 71 for 289 to nose out Ken Venturi, then an amateur, by a stroke. Venturi shot rounds of 66 and 69 before coming down to earth with a 75 and an 80 on the last two days. Burke was down eight strokes to Venturi going into the final day. Venturi played well behind Burke on the last day, who was comfortable in the clubhouse after shooting his 71 on the final round. After a front-nine score of 38, Venturi had a four-shot lead over Cary Middlecoff and a five-stroke lead over Burke. He was then sandbagged at "Amen Corner," where he bogeyed Nos. 11, 12, 14, and 15 to drop to even. Middlecoff, playing ahead of Venturi, three-putted his way out of the tournament on the seventeenth hole. Venturi broke his string of bogeys by parring the par-3 sixteenth. He needed a birdie and a par on the final two holes to win.

Venturi bogeyed seventeen after his overly aggressive approach rolled down the back slope of the green. He gamely landed his recovery shot to within eighteen feet on the eighteenth, but barely missed the putt to finish second. Venturi was that close to becoming the first amateur ever to win the Masters.

Burke's excellent play continued as he proceeded to win the PGA Championship at the Blue Hills Country Club in Canton, Massachusetts. Then a match-play event, it took Jack twenty-six holes to defeat Fred Haas Jr. in his second match. He was down five shots to Ed Furgol after fourteen holes, but finally won on the first extra hole (the thirty-seventh) with a birdie. In the 36-hole final, Burke was three down after nineteen holes, but later ran off four straight birdies and closed out Ted Kroll 3 and 2. Burke's first-place prize was $5,000 out of a total purse of $18,750.

Among Jack Burke's other golf achievements is his membership on the 1951, 1953,

1955, and 1957 Ryder Cup teams. He captained the team in both 1957 and 1973. He only lost one Ryder Cup match, 5 and 3 in singles match play in 1957, the first year Great Britain and Ireland had won the competition since 1933. Burke won the Texas Open in 1952 and 1963. He still holds the record, a 72-hole total of 260 (67, 65, 64, 64), for that tournament, whose other winners include Walter Hagen, Byron Nelson, Ben Hogan, Sam Snead, Arnold Palmer, and Lee Trevino.

# January 30

### 1957: Birthday of Payne Stewart, Winner of the 1989
### PGA Championship and 1991 U.S. Open

Payne Stewart won his first major title when he birdied four of the last five holes, shooting a 31 over the final nine, to edge Andy Bean, Mike Reid, and Curtis Strange by one stroke in the 1989 PGA Championship at 7,217 yard, par-72 Kemper Lakes, an excellent public golf course in Long Grove, Illinois. Mike Reid had a good chance to win the tournament but bogeyed the 469-yard, par-4 sixteenth, double-bogeyed the 203-yard, par-3 seventeenth, and missed a birdie putt on the 433-yard, par-4 final hole. This was the third time the medal-play-format PGA Championship was played at a course that was open to the public at the time the tournament was held. The others were Pebble Beach Golf Links (1977) and the Tanglewood Golf Club (1974) in North Carolina.

Payne Stewart is a native of Springfield, Missouri, and attended Southern Methodist University, where he majored in business and was an all-American golfer in 1979, the year he graduated. He won the Missouri State Amateur Championship in 1979, then turned professional and joined the Tour in 1981. He won another major, the 1991 U.S. Open, by defeating Scott Simpson 75–77 in an 18-hole play-off at Hazeltine National. He was a member of the 1987, 1989, 1991, and 1993 Ryder Cup teams and captained the victorious 1993 U.S. Dunhill Cup squad.

# January 31

## 1987: Judy Bell Becomes the First Woman Elected to the USGA Executive Committee

Judy Bell, a distinguished amateur American golfer, became the first woman elected to the USGA Executive Committee on January 31, 1987. She was a member of the Curtis Cup team in 1960 and 1962 and captained the team in 1986 and 1988. She has won numerous amateur tournaments and was elected treasurer of the USGA in 1990.

# February 1

## 1922: Amateur Public Links Championship Established

James D. Standish Jr., of Detroit, persuaded the USGA Executive Committee to establish an Amateur Public Links Championship and offered to donate a perpetual trophy. The event was awarded to the Ottawa Park Course in Toledo, Ohio, and a field of 136 players started the 36-hole qualifying round for thirty-two places of match play. George Aulbach, nineteen, a student at Boston University, won the qualifying medal with rounds of 70-69 for 139. The winner of the event was Edmund R. Held, nineteen, of St. Louis, who defeated Richard J. Walsh, eighteen, of New York, 6 and 5 to become the first Amateur Public Links champion on July 15, 1922.

The event, now called the USGA Men's Amateur Public Links, is held every year at various public golf courses throughout the United States. The only player to win the event three times is Carl F. Kauffmann, who won three years in a row beginning in 1927. The youngest champion was Les Bolstad, who won at age eighteen years, three months in 1926. Verne Callison, the oldest champion, was forty-eight when he won in 1967.

*Opposite:* Mickey Wright

# February 2

### 1975: Charles Sifford Wins the PGA Seniors' Championship

Charlie Sifford dropped a 22-foot birdie putt on the first extra hole to win a play-off from Fred Wampler in the PGA Seniors' Championship at the Walt Disney World Resort in Orlando, Florida. Sifford, the first African American to win the event, tied Wampler at 280 after 72 holes with a 69 on the final round. Sifford turned professional in 1948, joined the PGA Tour in 1960 at age thirty-seven, and won the Greater Hartford Open (1967) and the Los Angeles Open (1969). Sifford won the Negro National Open six times and joined the Senior Tour in 1980 at the age of 58. He has won over $850,000 in prize money since then.

# February 3

### 1941: Birthday of Carol Mann, Winner of 1965 Women's Open

At 6 feet 3 inches, Carol Mann is the tallest woman to successfully play tournament golf. From 1961 to 1975, she won thirty-eight tournaments, including two majors, the 1964 Western Open and the 1965 U.S. Women's Open. Her U.S. Open win was a two-stroke victory, 290 to 292, over Kathy Cornelius at the 6,220-yard, par-72 Atlantic City Country Club in Northfield, New Jersey. She won $4,000 for first prize in that event. In 1968, Carol Mann won ten tournaments and the Vare Trophy with a 72.04 per round scoring average. She was leading money winner on the LPGA Tour in 1969 with earnings of $49,152. She was elected to the LPGA Hall of Fame in 1977.

# February 4

### 1951: Lloyd Mangrum Takes Tucson Open, Wins
### Earnings Title in 1951

Lloyd Mangrum shot a 72-hole total of 269 to win his second tournament of the season at the 6,418-yard, par-70 El Rio Golf and Country Club in Tucson. Lloyd earned $2,000 for his efforts. He started off the 1951 Tour season with a tournament record 72-hole total of 280 to win the Los Angeles Open. Mangrum, who won five events in 1951, earned a total of $26,089 to head the PGA Tour earnings list for the only time in his career. His thirty-six career victories place him tenth on the all-time PGA Tour list.

# February 5

### 1971: Alan Shepard Lands on the Moon and Plays a
### 6-Iron

Adm. Alan Shepard and his crew landed on the moon February 5, 1971, after taking off from Houston on January 31. After the astronauts completed their work on the dusty surface, Shepard got out a 6-iron with a four-piece aluminum shaft and placed two golf balls on the "turf." He later explained to his friend Bob Hope, who allegedly inspired Shepard's secret mission, "Because of the cumbersome suit I was wearing, I couldn't make a very good pivot on the swing. And I had to hit the ball with just one hand." The 6-iron is now on display at Golf House, site of the USGA's museum and library, in Far Hills, New Jersey.

# February 6

## 1870: Birthday of James Braid, First to Win Five British Opens

James Braid, a member of golf's Great Triumvirate along with Harry Vardon and J. H. Taylor, was the first to win five British Open Championships, a feat he accomplished between 1901 and 1910. Braid won the first British PGA Matchplay Championship (then called the News of the World Matchplay Championship) in 1903 and followed with victories in 1905, 1907, and 1911. He won the French Open in 1910.

Braid was born in Elie, Scotland, the son of a ploughman, and left school at the age of thirteen to become a joiner in a nearby village. He became a golf professional in 1893 when a friend persuaded him to go to London as an apprentice clubmaker at the Army and Navy Stores. He played in his first British Open in 1893 and later gained a job at Romford in Essex. He won his first British Open at Muirfield with a 72-hole score of 309, defeating Harry Vardon by three strokes. Because there were few professional tournaments in those days, he made most of his money in challenge and exhibition matches.

In 1904, Braid became a professional at the Walton Heath Club and stayed there until his death in 1950. Just prior to his death he, J. H. Taylor, and Willie Auchterlonie were elected honorary members of the Royal and Ancient Golf Club of St. Andrews, the first professionals to receive such distinction.

# February 7

## 1954: Ed Furgol Wins Phoenix Open, 1954 PGA Player of the Year

Ed Furgol shot a 72-hole total of 272, then won the Phoenix Open in a play-off, at the 6,726-yard, par-71 Phoenix Country Club. He won the U.S. Open in 1954 and played on the Ryder Cup team in 1957. Furgol was named PGA Player of the Year in 1954.

Furgol's accomplishments in golf are remarkable because he had to overcome a handicap resulting from a childhood accident: his left arm was broken in a playground mishap and badly set. The muscles atrophied and the arm became rigid, bent at an angle; it was useless to his golf swing except to guide the club. Furgol developed a short, controlled backswing and had tremendous power from his body turn. He was an excellent amateur, winning the North and South Amateur at the age of twenty-six in 1945, shortly before he turned professional.

# February 8

## 1587: Mary, Queen of Scots, Early Lady Golfer, Beheaded

Mary, Queen of Scots, who was beheaded on February 8, 1587, was one of the earliest lady golfers to be mentioned by name. As evidence of her indifference to the fate of Darnley, her husband, who was murdered at Kirk O'Field, Edinburgh, she was charged at her trial with having played golf in the fields beside Seton "a few days after his death."

# February 9

## 1992: John Cook Wins the Hawaiian Open, Ties Hale Irwin's Record Score

John Cook shot a 72-hole total of 265 on the 6,975-yard, par-72 Waialae Country Club course to win the Hawaiian Open. Cook's 23-under-par score tied Hale Irwin's tournament record set in 1981. Cook won a $216,000 winner's share in this event, which has been held on the Waialae course since its inception in 1965. Gay Brewer won that first tournament with a score of 281.

John Cook joined the PGA Tour in 1980 and had his best year in 1992, when he won three events and finished third in money winnings with $1,165,606. Prior to joining the professional tour he was a three-time all-American at Ohio State (1977, 1978, 1979) and played on the 1979 Ohio State NCAA champion golf team. He was persuaded by Jack Nicklaus and Tom Weiskopf, both former members of the Ohio State golf team, to attend the university even though Cook grew up in southern California.

# February 10

## 1955: Birthday of Greg Norman, Golf's Leading All-Time Money Winner

Greg Norman was born in Queensland, Australia, and was sixteen years of age before he took up golf. His mother was an accomplished golfer, and after he caddied for her one day, he decided to play a few holes and, like millions before him, became hooked on the game. Within two years, Norman, an agile athlete at 6 feet 1 inch and 185 pounds, was a scratch golfer. Like Nicklaus, whose books he studied, Norman learned to hit the ball hard first and has been learning to control its flight ever since.

Norman turned professional in 1976 and won in Australia in his fourth start as a pro. He set out for Europe in 1977 and first played in the United States the same year. By 1979, he had won the Australian Open, finished second behind Sandy Lyle for the European money title, and was dubbed the Great White Shark by the press after he related some shark-hunting stories.

By the end of the 1993 season, he had won sixty-three tournaments worldwide, including eleven on the PGA Tour. He was rated second behind Nick Faldo in the worldwide Sony rankings and had won $2,285,280 that year, behind Nick Price. At this writing, Norman has won upward of $15 million in his career, putting him at the top of the World Money List.

A highlight of Greg Norman's career was his win in the 1993 British Open at Royal St. George's, where he finished with a strong 64 to shoot 267 and break Tom Watson's sixteen-year-old British Open scoring record. Defending champion Nick Faldo finished second at 269. Norman had previously won the Open at Turnberry in 1986. The other majors have eluded him. He, along with Craig Wood, are the only golfers to have lost four majors in play-offs. The most memorable of these losses was in the 1987 Masters, when Larry Mize chipped in from 140 feet for a birdie 3 after Norman had reached the green in regulation 2 and seemed a certain winner.

Greg Norman was the leading money winner on the U.S. Tour in 1986 ($653,296) and 1990 ($1,165,477). He won the Vardon Trophy in 1989 (69.49 scoring average per round), 1990 (69.10), and 1994 (68.81).

# February 11

## 1951: Dutch Harrison Wins the Texas Open in Play-off

Ernest Joe "Dutch" Harrison, a native of Conway, Arkansas, tied with Doug Ford with a 72-hole total of 265, then won an 18-hole play-off 67 to 68 to win the Texas Open. It was only the second play-off in the Open since its inception in 1922. Harrison won $2,000 in first-prize money. He had previously won the Open in 1939. Arnold Palmer tops the Texas Open win list with three consecutive victories from 1960 through 1962.

Harrison began his long career as a caddie at the Little Rock Country Club in 1925, chipping with a club fashioned from a cypress root. Turning professional in 1930, he played left-handed for two years and won a local tournament before changing to right-handed golf. After struggling, he finally won some important tournaments in 1939, including the Bing Crosby Tournament and the Texas Open. He served in the Air Corps as a staff sergeant in World War II, then rejoined the Tour. He won the Vardon Trophy in 1954 with a 70.22 stroke average.

# February 12

## 1993: Tom Kite Shoots 64, Goes On to Win Bob Hope Chrysler Classic With Record 325

Tom Kite shot a 64 in the third round of the Bob Hope Chrysler Classic after shooting a pair of 67s on the first two rounds. He then posted scores of 65 and 62 for a 35-under-par total of 325, a PGA Tour 90-hole record. Kite won the tournament by six shots over Rick Fehr and ten shots over third-place finisher Scott Simpson. The tournament was played over four golf courses, the Bermuda Dunes Country Club (6,927 yards, par 72), Indian Wells Country Club (6,478 yards, par 72), Tamarisk Country Club (6,881 yards, par 72), and the PGA West Palmer Course (6,931 yards, par 72). Kite won $198,000 for his eighteenth win since he joined the PGA Tour in 1972. He won the Nissan Los Angeles Open and then his first major, the U.S. Open (at Pebble Beach), in 1992.

The Bob Hope Chrysler Classic dates back to the Palm Springs Golf Classic, which Arnold Palmer won with a score of 338 in 1960. Palmer's prize was $12,000. The tournament was renamed the Bob Hope Desert Classic in 1965, the Bob Hope Classic in 1984, and then became the Bob Hope Chrysler Classic in 1986. Arnold Palmer has won this event a record five times (1960, 1962, 1968, 1971, and 1973).

# February 13

## 1918: Birthday of Patty Berg, Winner of First U.S. Women's Open

The first Women's Open Championship, a match-play competition, was held at the Spokane Country Club in Washington and was conducted by the Women's PGA and the Spokane Athletic Round Table. Patty Berg, representing Minneapolis, won the qualifying medal with a 73-72 for 145 and defeated Betty Jameson of San Antonio, Texas, 5 and 4 in the final. The purse was $19,700 in war bonds, and Miss Berg won $5,600 in bonds. The Open became a 72-hole medal-play event the following year, and after the 1948 tournament, the LPGA managed the event. Since 1953 it has been conducted by the USGA.

Patty Berg, who was a member of the Curtis Cup team in 1936 and won the U.S. Amateur in 1938, turned professional in 1940. When Miss Berg turned professional, there were few notable lady professionals. Among them were Babe Didrickson, Helen Hicks, and Helen Dettweiler. By 1941 there were only four tournaments on the fledgling women's pro circuit: the Western, the Titleholders, the Asheville Invitational, and the Women's Texas Open. In 1944 the Women's Professional Golf Association was formed, and by 1946 the U.S. Women's Open was established. A former PGA tour officer, Fred Corcoran, was brought in to organize the Women's Professional Golf Association, then presided over by Miss Berg, to develop a complete women's professional golf circuit. The organization was renamed the Ladies' Professional Golf Association in 1949. The LPGA Tour has had its ups and downs ever since.

Patty Berg won forty-one LPGA events and was the first winner of the Glenna Vare Trophy, named in honor of the great American amateur golfer Glenna Collett Vare and awarded to the Tour player with the lowest scoring average. Berg's 75 average for sixty-five rounds won the award in 1953, and she won it again in 1955 (74.47) and 1956 (74.57). She was the leading money winner on the Tour in 1954, 1955, and 1957. Miss Berg was named a charter member of the LPGA Hall of Fame in 1951.

# February 14

## 1935: Birthday of Mickey Wright, Winner of Four Women's Opens

Betsy Rawls, an LPGA Hall of Fame golfer, described Mickey Wright as follows: "She set a standard of shot-making that will probably never be equaled. Mickey's swing was flawless as a golf swing can be—smooth, efficient, powerful, rhythmical, and beautiful." Wright won eighty-two LPGA tournaments in her professional career, which began in 1956. She won four Women's Opens, four LPGA Championships, was the leading money winner four times, and won the Vare Trophy five times. She is the only woman to have held the four major titles at one time. In 1961, she won the U.S. Women's Open and the LPGA Championship, then began the 1962 season by winning the Titleholders and the Western Open. In 1963, she won four tournaments in a row, a record she shared with Kathy Whitworth, the only professional to have won more Tour events than Mickey Wright. Nancy Lopez won five consecutive tournaments in 1978 to set the new record. Mickey Wright won thirteen tournaments in 1963, or more than 40 percent of the events she entered. She still holds the LPGA 18-hole scoring record, 62, which she achieved twice.

Mickey Wright retired in 1971, but did return to play a light tournament schedule. She won the Colgate–Dinah Shore Winner's Circle in 1973, her last LPGA tournament win. Miss Wright was inducted into the LPGA Hall of Fame in 1964. She is considered, along with Joyce Wethered, Kathy Whitworth, and Babe Zaharias, to be among the best women golfers of all time, and maybe the best ever.

# February 15

### 1987: Chi Chi Rodriguez Wins the PGA Seniors' Championship

Juan "Chi Chi" Rodriguez (at 5 feet 7 and 132 pounds) is one of the most popular golfers in the game today. Born in 1935 in Bayamón, Puerto Rico, he joined the PGA Tour in 1960 and won eight tournaments and just over $1 million in his Tour career. The Senior Tour, which he joined in 1985, provided his golf career with a second life. He was second in Senior Tour earnings in 1986 with $399,172 and then won seven tournaments, including the PGA Seniors' Championship, in 1987 to become the leading money winner with $509,145.

Chi Chi won the PGA Seniors' with a dramatic come-from-behind win over Dale Douglass, who led by six strokes going into the final round. Rodriguez bought a new set of golf clubs at the host PGA National Golf Club pro shop after shooting a 76 on the third round. He went out and shot a 67 on the 6,520-yard, par-72 Championship course on the final day to post a 282 and win by one stroke over Douglass. Chi Chi earned $47,000 that day and has made well over $4 million on the Senior Tour.

Now a resident of Florida, Chi Chi has contributed significantly to Junior golf through his Chi Chi Rodriguez foundation and has won numerous humanitarian awards. He was inducted into the World Golf Hall of Fame in 1992.

# February 16

## 1941: Henry Picard Wins His Second New Orleans Open

Henry Picard shot a tournament record 276 on the 6,656-yard, par-72 City Park Golf Course to win his second Greater New Orleans Open Invitational Tournament. Picard earned $1,200 in first-prize winnings out of a purse of $5,000. Picard had also won the event in 1939 when he had a 72-hole score of 284.

The Greater New Orleans Open, which began in 1938 and was first won by Harry Cooper, is one of the oldest events on the PGA Tour. It was renamed the First NBC New Orleans Open in 1975, the Greater New Orleans Open in 1980, the USF&G New Orleans Open in 1981, the USF&G Class in 1982, and is currently known as the Freeport-McMoran Classic. Chip Beck holds the tournament-record low score, 262, which he shot at the 7,080-yard, par-72 Lakewood Country Club in 1988. The event is now held at the 7,106-yard, par-72 English Turn Golf and Country Club.

Henry Picard was born in Plymouth, Massachusetts, in 1907. His professional career began in 1925, and he was noted for his excellent golf-course management and his smooth swing. He won the 1938 Masters and the 1939 PGA Championship among his twenty-six professional wins. He was one of the early pioneers of the professional tour and is ranked nineteenth on the all-time winners' list. Picard was a member of the Ryder Cup team in 1935, 1937, and 1939. The 1939 team did not play because of World War II.

# February 17

## 1955: Mike Souchak Shoots 60 in First Round of Texas Open

Mike Souchak fired an 11-under-par 60 to take the lead in the first round of the Texas Open held on the 6,185-yard, par-71 Breckenridge Park Golf Course in San Antonio. Souchak shot 33 on the par-36 front nine and 27 on the par-35 back nine and then went on to register 257 for the 72-hole event to earn the $2,000 winner's share. Only Al Geiberger (59, in 1977 at the Colonial Country Club, Memphis, Tennessee, in the second round of the Memphis Classic) and Chip Beck (59, 1991 at the Sunrise Golf Club, Las Vegas, Nevada, in the third round of the Las Vegas Invitational) have bettered 60 in an 18-hole round on the PGA Tour. Souchak's 27-under-par 257 (60, 68, 64, 65) is the best 72-round total recorded since the Texas Open began in 1922 and it is still the best 72-hole total shot in any PGA Tour event.

Mike Souchak was born in Berwick, Pennsylvania, in 1927 and was a member of the 1959 and 1961 Ryder Cup teams. A large man with a smooth swing, Souchak won sixteen PGA tournaments in a professional career that began in 1952. His win in the Texas Open was his first PGA Tour victory. Souchak joined the Senior Tour in 1980 and had moderate success.

# February 18

## 1944: Alexander "Sandy" Herd Dies, Won British Open in 1902

Alexander "Sandy" Herd, just slightly below the Triumvirate of Vardon, Braid, and Taylor in his prime, died in London at the age of seventy-six. Herd, who was born in St. Andrews, Scotland, was the first player to win the British Open using the new rubber Haskell ball, which replaced the gutta-percha. He shot a 72-hole total of 77, 76, 73, and 81 for 307 to win the championship by one stroke over Harry Vardon and James Braid at Hoylake. Herd finished in the top five in the Open on twelve other occasions, including second-place finishes in 1895 and 1910 at St. Andrews and 1920 at Deal. Herd took part in his last Open at St. Andrews in 1939 when he was seventy-one years old. He had participated in the Open over a span of fifty-four years.

Herd was known as an excellent shotmaker. He was considered too eager in temperament in his earlier years, and his lack of patience cost him some tournaments down the stretch, including at least two of his second-place finishes in the British Open. He acquired the right temperament later in his career and won the British Professional Matchplay Championship at the age of fifty-eight. Herd used an old-fashioned palm grip, sat well down in his stance, and was noted for the number and ferocity of his waggles.

# February 19

## 1901: Birthday of Ed Dudley, Member of PGA Hall of Fame

Born in Brunswick, Georgia, Ed Dudley was a PGA Tour member from 1929 through 1939 and was on three Ryder Cup teams (1929, 1933, 1937). He served as head professional at Augusta National for more than twenty years. An active member of the PGA, Dudley served as its president from 1942 to 1948. He won sixteen PGA tournaments in his professional career including the Los Angeles Open (1931) and the Western Open (1931). Dudley never won a major tournament, although in the 1932 PGA Championship he reached the 36-hole match-play semifinal before losing to Olin Dutra, the champion, 3 and 2. Ed Dudley, who died in 1963 at age sixty-two, was inducted into the PGA Hall of Fame in 1964.

# February 20

## 1915: Birthday of Chick Harbert, 1954 PGA Champion

Chick Harbert was born in Dayton, Ohio, and made his first impression on the golf world by winning the 1937 Michigan Open, as an amateur, at age twenty-two. He attended Michigan State and won the Michigan Open again in 1942 and 1949, making him a popular figure in that state. Harbert was a long if somewhat erratic hitter off the tee and a strong match-play competitor.

He lost two PGA Matchplay Championship finals in close matches (2 and 1 to Jim Ferrier in 1947 and 1-up to Jim Turnesa in 1952) before breaking through with a 4-and-3 victory over defending champion Walter Burkemo, another popular Michigander, at the Keller Golf Club in St. Paul, Minnesota, in 1954. After Burkemo won three of the first four holes, Harbert shot 8 under par over the next twenty-nine to dominate the match, which ended on the thirty-third hole. Harbert was a member of the victorious 1949 Ryder Cup team and was playing captain on the winning 1955 team.

# February 21

## 1993: Phil Mickelson Fires Final Round 65 to Win Buick Invitational of California

The Buick Invitational of California, not to be confused with the Buick Classic held at the Westchester Country Club, was first won by Ted Kroll in 1952 when it was held at the San Diego Country Club. The event was then called the San Diego Open and evolved through several name changes to become the Buick Invitational of California in 1992. Kroll won $2,000 in first-prize money in the inaugural event. Phil Mickelson, a young golf phenom out of Arizona State University, shot 75, 69, 69, and 65 for 278 to finish four strokes ahead of Dave Rummells and collect $180,000. The event is now held on the 6,659-yard, par-72 Torrey Pines North and the 7,021-yard, par-72 South courses overlooking the Pacific Ocean in San Diego. This is one of the few municipal courses where a PGA Tour event has been held in recent years.

Ted Kroll, born in New Hartford, New York, in 1919 had his best year in 1956 when he won $72,835 and led the PGA Tour in earnings. He also won the George May Championship that year, worth $50,000. He won the 1960 U.S. Open and was the Canadian Open champion in 1962. Mickelson won two tournaments in 1993, his second year on the Tour, netting $628,735 in Tour earnings. He was ninth on the World Money List with total earnings of $862,540. Before joining the Tour, Mickelson was a four-time all-American at Arizona State and won the NCAA singles title three of those years (1989, 1990, 1992). He is the only left-handed golfer to win the U.S. Amateur (1990) and the only golfer other than Jack Nicklaus to win the NCAA and U.S. Amateur titles the same year. Mickelson finished the 1994 season with $748,316 in earnings, fifteenth on the Tour.

# February 22

## 1956: Birthday of Amy Alcott, Winner of 1980 U.S. Women's Open

Amy Alcott has won more than thirty LPGA events including five majors—the 1979 Peter Jackson Classic, the 1980 U.S. Women's Open, and the Nabisco–Dinah Shore Invitational (1983, 1988, 1991). Born in Kansas City, Missouri, Alcott won the 1973 USGA Girls' Junior Championship, 6 and 5, over Mary Lawrence at the Somerset Hills Country Club in Bernardsville, New Jersey. She turned professional in 1975, won the Orange Blossom Classic, and was named LPGA Player of the Year. She has won over $3 million on the LPGA Tour, placing her among the top ten all-time.

# February 23

## 1941: Harold McSpaden, One of the Golddust Twins, Wins Thomasville Open

Harold "Jug" McSpaden, a pioneer on the professional golf circuit in the United States, won the Thomasville Open and collected $700. He had a 54-hole total of 207. Named one of the "Golddust Twins" when he teamed up with Byron Nelson to raise money for the World War II effort, McSpaden ruefully noted that "in 1944 I received $18,000 in war bonds. When I cashed them in, I cleared $134.55." McSpaden was rejected for military service because of sinusitis, and Byron Nelson because of a form of hemophilia. The drain of barnstorming to raise money for the war effort is one reason that Nelson, who won fifty-two PGA tournaments in an illustrious career, elected to retire from the "Golden Grind" at the age of thirty-four.

McSpaden, born in Rosedale, Kansas, in 1908, was one of the stars of the professional tour in the 1930s. In 1944, after steadily winning a few tournaments a year since 1934, he began to win more frequently. That year he won the Los Angeles Open, the Phoenix Open, the Gulfport Open, the Chicago Victory Open, and the Minneapolis Four Ball (with partner Byron Nelson). He won a total of seventeen tournaments in his career, including the Canadian Open in 1939. He was an excellent match-play competitor, finishing second in the PGA Championship in 1937 and reaching the semifinals in 1940 and 1946 (all match-play events).

# February 24

## 1952: Jack Burke Jr. Wins Houston Open, His Second
## PGA Tour Win in Two Weeks

Jack Burke, a native of Fort Worth, Texas, shot a 277 to win the Houston Open at the 7,212-yard, par-70 Memorial Park Golf Course. This was his second consecutive win following a record 72-hole round of 260 (67, 65, 64, 64) in the Texas Open the previous week. Burke, one of the finest golfers of the postwar era, went on to win his next two tournaments, the Baton Rouge Open and the St. Petersburg Open, in his best season since joining the Tour in 1950. He won the Vardon Trophy with a scoring average of 70.54 and tied Sam Snead for the lead in tournaments won (five). Burke won a total of seventeen Tour tournaments including the Masters and the PGA Championship in 1956. He was named PGA Player of the Year in 1956. His last Tour victory came in 1963.

# February 25

## 1957: Arnold Palmer Wins Houston Open, Led PGA Tour With Four Tournament Wins in 1957

Arnold Palmer, playing in his third year on the PGA Tour, won his fourth PGA tournament by shooting a 72-hole total of 279 to win the Houston Open on the 7,212-yard, par-70 Memorial Park Golf Course in Houston. Palmer won $7,500 on his way to winning $27,802 in regular PGA Tour events. He led the Tour with four tournament wins, including victories at Houston and in the Azalea, Rubber City, and San Diego events. Palmer was the leading money winner in 1958, 1960, 1961, and 1963. His best money year on the regular tour was 1971, when he won $209,603 and finished third in earnings behind Lee Trevino and Jack Nicklaus. He was in the top ten of the money list for fifteen years, as was Sam Snead. Only Jack Nicklaus, with eighteen years on that list, has had a better record. Palmer ranks fifth all-time in PGA Tour victories with sixty.

The Houston Open was originally called the Tournament of Champions and was first won by Byron Nelson when he shot a 274 on the 6,588-yard, par-71 River Oaks Country Club course in 1946. The name of the tournament was changed to the Houston Open in 1950 and has had various names, venues, and sponsors over the years. It is now played at the TPC at the Woodlands and is called the Shell Houston Open. Only Curtis Strange, who won the tournament in 1980, 1986, and 1988, has won it more than twice.

# February 26

## 1993: Tom Weiskopf Shoots Opening Round 66, Goes On to Win His First Senior Tour Event

Tom Weiskopf joined the U.S. PGA Senior Tour in 1993 and won his first tournament at the 6,763-yard, par-72 TPC at Prestancia Golf Course in Sarasota, Florida. Weiskopf shot 66 in the opening round, then finished with a 67 and a 69 to win by four strokes. The $55,000 prize money was more than he had won in any single regular Tour event. Weiskopf finished second to his old nemesis, Jack Nicklaus, losing by one stroke, at the U.S. Senior Open at the Cherry Hills Country Club in July. Weiskopf earned $72,830 in that event and $482,028 in all of his tournaments in 1993, placing him twenty-second on the Senior World Money List.

Tom Weiskopf sharply curtailed his PGA Tour appearances after 1983, due to a rotator-cuff injury in his shoulder. He still had a career total of fifteen PGA Tour victories and won $2,241,688. Tom has designed some excellent golf courses with his partner Jay Morrish, including the Troon Golf and Country Club (1985), Troon North Golf Club (1990), and the TPC of Scottsdale (Desert Course, 1987, Stadium Course, 1986) in Arizona and others. Weiskopf won the British Open in 1973 when he scored 276 at Troon to edge Johnny Miller and N. C. Coles by three shots.

# February 27

### 1941: War Department Surveys Golf Courses as Potential Airstrips

The U.S. War Department ordered the Air Corps to conduct a survey of two hundred golf courses in its search for potential military-aircraft emergency landing fields.

# February 28

### 1971: Jack Nicklaus Wins His Second PGA Championship

Jack Nicklaus won his second PGA title as he opened the tournament at the 7,096-yard, par-72 PGA National Golf Club (now the Ballenisles Country Club) in Palm Beach Gardens, Florida, with a 69. He was never headed as he finished with a 72-hole total of 281 to defeat Billy Casper by two strokes. Casper, who played in a group ahead of Nicklaus, finished his final round with a fine 68 to come within one stroke of Nicklaus as he walked off the tee at the 588-yard, par-5 seventeenth. Then Nicklaus hit a 1-iron short of the bunkers in front of the green, then hit a wedge to within five feet of the pin. His birdie putt sealed the tournament and made him the first golfer in history to win the Masters, U.S. Open, British Open, and PGA Championship twice.

# February 29

## 1992: Dawn Coe Wins Women's Kemper Open

Dawn Coe, now Dawn Coe-Jones, won the Women's Kemper Open on the Wailea Golf Club Blue Course in Kihei, Maui, Hawaii. Ms. Coe, a native of Campbell River, British Columbia, Canada, won $75,000 for her efforts, her first win since joining the LPGA Tour in 1983. Coe-Jones won the HealthSouth Palm Beach Classic in 1994 and finished the year with career earnings of over $1.5 million.

The 5 feet 7 inch Coe-Jones took up golf at the age of twelve and later won two British Columbia Junior Championships (1978, 1979). She won the British Columbia Amateur in 1982 and 1983 and the Canadian Amateur in 1983. Coe-Jones was first team all-American at Lamar University in 1983. She joined the LPGA Tour after earning a degree in elementary education.

# March 1

## 1931: Bobby Jones Goes to Hollywood

Bobby Jones, who retired at age twenty-eight in 1930 after winning the Grand Slam (British Amateur, U.S. Amateur, U.S. Open, British Open), a feat that has never been equaled, arrived in Hollywood, California, to begin work on *How I Play Golf*, an instructional film series featuring stars James Cagney, Edward G. Robinson, W. C. Fields, and Loretta Young. This film series was shown in entertaining, short segments in movie theaters throughout the country, no doubt popularizing the game of golf. Jones's books *Bobby Jones on Golf* and *Down the Fairway* (with O. B. Keeler) are considered classics. As the late great golf writer Charles Price noted in a preface to Jones's instructional book: "What really set him [Jones] apart was his insight into the game, gorgeous in its dimensions. . . ."

*Opposite:* Sam Snead (*left*) greets Ben Hogan (*right*) at the Los Angeles Open

# March 2

## 1958: Birthday of Ian Woosnam, Winner of the 1991 Masters

Before winning the Masters in a down-to-the-wire struggle against Jose Maria Olazabal and Tom Watson in 1991, Ian Woosnam had spent most of his thirteen-year professional career in Europe. Born in Oswestry, Wales, the five-feet-four-inch Welshman turned professional at age twenty and won his first significant tournament, the Swiss Open, in 1982. He then won numerous events on the European tour, including the Bell's Scottish Open (1987), Volvo PGA Championship (1988), and Suntory World Match Play Championship (1990). He won five events on the European tour in 1987 and 1989. He won the Order of Merit in 1990 and surpassed Seve Ballesteros as Europe's career money leader. Woosnam still plays relatively few tournaments in the United States. In 1993 he was twenty-third on the World Money List with over $1 million in earnings. Woosnam was ranked seventh in Worldwide Sony Rankings behind Faldo, Norman, Langer, Price, Couples, and Azinger. He has won over $10 million in purses in his career.

# March 3

## 1946: Ben Hogan Wins St. Petersburg Open, Wins Thirteen Tournaments in 1946

Ben Hogan won his third tournament of the young PGA season by firing a 269 to pick up the $2,000 winner's check at the St. Petersburg Open. Hogan went on to win a total of thirteen tournaments including the Colonial National Invitation, the Western Open, the PGA Championship, and the North and South. Ben led the tour in money winnings with $42,556. During his career, he won sixty-three tournaments, third to Sam Snead (81) and Jack Nicklaus (70), and was the leading money winner five times (1940, 1941, 1942, 1946, and 1948). Injuries caused by a severe car accident in February 1949 curtailed his play thereafter. Only Byron Nelson has more PGA Tour wins in a season than Hogan (eighteen in 1945). Hogan won ten tournaments in 1948.

Hogan's win in the inaugural Colonial National Invitation tournament in 1946 was the first of his five wins in that event. He won it again in 1947, 1952, 1953, and 1959. The event, now called the Southwestern Bell Colonial, is still part of the PGA Tour and continues to be played at the Colonial Country Club, a 7,096-yard, par-70 layout in Fort Worth, Texas. Hogan won $3,000 in 1946 for his first-place finish. When Fulton Allem won with rounds of 66, 63, 68, and 67 for 264 to win by one stroke over Greg Norman in 1993, he pocketed $234,000.

# March 4

## 1990: Beth Daniel Wins Women's Kemper Open, Has Seven Tournament Wins in 1990

Beth Daniel, a native of Charleston, South Carolina, had an outstanding amateur career after taking up the game of golf at the age of seven. She won several amateur events including the Twin States (North and South Carolina) Junior Girls' Championship (1973, 1974, 1975) and the 1975 U.S. Women's Amateur, which she won at age eighteen on her first attempt. Only seven other women have accomplished this feat since the tournament began in 1895. She won the U.S. Amateur again in 1977 and was a member of the Curtis Cup teams (1976, 1978) and the 1978 World Amateur team.

Beth turned professional in 1978 after attending Furman University. She joined the LPGA tour in 1979 and was named Rookie of the Year after earning $97,027. Daniel won four tournaments in 1980 and became the first woman player to win more than $200,000 in a single season. She was named LPGA Player of the Year. She led the Tour in earnings again in 1981 ($206,978), but slumped in the mid-1980s due to back problems and a bout with mononucleosis. Daniel came back in 1989 to win three tournaments and the Vare Trophy with a 70.38 per round scoring average. She won the Orix Hawaiian Ladies' Open on February 24, 1990, then won the $75,000 first prize in the Women's Kemper Open with a 72-hole total of 283. She won five more tournaments in 1990, led the tour in earnings ($863,578), and won the Vare Trophy again (70.54). Daniel was also named the LPGA Player of the Year.

Beth Daniel has won over $4.5 million on the LPGA Tour and ranks in the top three tour money winners all-time. The 5-feet-10-inch Daniel, who is noted for her distance off the tee, quality medium irons, and excellent putting, is well on her way to the LPGA Hall of Fame. She won four tournaments in 1994 and was again named LPGA Player of the Year.

# March 5

## 1972: Jack Nicklaus Wins Doral-Eastern Open, Wins Seven Tournaments in 1972

Jack Nicklaus had one of his better years in a superlative career in 1972. He won the Bing Crosby Pro-Am in January, captured the Doral-Eastern Open (renamed the Doral-Ryder Open in 1987), then proceeded to win the Masters, the U.S. Open, the Westchester Classic, the U.S. Professional Match Play Championship, and the Walt Disney World Open. He led the PGA Tour in money winnings with $320,542 and was named PGA Player of the Year.

Before the 1972 season began, there was much anticipation that Nicklaus would win golf's modern Grand Slam—the Masters, U.S. Open, British Open, and PGA Championship. He won the first two Slam tournaments in the same year for the first time in his career. He was ready to take on the course at Muirfield in the British Open, but after a third-day 71, he was six shots behind Lee Trevino and five behind Tony Jacklin, both former British Open champions. He had used a 1-iron off the tee and carefully managed his game the first three rounds, but when that strategy proved ineffective, he told his friends, "What the hell. I'm going for broke. I either shoot eighty-two or sixty-two." Nicklaus caught Trevino and Jacklin at the turn after playing 4 under on the front nine in the final round. After taking the lead with a birdie on ten, Nicklaus was startled as the crowd acknowledged both Jacklin's and Trevino's eagles on the par-5 ninth. Nicklaus got his birdie on eleven, where he had heard the roar, but then reverted to a conservative course-management style while Trevino chipped in to save par on the seventeenth, parred the last hole, and won the tournament by a stroke.

Nicklaus finished tied for thirteenth at the PGA Championship held at Oakland Hills that August. He was six strokes behind Gary Player, the winner. Many thought that had Jack won at Muirfield, he would have won the Slam. It turned out that 1972 was his last best chance. Nicklaus never again won the Masters and U.S. Open in the same year.

# March 6

## 1457: Golf Prohibited by the Scottish Parliament of King James II

There are various theories about where and how golf originated. It is clear, however, that golf became an extremely popular pastime in fifteenth-century Scotland. According to the authorities, the game began to threaten the national defense of the country because it interfered with compulsory archery training. The bow and arrow, at that time, was the principal weapon of defense. The Scottish Parliament of King James II thus issued a decree, dated March 6, 1457, that read in part "that Futeball and golfe be utterly cried down and not be used." In 1471 an act was passed forbidding golf. This act read in part, "Futeball and Golfe be abused in time cumming," with further mention that they interfered with essential archery training.

There was an ongoing effort over the next century to limit the play of golf. In 1592, the Town Council of Edinburgh prohibited the playing of golf on Sundays. Those who transgressed this rule were often made to confess their aberrant golfing behavior to church congregations. Luckily, the statutes prohibiting golf became obsolete when the invention of gunpowder and firearms rendered the bow obsolete.

King James VI appointed a Clubmaker in 1603 and a Ball-Maker in 1618. The Ball-Maker was supposed to help the balance-of-payments problem caused by the importation of balls from Holland. In 1633, King Charles I ratified a previous act and "commanded" that his loyal and dutiful people should not be molested in their "lawful" recreations. In other words, King Charles was a golfer, and golf was no longer illegal.

By 1744, the Honorable Company of Edinburgh golfers was established and its first annual tournament was held. In 1754, the St. Andrews Society of Golfers, now known as the Royal and Ancient Golf Club of St. Andrews, came into existence. The Royal and Ancient, along with the United States Golf Association, would one day become the international arbiter of the rules of golf.

# March 7

## 1993: Greg Norman Tournament Record 265 Wins His Second Doral-Ryder Open

Greg Norman shot rounds of 65, 68, 62, and 70 to post a record-breaking score of 265 to win his second Doral-Ryder Open. The previous tournament record in the event, held at the 6,939-yard, par-72 Doral Resort and Country Club in Miami, was 270, set by Hubert Green in 1976. Norman won a first prize of $252,000. He won his first Doral-Ryder in 1990 in a play-off. Norman almost won the tournament in 1995 but pulled a 6-iron into the water on his approach to the final hole and lost to Nick Faldo.

The first Doral-Ryder, then called the Doral Country Club Open Invitational, was won by Billy Casper, who shot 283 and won $9,000 in 1962. Casper won the event again in 1964. Raymond Floyd is the only golfer to win the event three times (1980, 1981, 1992). The tournament was renamed the Doral-Eastern Open Invitational in 1970 before it became the Doral-Ryder Open in 1987. The event has always been held on the Dick Wilson–designed Doral Blue Course.

# March 8

## 1992: Raymond Floyd Wins Doral-Ryder Open, First Player to Win Tour and Senior Tour Event in One Year

Raymond Floyd, forty-nine years of age, shot a 17-under-par 271 on the 6,939-yard, par-72 Blue Course at the Doral Country Club to win his third Doral Open in Miami. Floyd, who won $252,000, also captured the tournament in 1980 and 1981. Floyd, whose nearby home burned down shortly before the tournament, was a sentimental favorite as he picked up his twenty-second PGA Tour win. Floyd then went on to win $741,918 on the regular Tour, putting him over $4.9 million in career earnings. Raymond, who turned fifty in September of 1992, also won the GTE North Classic, making him the first player to win a tournament on both the PGA Tour and the Senior PGA Tour.

With his third Doral win, Floyd, who is tied for twenty-third on the all-time tournament win list and ranks in the top twenty in career PGA Tour money earnings, tied Sam Snead for the longest time interval between a player's first PGA Tour win (for Floyd, at age twenty in the St. Petersburg Open in 1963) and his last, twenty-nine years. Raymond Floyd still holds the honor of being the youngest post–World War II golfer to win a PGA event.

# March 9

## 1952: Jack Burke Jr. Wins Fourth PGA Title in Four Weeks

Jack Burke Jr. won the St. Petersburg Open for his fourth PGA title in as many weeks. Burke's three other wins during this period were at the Texas Open, the Houston Open, and the Baton Rouge Open. Burke won the Vardon Trophy in 1952 with a 70.05 per round scoring average on the PGA Tour. Burke won seventeen PGA tournaments in his career, including the Masters and PGA Championship in 1956, and was selected to five Ryder Cup teams: 1951, 1953, 1955, 1957 (captain), and 1973 (nonplaying captain). Jack Burke was elected to the PGA Hall of Fame in 1975.

# March 10

## 1914: Birthday of Chandler Harper, Winner of 1950 PGA Championship

Chandler Harper was born in Portsmouth, Virginia, and won his first Virginia State Amateur in 1930 at the age of seventeen. He also won that event in 1933 and 1934. Harper turned professional at age twenty. His only major championship win was the 1950 PGA Championship at the Scioto Country Club in Columbus, Ohio, where he defeated another long shot, Henry Williams Jr., 4 and 3, in the 36-hole match-play final. Harper defeated Fred Annon, Dick Metz, Bob Toski, Lloyd Mangrum, and Jimmy Demaret on his way to the finals.

In 1954, Harper shot final rounds of 63, 63, and 63 to finish with a winning total of 259 at the Texas Open. Only Mike Souchak (257) and Donnie Hammond (258) have bettered this total in a PGA Tour event. Tim Norris, Byron Nelson, Corey Pavin, and David Frost have equaled it. Harper was a member of the Ryder Cup team in 1955 and won the PGA Seniors' Championship in 1968. He was inducted into the PGA Hall of Fame in 1969.

# March 11

## 1945: Byron Nelson's Record of Eleven Consecutive Wins Begins at the Miami Four-Ball Championship

Byron Nelson teamed up with Harold "Jug" McSpaden to win the Miami Four-Ball Invitational. He went on to win the Charlotte Open, Greensboro Open, Durham Open, Atlanta Iron Lung Tournament, PGA Canadian Open, Philadelphia Inquirer Invitational, Chicago Victory Open, PGA Championship, Tom O'Shanter Open, and the Canadian National Open consecutively. The eleven-straight tournament win streak ended in early August. Nelson finished second in seven other tournaments that year and won a total of $63,335.66 in War Bonds. Byron Nelson had the lowest average scoring statistic in 1945 (68.33 per round). He had a record nineteen consecutive rounds under seventy. Nelson was named Male Athlete of the Year by the Associated Press for the second consecutive year.

Nelson later attributed his winning streak to an analysis that he did on detailed records of his rounds of golf in 1944 when he won eight tournaments. He noticed that the comments "poor chipping" and "careless shot" kept appearing in his 1944 golf logbook. Byron resolved to correct those problems. He also wanted to buy a ranch and retire to his native Texas with his wife, Louise. He purchased a ranch in Roanoke in 1946 and retired from the PGA Tour the same year.

# March 12

### 1961: Mickey Wright Wins LPGA Championship

Mickey Wright shot a 54-hole total of 220 to win her third LPGA Championship. She had previously won the title in 1958 and 1960. Wright won again in 1963 to become the only four-time winner in the history of the event, a major tournament on the LPGA Tour. Mickey led the LPGA in winnings with $22,236 in 1961 and won the Vare Trophy (73.55 strokes per round). Wright won ten of the twenty-five LPGA events that year, and eighty-two tournaments in her career. She won thirteen major tournaments, including four LPGA Championships, four U.S. Women's Opens, two Title holders, and three Western Opens.

# March 13

### 1960: Arnold Palmer Wins Pensacola Open, Third Consecutive Tournament Win

The year 1960 was a big one for Arnold Palmer, who won a total of eight tournaments including his second Masters victory. His win in the Pensacola Open was his third straight, after the Texas Open and Baton Rouge Open. Only Johnny Miller (1974) has since won as many as eight events in a single PGA Tour season. Palmer led the Tour in earnings with $75,263 in 1960. The award given to the leading money winner since 1981 is the Arnold Palmer Award. He was selected *Sports Illustrated* sportsman of the year in 1960.

# March 14

## 1929: Birthday of Bob Goalby, Winner of 1968 Masters

Born in Belleville, Illinois, Bob Goalby turned professional in 1952 and earned a total of eleven regular Tour victories before joining the Senior Tour in 1980. His first Tour victory was the Greater Greensboro Open in 1958. His one and only major victory came in the Masters in 1968, in one of the most hard-fought finishes in the history of that event.

At the end of the third round of the 1968 Masters, eight players, including Gary Player, Frank Beard, Bruce Devlin, Raymond Floyd, Bob Goalby, Don January, Roberto de Vicenzo, and twenty-eight-year-old Lee Trevino, were within two strokes of each other. On the final day, Bob Goalby and Robert de Vicenzo emerged from the pack to tie at 277. Goalby birdied the thirteenth with an 8-foot putt, birdied the fourteenth with a 15-footer, and eagled the fifteenth after a brilliant 3-iron approach to within eight feet of the cup, to record a final-round 66.

Roberto de Vicenzo started out his final round with a stunning eagle 2 on the 400-yard, par-4 first hole. At the end of the day, Roberto had apparently tied Goalby at 277 with a final round 65. But de Vicenzo had incorrectly recorded a 4 when he had actually shot a 3 on the 400-yard, par-4 seventeenth. Technically, de Vicenzo's playing partner, Tommy Aaron, recorded the score, but de Vicenzo signed the card, requiring him, under USGA rules, to take the higher score of 66. This cost him a chance for a Masters title, which would have been decided in a play-off with Goalby.

# March 15

## 1910: Birthday of Enid Wilson, Noted British Golfer and Journalist

Enid Wilson was one of women golf's contrarian free spirits. Before retiring from amateur competition at the young age of twenty-four, Ms. Wilson, who was born in Stonebroom, Derbyshire, England, had won the British Girls' (1925), English Ladies' (1928, 1930), and British Ladies' (1931, 1932, 1933) and was a member of the first British and Irish Curtis Cup team in 1932. She liked to wear trousers and smoke cigarettes at a time when that was considered controversial for women, and she was labeled a "nonamateur" by the British Ladies' Golf Union in 1934 and was thus no longer eligible to play amateur tournaments. She turned to journalism and for many years wrote golf articles for the *Daily Telegraph.* Her book, *A Gallery of Women Golfers,* is considered one of the best on the subject.

# March 16

## 1958: Beverly Hanson Wins the Titleholders Championship, LPGA Major Tournament

The Titleholders was one of the early mainstays of the women's professional Tour. It was founded by Mrs. Dorothy Manice in 1937 when there were few tournaments for women professionals available. The Titleholders was played at the Augusta Country Club, a Donald Ross layout adjacent to the Augusta National Golf Club. The event was a social gathering as well as a competition. Tea dances, card parties, a "Titleholders Talent Night," and a Calcutta were part of the event. It was at the Titleholders that Fred Corcoran announced plans for the nascent 1949–50 LPGA tournament circuit.

Fred Corcoran, born in Cambridge, Massachusetts, in 1905, was one of the early sports agents. Starting with Sam Snead, he advised celebrities such as Ted Williams, Ken Venturi, Babe Zaharias, and many others. He served as executive director of the PGA from 1936 through 1947 and as director of the LPGA from 1949 to 1961. He helped start the Golf Writers Association and managed the 1937, 1939, 1941, and 1953 Ryder Cup teams. The Titleholders, then considered a major, was part of the original LPGA Tour organized by Corcoran and the women professionals.

Patty Berg was the first winner of the Titleholders in 1937 and won six more times after that. Beverly Hanson, winner of the 1958 Titleholders, was a member of the 1950 Curtis Cup team and won the Women's Amateur in 1950. She also won the LPGA title in 1955. In 1958, besides winning the Titleholders, Hanson won the Vare Trophy with a 74.92 stroke average and led the LPGA in earnings with $12,639. The last Titleholders Tournament was held in 1972 and was won by Sandra Palmer.

# March 17

## 1985: Peter Thomson Wins Vintage Invitational, Won
## Nine Seniors' Events in 1985

Peter Thomson shot a 280 to win the Vintage Invitational at the Vintage Club in Indian Wells, California. Thomson won by a single stroke over Billy Casper and Arnold Palmer to collect the $40,000 first prize. Thomson led the 1985 Senior Tour in earnings ($386,724) and tournaments won (nine).

Born in Melbourne, Victoria, Australia, in 1929, Thomson gained distinction during his earlier career by winning five British Open championships (1954, 1955, 1956, 1958, 1965). Only Harry Vardon, with six victories, has won more, and only J. H. Taylor, Tom Watson, and James Braid have won as many. Thomson also won the New Zealand Open eight times, the Australian Open three times, and the British Professional Matchplay Championship on four occasions.

Enormously respected in the international golf community, his game is more suited to seaside courses than the heavily watered tracts in the United States. He designed the Kayak Point Golf Club in Washington State with Donald Fream and courses in Singapore, Australia, Tunisia, and thirteen other countries. He has written about golf in newspapers and has been a television commentator.

# March 18

## 1952: Two Women Killed on the Golf Course

Golf can sometimes be a dangerous game. Two women golfers were instantly killed March 18, 1952, in Jacksonville, Florida, when hit simultaneously by the whirling propeller of a navy fighter plane. They were playing together when the plane, with a dead engine and out of control, hit them from behind. In the summer of 1963, Harold Kalles of Toronto, Canada, died six days after his throat had been cut by a golf club shaft that broke against a tree as he was trying to play out of a bunker. Lightning storms are another source of danger on the links. One of the most famous golf incidents involving lightning occurred at the 1975 Western Open when Lee Trevino, Jerry Heard, and Bobby Nichols were all struck and had to be taken to the hospital.

# March 19

### 1871: Birthday of John H. Taylor, Winner of Five British Opens

John Henry Taylor, or J.H. as he was commonly referred to, left school at age eleven and worked as a caddie at the Westward Ho! Club in his native England. He also worked as a bootboy, gardener's assistant, and mason's laborer. At age seventeen he became a member of the greenskeeping staff at Westward Ho!

Taylor recorded his first British Open victory in 1894 at Royal St. Georges in England, shooting a 72-hole total of 326 to win by five strokes. Taylor won the Open again in 1895, 1900, 1909, and 1913. He was runner-up or tied for second five times in the Open and won the French Open (1908, 1909) and the German Open (1912). Part of the Great Triumvirate that included Harry Vardon and James Braid, the trio won sixteen British Opens and dominated professional golf for three decades prior to World War I.

Taylor had a strong, firm-footed stance and a short, punched swing that stood him well in the variable and often sterm weather conditions of British Open play. He was well respected by his fellow golfers and played a major role in the formation of the British PGA. In 1933, as nonplaying captain, he led the British team to victory in the Ryder Cup at Southport and Ainsdale. The British (and Irish) team would not win again until 1957.

# March 20

## 1941: Sam Snead Wins North and South Open, Led
## PGA in Tournament Victories in 1941

Sam Snead shot a 277 to collect $1,000, the winner's share at the North and South Open Tournament held at the Pinehurst Country Club in Pinehurst, North Carolina. Snead won a PGA-leading total of seven tournaments in 1941 including the Bing Crosby, St. Petersburg Open, St. Augustine Pro-Am, North and South Open, Canadian Open, Rochester Times Union Open, and the Henry Hurst Invitational. The most tournaments Snead won in any year was eleven in 1950.

The first North and South Open was held in 1903 and was won by Donald Ross, a Scotsman born in Dornoch who had learned golf as an apprentice to Old Tom Morris. Ross had also served as greenskeeper at the Dornoch Golf Club. He won the North and South Open three times, and it was won by his brother, Alec, five times. American-born golfers, including Walter Hagen, Byron Nelson, Ben Hogan, and Cary Middlecoff, later won the event, which was then an important part of the professional circuit. Sam Snead won the tournament three times (1941, 1949, 1950) and finished second to Ben Hogan three times (1940, 1942, 1946). Tommy Bolt was the last golfer to win the North and South Open before it was discontinued in 1952.

# March 21

### 1993: Ben Crenshaw Wins the Nestlé Invitational

Ben Crenshaw shot 71, 70, 69, and 70 for 280 on the 7,114-yard, par-72 Bay Hill Club Course to win the Nestlé Invitational in Orlando. It was Crenshaw's seventeenth PGA Tour win. He joined the circuit in 1973 after winning the 1973 Qualifying Tournament by a then-record twelve strokes.

# March 22

### 1992: Fred Couples Wins Nestlé Invitational, Named
### PGA Player of the Year in 1992

The Nestlé Invitational was initially called the Florida Citrus Open Invitational and was first held at the Rio Pinar Country Club in 1966 in Orlando, Florida. Lionel Hebert shot a 279 to win the first contest, whose first-prize money was $21,000 out of a total purse of $110,000. The event was moved to the 7,103-yard, par-71 Bay Hill Club, now owned by Arnold Palmer, and renamed the Bay Hill Citrus Classic in 1979. After being dubbed the Bay Hill Classic (1980) and Hertz Bay Hill Classic (1985), it is now called the Nestlé Invitational. Arnold Palmer won this event in 1971. One of the more memorable finishes occurred in 1990, when Robert Gamez holed an eagle 2 with a 7-iron from just over 176 yards to win the tournament by one stroke over Greg Norman. To date, no one has won this tournament more than once.

Fred Couples won the Nestlé Invitational in 1992 with a 72-hole score of 269. He picked up a check for $180,000 on his way to $1,344,188 in Tour earnings, ranking him first for the year. Couples had previously won the Nissan Los Angeles Open and would later win his first Masters and only major tournament to date. Couples won his second Vardon Trophy in a row in 1992 with a stroke average of 69.38 per round. Freddy was named PGA Player of the Year for the second consecutive year.

# March 23

## 1986: Dale Douglass Wins Vintage Invitational, Wins Four Senior Tournaments in 1986

Dale Douglass, a journeyman from the PGA Tour who has found new life on the Senior PGA Tour, fired a 16-under-par 272 to win by four strokes over Gary Player at the Vintage Club in Indian Wells, California. Douglass, fifty, playing in his first year on the Senior Tour, went on to win three more tournaments in 1986 (Johnny Mathis Senior Classic, U.S. Senior Open, Fairfield-Barnett Senior Classic) and earned $309,760, third on the Tour. On the PGA Tour, which he joined in 1963, the native of Wewoka, Oklahoma, earned $577,951 in his career and won three tournaments. By the end of 1994, Douglass had earned over $3.6 million on the Senior circuit. Dale was a member of the 1969 Ryder Cup team.

# March 24

## 1951: Birthday of Pat Bradley, Member of LPGA Hall of Fame

Pat Bradley had her best year in 1986, when she won three of the LPGA majors—the LPGA Championship, the du Maurier Classic, and the Nabisco–Dinah Shore. She finished tied for fifth, three strokes back, in the Women's Open that year, barely missing a Grand Slam. The only other women golfers to win three majors in a year are Mickey Wright (1961) and Babe Zaharias (1950). Pat Bradley's 1986 efforts earned her $492,021, then an LPGA record. Bradley had the lowest Tour scoring average with 71.10 strokes per round, led in Tour earnings, and was named the LPGA Player of the Year.

After coming back from hyperthyroidism, diagnosed in 1988, she reached thirty LPGA Tour wins and was inducted into the LPGA Hall of Fame after winning Player of the Year honors again in 1991. Bradley won the Vare Trophy for the second time (70.63 strokes per round), won four tournaments, and led the LPGA Tour in earnings with $763,118. By the end of 1994, Miss Bradley was second on the all-time money winners list in official LPGA Tour events with over $4.7 million in winnings.

# March 25

## 1934: Horton Smith Wins the First Masters

Horton Smith, an American professional from Springfield, Missouri, won the first Masters tournament, held at Augusta National in Georgia in 1934, by one stroke over Craig Wood. The noted British golf writer Bernard Darwin wrote that Smith's short game was "a joy to watch, easy, elegant, and a horrid certainty. The United States have sent us a number of great putters from whom to choose models, but I am disposed to doubt if they have sent a better than Horton Smith." Smith entered the professional tournament scene in 1928, at the age of twenty, and was the leading money winner at the end of 1929. He went on to win another Masters in 1936 and was a member of the Ryder Cup team in 1929, 1933, and 1935.

Augusta National is the dream realized of Robert Tyre Jones, considered by many to be the best golfer of all time. Jones grew up in Atlanta and played tournament golf as an amateur, winning the Grand Slam of golf—the British Amateur, the British Open, the U.S. Open, and the U.S. Amateur—in 1930. He then retired to Atlanta at the age of twenty-eight to practice law and raise a family. One of his goals was to build a golf course where he could play with his friends. An old acquaintance, Clifford Roberts, a successful Wall Street banker, was aware of 365 acres of beautiful rolling pinelands that might fit Jones's golf-course-building plans. It was in Augusta, where Roberts often wintered and Jones's wife was raised. The property had been in the hands of a famous horticulturist and nursery owner, a Belgian baron named Prosper Jules Alphonse Berckmans, who established one of the foremost nurseries in the United States.

In the catalog of Berckmans's nursery for 1861 there were 1,300 varieties of pears, 900 of apples, 300 of grapes, and over 100 each of azaleas and camellias. Bob Jones recorded these words as he turned off the highway and rode down the long archway of magnolias to Berckmans's manor house:

I stood at the top of the hill before that fine old house and looked at the wide stretch of land rolling down the slope before me. It was cleared land for the most part, and you could take in the whole vista all the way down to Rae's Creek. I know instantly it was the kind of terrain I had always hoped to find. I had been told, of course, about the marvelous trees and plants, but I was still unprepared for the great bonus of beauty Fruitlands offered. Frankly, I was overwhelmed by the exciting possibilities of a golf course set in the midst of such a nursery.

Clifford Roberts and Bob Jones organized the new golf club membership after purchasing the land. Dr. Alister Mackenzie, whose golf-course architecture Jones always admired, was retained in 1931 to lay out the course. Mackenzie, the son of Scottish Highland parents, graduated from Cambridge University with degrees in medicine, natural science, and chemistry. He served in the Boer War as a surgeon, returned to Britain to practice medicine, and became interested in golf-course design in the early 1900s. He collaborated with the noted golf-course architect H. S. Colt on the design of the Alwoodley Golf Club in England, and gradually he became a full-time golf-course architect. By the time Mackenzie arrived in Augusta in 1931, he had designed such timeless golf classics as Cypress Point (1928, with Robert Hunter) and Pastiempo (1929) in California. Augusta National opened in 1933.

The course was planned as a "wide-open" one to accommodate the average golfer. To challenge the good golfer, the large greens were made difficult with tricky pin placements, subtle and dramatic undulations, and strategic bunker placements. Alister Mackenzie later wrote that he and Jones were in complete agreement on the basic principles of what constitutes a "great golf course":

1. A really great course must be pleasurable to the greatest possible number.
2. It must require strategy as well as skill or it cannot be enduringly interesting.
3. It must give the average player a fair chance and at the same time require the utmost from the expert who tries for subpar scores.
4. All natural beauty should be preserved, natural hazards utilized, and a minimum of artificiality introduced.

The golf course has been modified over the years by such architects as Perry Maxwell,

Robert Trent Jones Sr., George W. Cobb, John La Foy, George Fazio, Joe Finger, Byron Nelson, Jay Morrish, Robert Cupp, and Jack Nicklaus. The classic design and natural beauty of the course remain.

Augusta National was conceived and built in the early stages of the Great Depression. There were preliminary discussions about holding the U.S. Open at Augusta, but for various reasons that idea was dropped and it was decided to host a new tournament. The event was originally called the "First Annual Invitation Tournament" at Augusta National Golf Club. The total purse was $5,000, the same amount as the 1934 U.S. Open, and seventy-two players were in the original field. The front and back nines were played in reverse order from today's. Bobby Jones came out of retirement to play in this inaugural event. He shot a 7-under-par 65 in a practice round but eventually finished well behind the winner, Horton Smith, who shot 70, 72, 70, and 72 for 284 to win by a single stroke.

Over the years, the Masters has reached the status of being considered a "major" tournament along with the U.S. Open, British Open, and PGA Championship. The reputation and charisma of Bobby Jones, the iron-fisted management style of Clifford Roberts, both now deceased, and the age of golf television and the advent of Arnold Palmer, who won Masters titles in 1958, 1960, and 1962 before millions of television viewers, put the tournament in a class all by itself.

# March 26

## 1951: Patty Berg Wins Sandhills Open, Member of LPGA Hall of Fame

Patty Berg shot a 54-hole score of 221 to win the Sandhills Open and pocket $750 in prize money. Miss Berg, playing in the second year that the women's professional Tour was managed by the LPGA, won three—the Sandhills Women's Open, the Weathervane Women's Open (Pebble Beach), and the Women's Western Open—of the sixteen scheduled events. Babe Zaharias dominated the Tour with seven wins and led in earnings with $15,087 that year. Patty Berg finished second with $13,237 in prize money. Miss Berg was the leading money winner in 1954, 1956, and 1957. She won fifty-seven professional events in her career, including forty-four LPGA titles. Only Kathy Whitworth (88) and Mickey Wright (82) have won more pro tournaments on the women's Tour.

# March 27

## 1966: Marilynn Smith Wins Louise Suggs Delray Beach Invitational, Second Consecutive Victory

Marilynn Smith fired a 54-hole score of 211 to capture first-prize money of $1,275 in the Louise Suggs Delray Beach Invitational. The previous week Ms. Smith won the St. Petersburg Women's Open with a 72-hole score of 285. Up until 1968, many of the LPGA events were 72-hole events, including the Western Open, St. Petersburg Orange Classic, Dallas Civitan Open, Milwaukee Jaycee Open, and others. There is still a mix of 54- and 72-hole events on the Tour, with the longer events, headed by the U.S. Women's Open, Nabisco–Dinah Shore, du Maurier, and LPGA Championship, the "majors" on the ladies' Tour.

Marilynn Smith was a pioneer of the early LPGA Tour. And there were many hazards in those early days, as Smith related to Rhonda Glenn, author of *The Illustrated History of Women's Golf*. Marilynn Smith escaped injury at the rain-delayed 1967 Babe Zaharias Open at the Bayou Din Country Club in Beaumont, Texas, when water moccasins wriggled onto the course. Ms. Smith found one in a ball washer but managed to win the tournament anyway. She remembered a more difficult situation at an earlier tournament in Florida: "We were playing the second round. I was preparing my second shot on the fourteenth hole when, with a kind of whine and swoosh, this bullet flew past my head! A sniper was hiding in nearby bushes, shooting at us. We delayed play for forty-five minutes while tournament officials tried to find the villain. They never could."

# March 28

## 1877: Birthday of Ted Ray, Winner of 1920 U.S. Open

Ted Ray was born in Jersey, England, and was noted for his long drives and his powers of recovery. He was prone to wild, disastrous shots because he swayed and sometimes lunged at the ball in his quest, as he would say, to "hit it a bloody sight harder, mate." He did have a dependable rhythm to his swing and had a fine touch around the greens, which stood him well over the years. He won the British Open in 1912 and took the then bold step of traveling to the United States to play in the U.S. Open. Ray became famous, along with Harry Vardon and Francis Ouimet, when they tied in regulation and Ouimet, a twenty-year-old amateur, shocked the golf world and became an American national hero when he defeated the two seasoned British professionals in the 18-hole play-off at the Country Club.

Ted Ray returned to the United States after the war and, at the age of forty-three, won the U.S. Open at Inverness in 1920. He was the last Britisher to win the Open until Tony Jacklin triumphed in 1970. Ray was the captain of the 1927 Great Britain and Ireland team, which lost 9 to 2 to the U.S. team in the first Ryder Cup match held in Worcester, Massachusetts.

# March 29

### 1992: Dottie Mochrie Wins Nabisco–Dinah Shore

Dottie Mochrie fired a 279 to win the Nabisco–Dinah Shore and earn $105,000 in prize money. Mrs. Mochrie went on to win four LPGA tournaments that year and pick up the LPGA Player of the Year award. She won the Vare Trophy (70.80 strokes per round) and earned $693,335 in tour winnings to raise her total to $1,670,635 since joining the Tour in 1988. Mrs. Mochrie was a three-time all-American at Furman before turning professional in 1987. By the end of 1994, Mochrie had eight LPGA victories and over $2.5 million in official earnings.

# March 30

### 1920: Birthday of Julius Boros, Winner of Two U.S. Opens

Julius Boros made golf look easy as he repeated his effortless, fluid, long swing in a variety of critical tournament situations. He won the U.S. Open in 1952, three years after he joined the tour at the age of twenty-nine. He led the tour in earnings that year with $37,033 in prize money. Boros won the PGA Championship in 1968 at age forty-eight and remains the oldest golfer ever to win that event. He won a total of eighteen Tour tournaments and played on four Ryder Cup teams (1959, 1963, 1965, 1967). Boros joined the Senior Tour in 1981 and won the PGA Seniors' Championship twice (1971, 1977). He was inducted into the PGA Hall of Fame in 1974 and the World Golf Hall of Fame in 1982. Julius Boros died at the age of seventy-four in 1994.

# March 31

### 1985: Calvin Peete Wins Tournament Players Championship

Calvin Peete, who didn't learn how to play golf until he was twenty-three years old, shot a 274 to win the Tournament Players Championship on the 6,857-yard, par-72 TPC at Sawgrass in Ponte Vedra, Florida. Peete collected $162,000 and went on to finish third that year in PGA Tour earnings with $384,489. He won over $2.3 million and twelve tournaments on the PGA Tour; since 1987, his activity has been curtailed because of back injuries. One of the best African-American players ever to play the Tour, Peete was presented the Golf Writers' Ben Hogan Award in 1983, which goes to an individual who has overcome a physical handicap or illness to play golf. As a child, Peete suffered a broken left elbow and still can't fully extend his arm.

Calvin Peete was a member of 1983 and 1985 Ryder Cup teams. He won the Vardon Trophy in 1984 for low stroke average (70.56 strokes per round) and won the Tour driving-accuracy title ten straight years from 1981 through 1990.

# April 1

## 1901: Birthday of Johnny Farrell, Winner of 1928 U.S. Open

Johnny Farrell played on the PGA circuit from 1922 through 1936 and won twenty-two tournaments, placing him twenty-second on the all-time list along with Raymond Floyd. Farrell, a native of White Plains, New York, and a PGA Hall of Famer, won eight events in 1927. The following year he tied Bobby Jones at 294 after 72 holes of regulation play in the U.S. Open at Olympia Fields in Matteson, Illinois. Farrell, a short hitter with an excellent game around the greens, won the 36-hole play-off by a single stroke, 143 to 144.

Farrell was a member of the first Ryder Cup team in 1927 and was again selected in 1929 and 1931. Walter Hagen was the captain of those teams and continued to captain the Ryder Cup team until 1947, when Ben Hogan had the honor. Johnny Farrell, who started as a caddie in Westchester County, eventually became the head professional at Baltusrol.

*Opposite:* Bobby Jones and Harry Varden

# April 2

## 1951: Birthday of Ayako Okamoto, 1987 LPGA Player of the Year

Ayako Okamoto was one of Japan's foremost women's softball pitchers before she took up golf at the age of twenty-three. She turned professional in 1975 and won twenty Japanese LPGA events before winning her first U.S. LPGA event, the Arizona Copper in 1982, when she was thirty-one. Through 1994, she had won seventeen Tour events. Okamoto had her best year in 1987, when she became the first foreign-born player to win LPGA Player of the Year honors. She won the Lady Keystone Open and Nestlé World Championship that year and led the Tour with $466,034 in winnings. Ms. Okamoto ranks among the top ten all-time winners on the LPGA tour.

According to the Women's World Money List, which includes official earnings on the U.S. LPGA Tour, Women's European Tour, Women's Asian Tour, Japan LPGA Tour, and other established unofficial events, three Japanese golfers were among the top worldwide money winners in 1993. They were Mayumi Hirase (1), Toshimi Kimura (2), and Mayumi Murai (4). Betsy King was third and Patty Sheehan ranked fifth.

# April 3

## 1966: Doug Sanders Wins His Second Greater Greensboro Open, Second Straight PGA Tour Win

Doug Sanders fired a 276 to win $20,000 in first-prize money in the Greater Greensboro Open. Sanders had won the Jacksonville Open and $13,000 the previous week. Sanders, a flashy dresser from Cedartown, Georgia, and one of the more colorful players on the PGA Tour, also won the Bob Hope Classic in 1966 and finished fourth in earnings with $80,096. Sanders finished in the top ten money winners in 1965, 1966, and 1967 and won nineteen tournaments and $722,444 in his PGA Tour career. Sanders, who won his first professional tournament as an amateur in 1956 (the Canadian Open), also won the Greater Greensboro Open in 1963.

Many golf observers consider Sanders's 18-hole play-off contest against Jack Nicklaus on the Old Course in the 1970 British Open at St. Andrews a classic. Sanders played his fourth round in colorful purple attire and needed a 3½-foot putt to win in regulation on the eighteenth. He missed to the right and, after thirteen holes in the play-off, found himself four shots down. Sanders fought back to one shot back going into the final hole. Both men birdied the hole, and in a rare display of exhilaration, winner Nicklaus tossed his putter high in the air. At the presentation ceremony, William Whitelaw, the captain of the Royal and Ancient, commented, "We have been privileged to watch one of the great golf matches of all time."

# April 4

## 1937: Byron Nelson Opens With Record 66, Then Wins His First Masters

Byron Nelson, a native of Fort Worth, Texas, who worked his way up from the caddie ranks as did his counterpart Ben Hogan, won his first Masters, or the "Annual Invitation Tournament" as it was then called, in a field of thirty-eight professionals and seven amateurs at Augusta National. Nelson fired a record 66 the opening round, then followed with rounds of 72 and 75 to trail the leader, Ralph Guldahl, by four strokes.

Both Guldahl and Nelson shot 38s on the final front nine, but Guldahl double-bogeyed the par-3 twelfth and then bogeyed the par-5 thirteenth after hitting a ball into Rae's Creek. Guldahl finished with another 38 to post a 72-hole total of 285. Nelson, in his biography, *How I Played the Game*, recalled his reaction to Guldahl's misfortunes, as he stood on the tee of the par-3 twelfth watching his opponent, who was playing one twosome ahead of him:

> Standing on the tee, I saw Guldahl drop a ball short of the creek, which meant he'd gone in the water from the tee. If he got on and 2-putted, he'd have a 5. Watching his misfortunes, I suddenly felt like a lightbulb went off in my head. . . . I realized then that if I could get lucky and make a 2, I'd catch up with Guldahl right there. Fortunately, I put my tee shot six feet from the hole with a 6-iron into the wind, and holed it.

Nelson then chipped in for a 3 after hitting a 3-wood to the left edge of the green on the par-5 thirteenth and went ahead of Guldahl by three strokes. Byron went on to shoot a 32 on the back nine to win the tournament by two shots with a 283.

Nelson considers this the most important victory of his career because it gave him confidence in his game under difficult tournament pressure. Nelson was awarded a medal by tournament host Bobby Jones and a check for $1,500 as a reward for winning the 1937 Masters.

# April 5

## 1987: Betsy King Wins Nabisco–Dinah Shore, 1987
## Winner of LPGA Vare Trophy

Betsy King won her second tournament of the young season by shooting a 283 to win the Nabisco–Dinah Shore, one of the LPGA Tour's major championships. King won three more tournaments in 1987: the Circle K Tucson Open, the McDonald's Championship, and the Atlantic City LPGA Classic. King won a total of $460,385 to finish second on the Tour to Ayako Okamoto. King, a native of Reading, Pennsylvania, won the LPGA Vare Trophy (71.14 strokes per round average).

Betsy King, who turned professional in 1977, has become one of the most formidable competitors on the LPGA tour. She ranks first in all-time LPGA earnings and will undoubtedly become a member of the LPGA Hall of Fame. King was named Player of the Year in 1984 and 1989 and led the earnings list both of those years. After failing to win a tournament her first seven years on the tour, she won twenty-three events from 1984 through 1990, more than any other LPGA player. She won the U.S. Open, her second major, in 1989, when she won six tournaments and earned $654,132. After King's early Tour dry spell, she took instruction from Ed Oldfield, who reworked her swing and helped her correct a tendency to hook. Now she is considered one of the best drivers on the Tour, characterized by high shots off the tee.

Since 1983, Betsy King's scoring average has been a bit over 71 strokes per round. A quiet perfectionist, she is also an excellent putter.

# April 6

## 1958: Arnold Palmer Wins the Masters, His First Major

Arnold Palmer, age twenty-nine, won his first Masters and first major tournament with a 70, 73, 68, and 73 for 284 at Augusta National in 1958. Doug Ford and Fred Hawkins tied for second at 285. Palmer led by two strokes going into the last day. A drenching overnight rain prompted the tournament officials to permit the players to lift, clean, and drop any ball that became embedded in its own divot mark "through the green"—on all the areas of the golf course except the hazards.

Palmer was paired with Ken Venturi, who had turned professional after he almost won the 1956 Masters as an amateur. Venturi was only one stroke behind Palmer after ten holes. Palmer got a break on the par-3 twelfth when he embedded a ball in a bank above a greenside bunker. Because of the "embedded ball" rule, he was allowed to play a provisional ball, having recorded a 5 with his first ball after hacking out of the wet sod. Palmer proceeded with his round while waiting for a ruling after he parred the twelfth with his provisional ball.

Palmer eagled the par-5 thirteenth after hitting a 3-wood to within eighteen feet of the hole. Venturi got up and down with a wedge and a putt for his birdie to stay close.

Before teeing off on fourteen, both players learned that Palmer was credited with a par 3 on the twelfth by the officials. Venturi then three-putted each of the next three holes while Palmer bogeyed sixteen and eighteen to stagger in with a final round of 73 and a total of 284. Venturi finished two strokes back at 286. Arnold Palmer was the new Masters champion, and the "era of Arnold Palmer," the most exciting golf personality since Walter Hagen, began.

# April 7

## 1935: Gene Sarazen Sinks 230-Yard Approach Shot for Famed Double Eagle, Wins the Masters

A field of sixty-three entered the "2nd Annual Invitation Tournament," now called the Masters, at the Augusta National Golf Club. For the first time, the two nine-hole layouts were reversed from the inaugural tournament to play in the current sequence. Henry Picard, an American professional from Plymouth, Massachusetts, led after the first round with a 67. He fired a 68 on the second day to lead Gene Sarazen and Ray Mangrum by four. Craig Wood then shot a third-round 68 in a blustery rainstorm to lead by one stroke at 209, seven under par.

The course was rain-soaked and the weather near freezing for the final round as Craig Wood and Gene Sarazen dueled each other on the back nine. Wood, playing ahead of Sarazen, birdied the par-4 final hole to post a 72-hole score of 282. As Sarazen approached the fifteenth tee, he would need three birdies on the last four holes to tie. The par-5 fifteenth then measured 485 yards. Sarazen hit an excellent 255-yard drive to leave him a 230-yard shot that would have to negotiate the pond, then approximately thirty feet wide, guarding the front of the green. Walter Hagen was in Sarazen's twosome as he reached for a 4-wood. He caught the ball square. It sailed toward the green, skipped low on the putting surface, rolled straight toward the flag, and miraculously dropped in. Sarazen had scored a double eagle, or albatross as it is sometimes called, and captured the national golf imagination. This was later called "the shot heard round the world," and in 1955 a bridge named for Sarazen was erected across the pond to commemorate the twentieth anniversary of Gene's famed shot. Sarazen parred the final holes, forcing a play-off with Craig Wood.

The following day, Sarazen and Wood teed it up for a 36-hole play-off. Buoyed by his comeback the previous day, Sarazen shot 144 against Wood's 149 to win the second "Masters." Sarazen, an aggressive streak player, was difficult to stop once he gained momentum on a golf course. Jones commented on Gene's play after he holed his double eagle: "What impressed me most was his absolute confidence. He walked right up and struck them [three difficult putts for pars on the final holes] solidly and quickly. Every one of them went into the center of the hole. Gene was one of those players who, when he got on a hot streak, charged around the course like a tiger."

# April 8

## 1951: Ben Hogan Wins His First Masters

The white cap, the cold stare from steely competitive eyes, and the desire for golf perfection were Ben Hogan's trademarks. Nicknamed Bantam Ben, he weighed less than 140 pounds during the prime of his career, which was in the 1940s and early 1950s. He is considered among the best golfers of all time along with Bobby Jones, Sam Snead, Jack Nicklaus, and perhaps a few others.

Hogan entered his first Masters in 1939 but finished ninth, eleven shots behind the winner, Ralph Guldahl, who shot a 279 to defeat Sam Snead by one stroke. Prior to 1951, Hogan's highest finish in the Masters was a first-place tie with Byron Nelson in 1942. Nelson won the 18-hole play-off by one stroke with a 69, the only time the two natives of Texas, who had known each other since they were teenage caddies, ever faced each other in a play-off.

By the time Hogan reached the 1951 Masters, he had won the U.S. Open (1948, 1950), the PGA Championship (1946, 1948), and had been the leading PGA Tour money winner in 1940, 1941, 1942, 1946, and 1948. He won the Vardon Trophy for the best stroke average in 1940, 1941, and 1948. He is only one of four players (along with Gene Sarazen, Gary Player, and Jack Nicklaus) to have won modern golf's four major titles (the Masters, U.S. Open, British Open, PGA).

Hogan's career was interrupted by World War II when the major tournaments were discontinued. Then a near-fatal car accident in 1949 almost ended his career at age thirty-six. After a painful rehabilitation, Hogan's iron will and resolve to be the world's best golfer brought him back to the Tour and the Los Angeles Open in January of 1950. He tied Sam Snead for first place in regulation play in that tournament before losing the play-off. He won the U.S. Open in 1950 and was named PGA Player of the Year, an honor he also earned in 1948, 1951, and 1953.

Although Hogan had not totally regained his pre-accident body strength, especially in his legs, he was ready to play the 1951 Masters. After a first-round 70, he trailed George Fazio by two strokes. At the end of three rounds, Hogan had scores of 70, 72, and 70 to trail Sam Snead and "Skee" Riegel by only one stroke. After a 33 on the final front nine, Hogan closed with a 35 and a 72-hole total of 280 to defeat Riegel by two strokes. Snead had a disastrous 80, dropping him to 291. He had taken a quadruple-bogey 8 on the eleventh, a long par-4 protected by water to the left front of the green. Sam found the water, ending his chances to win his second Masters.

Hogan set a new Masters 72-hole scoring record when he won his second title in 1953. His 70, 69, 66, and 69 for 274 defeated Ed "Porky" Oliver by five strokes.

# April 9

## 1950: Jimmy Demaret Wins Record Third Masters

Jimmy Demaret shot a final-round 69 to close with a 72-hole score of 283 to win the Masters by two strokes over Jim Ferrier. Ferrier managed only one par on the last six holes where he lost seven strokes to shoot a final round of 75. Demaret became the first three-time Masters winner. He had also won in 1940 and 1947. Demaret won a total of thirty-one PGA Tour events in a playing career that spanned from 1935 to 1957.

# April 10

## 1949: Sam Snead Wins First Masters, Fires Final Rounds of 67 and 67

Sam Snead shot two final rounds of 67 to win his first Masters title after starting out with 73 and 75. His 72-hole total of 282 gave him a three-stroke margin over Johnny Bulla and Lloyd Mangrum, who tied at 285. Snead's highest finish in eight previous Masters tournaments was a second-place finish behind Ralph Guldahl in 1939. In the past, Snead had often had putting problems on Augusta's slippery, tricky greens. Snead was down five strokes going into the third round but began to sink putts with a new putter. Sam's third-round 67 put him one stroke off the pace.

Snead's putting helped him build a 33 on the front nine of the final round as he dropped a 20-footer on the par-4 first, birdied the par-5 second after reaching the green in two with a 1-iron, dropped a 15-foot birdie putt on the par-3 twelfth, and birdied the two par-5 holes, eleven and fifteen, on the back nine to finish with 34 and an 18-hole total of 67.

Sam Snead was awarded the first green Masters coat as tournament winner. Coats were ordered for past champions Horton Smith (1934, 1936), Gene Sarazen (1935), Bryon Nelson (1937, 1942), Henry Picard (1938), Ralph Guldahl (1939), Jimmy Demaret (1940, 1947), Craig Wood (1941), Herman Keiser (1946), and Claude Harmon (1948). These gentlemen were all members of the exclusive Masters Champions Club. Snead would win again in 1952 and 1954 to join Jimmy Demaret as the only three-time Masters champions up until that time.

# April 11

### 1993: Bernhard Langer Wins Second Masters
### Championship

Bernhard Langer, the best golfer Germany has ever produced, won his second Masters as he finished with a final-round 70 for a 72-hole total of 277 on the 6,905-yard, par-72 Augusta National layout. Langer defeated Chip Beck, who also had a 70 on the final round, by four strokes. A critical point in the tournament came when Beck was on the green of the 485-yard, par-5 thirteenth in two shots and Beck two-putted for birdie while Langer eagled. When Beck and Langer reached the par-5 fifteenth, Beck was three strokes behind Langer but elected not to go for the green on the second shot. He parred the hole and Langer birdied, then coasted to his second Masters win. Bernhard won his first Masters in 1985 and has won forty-one international events, including the German Open (five times), through 1993.

At the end of 1993, he was second on the Career World Money List with $11,211,053 in tournament earnings. Greg Norman was ranked first with $12,294,529. Langer finished fifteenth on the 1994 World Money List with $1,333,036. He was fourth in the Sony Rankings, behind Nick Price, Greg Norman, and Nick Faldo.

# April 12

## 1987: Larry Mize Stuns Greg Norman in Play-off, Chips in From 140 Feet to Win Masters

No matter what Larry Mize does the rest of his golfing career, which began on the PGA Tour in 1982, he will always be remembered for the sand wedge he used to sink a 140-foot chip shot on the second overtime hole of the 1987 Masters. Mize, who was born in Augusta and whose middle name is Hogan, had won only one PGA Tour event before reaching the Masters. He finished regulation in a three-way tie with Greg Norman and Seve Ballesteros at 285 (3 under par). Ballesteros was eliminated on the first play-off hole after he missed a short putt for par.

Norman and Mize then advanced to the tee on the 445-yard, par-4 eleventh hole, the most difficult hole on the course. Both golfers drove well. Mize, 194 yards out, played a 5-iron but pushed his shot to the right of the green. Norman, with 164 yards left to the hole, slightly pushed a 7-iron to the right fringe. Using his sand iron, Mize's shot flew low, bounded twice before hitting the slippery green, and went straight into the hole. A jubilant Mize gave way to the stunned Greg Norman, who needed to hole his long putt to halve. Norman couldn't do it and Mize had made Masters history. Through 1994, Larry Mize had won four Tour victories and had earned over $4 million in Tour prize money.

# April 13

## 1986: Jack Nicklaus Fires Final-Round 65 to Win His Sixth Masters at Age 46

One of the most dramatic finishes in golf history occurred at the fiftieth Masters when Jack Nicklaus, forty-six years old and five shots back going into the final round, came back to win his record sixth Masters. Nicklaus played the last ten holes in 7 under par, including a record-tying thirty strokes on the back nine. Nicklaus's putting made the difference as he took only thirteen putts on the last ten holes. Tom Kite and Greg Norman had a chance to catch him at the seventy-second hole, but couldn't prevent Jack from winning his twentieth major tournament. Jack Nicklaus had transformed himself from a portly pretender to Arnold Palmer's throne in the early 1960s to a revered champion who marched up the final fairway to thunderous applause in the cathedral of pines at Augusta. When Jack won his first Masters in 1963 at age twenty-three, his green jacket was a 44 long. The trimmed down Nicklaus of the eighties put on a 42 regular green jacket to accept what would doubtless be his last major Tour victory trophy.

# April 14

## 1936: Birthday of Bobby Nichols, Winner of 1964 PGA Championship

A near-fatal car accident almost ended Bobby Nichols's golf career before it began. He injured his pelvis, spleen, liver, and one kidney when he was a junior in high school and, after receiving inspirational letters from Ben Hogan, who almost met his own end in a 1949 automobile collision, won two state high-school golf championships, then went to Texas A&M on a football scholarship. The native of Louisville, Kentucky, turned professional in 1959 and joined the PGA Tour in 1960, where he won over $1.47 million, including an $18,000 payday when he won the PGA Championship at the 6,851-yard, par-70 Columbus Country Club in Columbus, Ohio, in 1964.

Nichols opened that tournament with a round of 64, then shot rounds of 71, 69, and 67 to win by three strokes over Jack Nicklaus, who shot a final-round 64, and Arnold Palmer. Nichols's 72-hole total of 271 is still the lowest 72-hole total in PGA Championship history.

Nichols was named to the 1967 Ryder Cup team and won the Canadian Open in 1974. He joined the Senior Tour in 1986 after winning seven Tour victories from 1962 through 1970. In 1962, Nichols received the Ben Hogan Award for his courageous recovery from the severe injuries he had incurred as a teenager.

# April 15

### 1990: Gary Player Wins His Third PGA Seniors' Championship

Gary Player shot a 7-under-par 281 at PGA National to win his third PGA Seniors' Championship over a strong field that included Chi Chi Rodriguez, Jack Nicklaus, Lee Trevino, Arnold Palmer, and Bob Charles. Player won the event in 1986 and 1988, the only golfer to win three Senior PGA titles since the Senior Tour began in 1980. Sam Snead won a record six titles and Eddie Williams three straight, prior to 1980.

Player won twenty-one regular Tour events after joining in 1957. He had $1,811,251 in career earnings, then joined the Senior Tour in 1985 and has won over $3 million. Player, who has won over 125 tournaments worldwide, was the leading PGA money winner in 1961.

# April 16

### 1972: Jane Blalock Wins Colgate–Dinah Shore

Jane Blalock won the richest tournament on the LPGA Tour by shooting a 54-hole total of 213 to pick up $20,000 at the Colgate–Dinah Shore Winner's Circle. Blalock, also won the Suzuki International, Angelo's 4-Ball Championship, the Dallas Civilian Open, and the Lady Errol Classic and won a total of $57,323 in 1972.

Miss Blalock attended Rollins College before joining the Tour in 1970 and being named Rookie of the Year. She won twenty-nine LPGA events and over $1 million in her professional career. In 1969 she began an incredible streak of 299 tournaments without missing a cut. The streak ended in 1980.

# April 17

### 1960: Sam Snead Wins Seventh Greater Greensboro Open

Sam Snead shot a 72-hole score of 270 to win the Greater Greensboro Open for the seventh time. The event was held at the 6,630-yard, par-71 Starmount Forest Country Club, where Snead had won the first Greater Greensboro Open in 1938. He also won it in 1946, 1949, 1950, 1955, and 1956. He won the tournament again in 1965 at the age of fifty-two years and ten months, making him the oldest golfer to win a regular PGA Tour event. He holds the record for wins in a single tournament (eight) and is also credited with six wins in the Miami Open.

# April 18

### 1993: Tom Wargo Wins PGA Seniors' in Play-off With Bruce Crampton

Tom Wargo defeated Bruce Crampton on the second play-off hole after they tied at 275 in the PGA Seniors' Championship on the 6,718-yard, par-72 Champion Course at the PGA National Golf Club. The fifty-year-old Wargo, the 1992 PGA Club Pro of the Year from Centralia, Illinois, was a surprise winner in a field that included Tom Weiskopf, Jack Nicklaus, and Lee Trevino. Wargo, a steel and auto worker before turning to golf in the early 1970s, used a hot putter to move ahead after the third round. Crampton birdied the last two holes on the final round to fire a 66 and force a play-off. Crampton put his tee shot in the water on the second extra hole and Wargo went on to win. He continues to thrive on the Senior Tour and was sixth for the year in 1994 with over $1.1 million in earnings.

# April 19

### 1992: Lee Trevino Shoots a Second-Round 64 and
### Goes On to Win His First PGA Seniors' Championship

Lee Trevino shot a tournament-low 64 during the second round of the PGA Seniors' Championship on the Champion Course at PGA National and went on to win the event by one stroke over Mike Hill with a 10-under-par 72-hole total of 278. Trevino, fifty-two years old, earned the first $100,000 winner's share in PGA Senior Tour history. When the first PGA Seniors' Championship on the Senior Tour was held in 1979, the total purse was $100,000 and winner Don January's first prize was $15,000.

Trevino became the first player to win over $1 million in a year on the Senior Tour by winning the Vantage at the Dominion, the Tradition, the PGA Seniors' Championship, the Las Vegas Senior Classic, and the Bell Atlantic Classic. Besides being first in money winnings, he was first in scoring with a 69.46 average. By 1993, he had won more money in his five years on the Senior Tour than he had in twenty-two years on the regular PGA Tour.

# April 20

### 1969: Kathy Whitworth Wins Lady Carling Open, Her Fourth Consecutive LPGA Tournament Win

Kathy Whitworth shot a 54-hole total of 210 to win the Lady Carling Open in Georgia, her fourth consecutive LPGA Tour win. She had previously won the Orange Blossom Open, Port Charlotte Invitational, and Port Malabar Invitational. Miss Whitworth won six tournaments in 1969, the others being the Patty Berg Classic and Wendell-West Open. In 1965 and 1967, she was Associated Press Woman Athlete of the Year. Whitworth won a total of eighty-eight Tour victories, the most of any golf professional. She was inducted into the LPGA Hall of Fame in 1975.

# April 21

### 1991: Jack Nicklaus Wins His First PGA Seniors' Championship

Jack Nicklaus, age fifty-one and playing in his second PGA Seniors' Championship, shot a 17-under-par 271 to win by six strokes over Bruce Crampton. Since turning fifty in January of 1990, Nicklaus, who continues to play the regular PGA Tour, had won four of his six senior events up to this point. This was the fifth time Bruce Crampton had finished runner-up in a major championship—each time to Nicklaus. Nicklaus's 66, 66, 69, and 70 for 271 was ten strokes less than the previous tournament best on the PGA National Golf Club's Champion Course. The 1991 event was played from a distance of 6,630 yards, and the first prize was $85,000 out of a purse of $550,000.

# April 22

## 1984: Billy Casper Wins Senior PGA Tour Roundup, Fourth Career Senior Tour Win

Billy Casper, a native Californian who won fifty-one PGA Tour victories and $1,691,584 before joining the Senior Tour in 1981, won his fourth Senior Tour event by shooting a 14-under-par 54-hole total of 202 to win $30,000 at the Hillcrest Golf Club in Sun City West, Arizona. Casper won a total of $170,796 in 1984 to place him seventh in Senior Tour earnings. By 1984 the Senior Tour had grown from two events in its inaugural year in 1980 to twenty-four events. Total prize money had risen from $250,000 in 1980 to $5,156,000. By 1994 there were forty-four PGA Senior Tour events and total official prize money was $28,850,000. Through 1993, Billy Casper had won nine tournaments and $1,581,203.

Casper's fifty-one PGA Tour victories places him in an elite group behind Sam Snead (81 Tour wins), Jack Nicklaus (70), Ben Hogan (63), Arnold Palmer (60), and Byron Nelson (52). Billy had his best Tour earnings years in 1966 and 1968 when he led in winnings. He tied for the lead in number of tournaments won in 1964 with Jack Nicklaus and Tony Lema (4 wins) and led in 1966 (4), 1968 (6), and 1970 (4). He also tied in 1969 when he, Dave Hill, Jack Nicklaus, and Raymond Floyd each won three PGA Tour events. Casper was named PGA Player of the Year in 1966 and 1970. He won the Vardon Trophy for the least strokes per round average in 1960, 1963, 1965, 1966, and 1968. He was a member of the Ryder Cup team in 1961, 1963, 1965, 1967, 1969, 1973, and 1975 and was nonplaying captain in 1979. He won the U.S. Open in 1959 and 1966 and was inducted into the PGA Hall of Fame in 1982.

# April 23

### 1993: Sean Murphy Opens With a 73, Then Rallies
### to Win Central Georgia Open on the Nike Tour

Sean Murphy opened with a 73, then smoked a 61 on the second round, and finished with a 71 and a total of 205 to win the Nike Tour's Central Georgia Open at the River North Country Club, a 6,714-yard, par-72 layout in Macon. By year's end the twenty-eight-year-old Murphy regained his right to play on the PGA Tour by finishing among the top five money winners on the Nike Tour. Murphy had played on the PGA Tour in 1991 but lost his card and had to go back down to golf's "minor leagues," a circuit originally set up as the Hogan Tour. Nike took over sponsorship of this satellite tour in August of 1992.

# April 24

### 1975: Duck!

On this date in 1975, Jim Tollan's drive at the fourteenth hole, called the Mallard, of England's Scunthorpe Golf Club struck and killed a female mallard duck in flight. In another, more bizarre incident, W. S. Robinson, the professional, killed a cow with his tee shot at the eighteenth hole at the St. Margaret's-at-Cliffe Golf Club, Kent, England, on June 13, 1934. The cow was standing in the fairway about one hundred yards from the tee.

# April 25

## 1916: Birthday of Jerry Barber, Winner of 1961 PGA Championship

Jerry Barber, at 5 feet 5 inches tall, was one of the smallest players on the PGA Tour, which he joined in 1948 after turning professional in 1942. He won a total of eight Tour victories before joining the Senior Tour in 1980. Barber's best year was 1961, when he won the PGA Championship at the Olympia Fields Country Club in his native Illinois. He was voted PGA Player of the Year and captained the 1961 American Ryder Cup team, which defeated Great Britain at Royal Lytham and St. Annes in St. Annes, England. The format of the Ryder Cup was changed for the first time that year, as the traditional 36-hole matches were changed to 18-hole matches, thus doubling the number of total points to 24. The U.S. team won 14½ to 9½.

In the final round of the PGA Championship on the 6,722-yard, par-70 Olympia Fields layout, the forty-five-year-old Barber trailed Don January by four shots with three holes remaining. Barber, playing in the same group as January, sank putts of twenty feet for a birdie, forty feet for a par, and sixty feet for a birdie to tie at 277. In the 18-hole play-off, Barber shot a 67 to defeat the thirty-one-year-old January by a single stroke to win the $11,000 winner's share.

Jerry Barber died of heart failure on September 23, 1994. One of his quips as he continued to play competitive golf: "The older you get, the easier it is to shoot your age."

# April 26

## 1992: Lee Trevino and Mike Hill Win Second Straight Legends

Lee Trevino teamed with Mike Hill to win their second consecutive Liberty Mutual Legends of Golf title. Thirty PGA Senior Tour teams competed for $770,000 in prize money at the Barton Creek Country Club in Austin, Texas. Trevino and Hill fired a 62, 64, 60, and 65 for 251 to win by two strokes over S. C. Snead and Bobby Nichols. Bob Toski and Mike Fetchik shot 66, 68, 66, and 68 for 268 to win the Legendary Champions (sixty-and-over division) title. Trevino and Hill had won the previous year with a score of 252.

# April 27

## 1899: Birthday of Leo Diegel, 1928 and 1929 PGA Champion

Leo Diegel, a native of Detroit, Michigan, was sometimes called Third Round Diegel because of his tendency to fade in the later stages of critical tournaments. He did win consecutive PGA Championship titles in 1928 and 1929 and won thirty tournaments on the PGA Tour, placing him fifteenth on the all-time list. Diegel led the PGA Tour in wins in 1925 (5) and was selected to the Ryder Cup team three times (1927, 1929, 1931). Considered one of the best golfers of his day, he was noted for his unorthodox ball-striking styles, especially his putting stroke, where his elbows were bent to an extreme gull-winged position with forearms horizontal. Diegel, who died in 1951, was elected to the PGA Hall of Fame in 1955.

# April 28

## 1966: Birthday of John Daly, Surprise Winner of 1991 PGA Championship

John Daly came out of nowhere to capture the imagination of the golf world by winning the 1991 PGA Championship on the Pete Dye–designed, 7,295-yard, par-72 Crooked Stick golf course in Carmel, Indiana. Daly, then only twenty-five years old, was an alternate when he was notified the day before the tournament that Nick Price had dropped out to attend the birth of his child. Other alternates preceding Daly had declined the last-minute invitation. Daly drove all night to reach the tournament, had no time for a practice round, had never played Crooked Stick, and promptly shot a 69. He then fired rounds of 67, 69, and 71 to post a 12-under-par total of 276, which earned him a 3-stroke win over Bruce Lietzke.

Daly, who was born in Sacramento, California, but grew up in Arkansas, attended the University of Arkansas, turned professional in 1987, and completed Qualifying School in 1990. He won the only Ben Hogan Tour Qualifying Tournament in 1990 and finished ninth in Hogan Tour earnings with over $64,000 in purses. For his efforts in 1991, Daly was named PGA Tour Rookie of the Year. Daly, a big hitter who often drives the ball well over three hundred yards, draws huge galleries wherever he plays. Time will tell whether his early promise is realized as he attempts to overcome problems with alcohol and other personal issues.

# April 29

### 1947: Birthday of Johnny Miller, Player of the Year in 1974

Johnny Miller planned to caddie at the U.S. Open in 1966, but due to a last-minute withdrawal by one of the players, he was able to play. The nineteen-year-old finished eighth and was low amateur. After attending Brigham Young, he turned professional in 1969 and made his professional breakthrough in 1973 with a dramatic 63 on the last day to win the Open at Oakmont.

The year 1974 was a great one for Miller. He started out the year by winning the first three PGA events—the Bing Crosby Pro-Am, Phoenix Open, and Dean Martin–Tucson Open. He later won the Heritage Classic, Tournament of Champions, Westchester Classic, World Open, and Kaiser International to lead the Tour in earnings ($353,021) and tournaments won (8). Miller was named the PGA Player of the Year. No one has won as many events in one PGA Tour season since.

In 1976, Miller staged a dramatic comeback in the British Open at Birkdale. He shot a 66 on the final round to pass Seve Ballesteros and win by six strokes. By this time, Johnny was twenty-nine years old and had seventeen Tour victories. The combination of a major slump from the end of 1976 to 1980, when he won the Inverrary, and injuries, which forced Miller off the Tour by 1990, kept him from greater achievements. His last Tour victory was at the 1994 AT&T Pebble Beach National Pro-Amateur, which he also won in 1974 and 1987. Recurring knee problems requiring arthroscopic surgery are likely to limit future play.

# April 30

## 1950: Babe Zaharias Wins Weathervane Women's Open at Pebble Beach

Babe Zaharias fired a 36-hole total of 158 to win the Weathervane Women's Open at Pebble Beach. The Weathervane was part of a series of events called the Weathervane Transcontinental Tournament with stops in San Francisco, Chicago, Cleveland, and New York. These tournaments, comprising five of the eleven LPGA tournaments in 1950, were sponsored by Weathervane Sports Clothes for women. Alvin Handmacher, who owned the company, agreed to put up a total of $15,000 in prize money and an additional $5,000 bonus incentive for the Weathervane series winner.

Rhonda Glenn, in her account at the nascent LPGA in *The Illustrated History of Women's Golf,* detailed the reaction of Bettye Mims Danoff: "I loved that Weathervane Tour. Mr. Handmacher organized that Tour and flew me to New York to model his golf clothes. I stayed in the Pierre Hotel and went to Broadway shows. That was quite a thrill."

But Babe Zaharias was the star of the LPGA Tour. She won five events in 1950 and led the Tour in winnings with $14,800. She made much more than that in off-the-course revenues from exhibitions, endorsements, and other business dealings.

Byron Nelson recalled Babe Zaharias, a great natural athlete, in his biography, *How I Played the Game:* "In Texas we call someone like Babe Zaharias 'a piece of work,' but brash as she could be at times, she sure did have the talent to back it up. . . . When she took up golf, people said, 'This is one game the Babe won't be so good at.' But they didn't know her. She practiced till her hands bled and goodness alive, she could play."

The LPGA Tour, with the possible exception of Nancy Lopez, has never had another gate attraction like Babe Zaharias, who died of cancer in 1956. While fighting the disease, she received the first Ben Hogan Trophy in 1954, awarded annually by The Golf Writers Association of America to the individual who has continued to be active in golf despite a physical handicap.

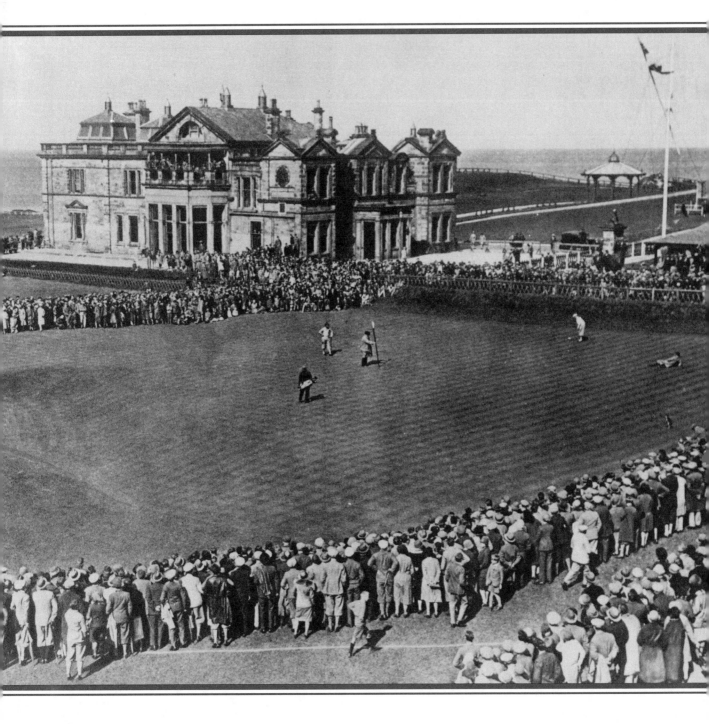

# May 1

## 1977: Gene Littler Wins the Houston Open, His Last Win on the PGA Tour

Gene Littler fired a 72-hole total of 276 on the 6,939-yard, par-72 Woodlands Country Club course to win the Houston Open in Woodlands, Texas. Littler, a smooth-swinging San Diegan, joined the Tour in 1954 and had twenty-eight wins prior to this event, his last Tour victory. He joined the Senior Tour in 1981 and has won over $2 million, more than he earned in twenty-six years on the regular professional circuit. Littler was inducted into the World Golf Hall of Fame in 1990 and the PGA Hall of Fame in 1982.

In his early days, after winning the 1953 U.S. Amateur and then the San Diego Open, Littler was heralded by some as the next Ben Hogan. The noted golf writer Herbert Warren Wind observed: "Littler had his critics, who felt that he did not hit the ball long enough and that he also lacked the inner fire to become an outstanding champion, but his supporters believed that his pacific temperament was actually one of his most reliable assets, as intrinsic to his success as the beautifully slow tempo of his simplified, grooved swing and his unhurried putting stroke."

Littler had a fine career, but he never reached the pantheon of great golfers such as Snead, Hogan, Nelson, Nicklaus, Jones, and Palmer.

*Opposite:* Saint Andrews Club House, circa 1927

# May 2

## 1904: Birthday of Bing Crosby, Benefactor of American Golf

Bing Crosby was born in Tacoma, Washington, and became addicted to golf when he was making a film called *The King of Jazz* in 1930. With other musicians, he played at Lakeside in Los Angeles, a club where he eventually won many championships. Crosby reduced his handicap to 2 and played in the 1952 British Amateur at St. Andrews. He started out with two 3s on his first round.

The Bing Crosby Pro-Am Tournament is now a fixture on the PGA Tour. The event, sponsored by Crosby, started out in Rancho Santa Fe in 1937 but was moved to the Monterey Peninsula when Crosby moved north and joined the Cypress Point Club after World War II. Crosby is one of the few golfers to have scored a hole in one on the 233-yard, par-3 sixteenth hole at Cypress Point, one of the best golf courses in the world. A carry over the Pacific Ocean on the tee shot, the sixteenth at Cypress Point is described in *The World Atlas of Golf*, edited by Pat Ward-Thomas and Iain Parsons: "Requires a full driver off the back tee and carry all the way; the sixteenth at Cypress Point strikes fear into the hearts of the greatest golfers, and even pros play safely to the left." The crooner could not only sing "White Christmas," but he could also play golf.

The spectacular setting of the Monterey Peninsula and the celebrities who played in the tournament provided a perfect format for television. The Crosby was one of the first tournaments to be televised in the United States, and with the advent of the charismatic Arnold Palmer in the late 1950s, golf had a major box-office attraction. Not only did the Dodgers and the Giants seek their manifest destiny in California beginning in the late 1950s, many golfers did too.

Today the Crosby is still played on the Monterey Peninsula on a rotation of courses including Pebble Beach, Spyglass, and Poppy Hills. The event was renamed the AT&T Pebble Beach National Pro-Am in 1986. In the quaint old days when the tournament began, the first tournament was canceled for three days because of heavy rains, and only one round could be played. Sam Snead won with a score of 68 and Crosby took a financial beating. Bing still wrote a check for the entire purse, endearing him to the assembled participants.

Bing Crosby died of a heart attack on a golf course in Spain on October 14, 1977. An appropriate place of departure for a class act.

# May 3

## 1992: Danielle Ammaccapane Takes Centel Classic, Wins Three Tournaments in 1992

Danielle Ammaccapane shot a 275 to win the $180,000 first prize in the Centel Classic, the richest tournament on the LPGA Tour in 1992. Ammaccapane, winner of the 1985 U.S. Public Links title and a member of the 1986 Curtis Cup team, attended Arizona State where she won the 1985 NCAA Women's Championship. Danielle turned professional in 1987. She also won the Standard Register Ping and Lady Keystone Open in 1992 and in 1993 finished with $191,165 in earnings in all events. Ammaccapane's first tournament win came in 1991 in the Standard Register Ping. By the end of 1994 she had won four LPGA tournaments and over $1.6 million.

# May 4

## 1959: Birthday of Bob Tway, Winner of 1986 PGA Championship

Bob Tway had a dream season in 1986, his second year on the PGA Tour, when he won four tournaments, including the PGA Championship, and finished second in money winnings with a total of $652,780. He was named PGA Player of the Year and finished first in total wins.

Tway shot 64 in the third round of the 1986 PGA Championship, held at the 6,982-yard, par-71 Inverness Club in Toledo, Ohio. This put him in contention with Greg Norman, who had shot 65, 68, and 69 the first three rounds. Tway began the final round four strokes behind Norman, caught him on the back nine, and became the first player in modern history to win the PGA Championship with a birdie on the seventy-second hole when he holed a shot from a greenside bunker. Tway shot a 1-under-par 70 to Norman's 76 on the final round to win by two strokes.

Bob Tway, a native of Oklahoma City, attended Oklahoma State University, where he was a three-time golf all-American. He was a member of the 1978 and 1980 Oklahoma State NCAA Golf Championship teams and the 1981 winner of the Fred Haskins trophy as outstanding collegiate player.

# May 5

## 1976: Fred McLeod, Winner of 1908 U.S. Open, Dead at the Age of 94

Fred McLeod was born in North Berwick, East Lothian, Scotland, in 1882 and emigrated to the United States in 1903. He won the Western Professional tournament in 1905 and 1907, then, carrying only seven clubs, won the U.S. Open at the Myopia Hunt Club in South Hamilton, Massachusetts in 1908. McLeod and Willie Smith tied at 322 during regulation play, but McLeod bettered Smith in the 18-hole play-off, 77 to 83. The high scores were indicative of Myopia's difficulty. The course, designed by club member Herbert Leeds, was the site of the Open in 1898 and 1905 also. No one ever scored better than 314 for seventy-two holes in a U.S. Open at Myopia.

McLeod, a small man at 118 pounds, won the St. Petersburg Open in 1924, the Maryland Open in 1927, and the PGA Seniors' in 1938. McLeod played in twenty U.S. Opens and finished in the top ten eight times. He had an excellent short game and continued to use a 9-iron out of the bunkers even after the wedge became popular. Fred McLeod and Jock Hutchison were the traditional starting twosome at the Masters for many years. This, along with the green coat, par-3 tournament, and other traditions helped make the Masters a colorful and memorable event.

# May 6

## 1936: Great Britain and Ireland Tie the United States in the International Match for the Curtis Cup

The first tie occurred in the Curtis Cup match, 4½ to 4½ as Miss Jessie Anderson of the British Isles sank a 21-foot putt on the last hole to defeat Mrs. L. D. Cheney, 1-up in the final match. The teams had tied in the foursomes with 1½ points each. In the singles, Glenna Collett Vare, Charlotte Glutting, and Maureen Orcutt won for the United States. Mrs. Andrew Holm and Mrs. Marjorie Ross Garon scored for the British Isles. All the matches were played in a single day, at the King's Course, Gleneagles, Scotland. Miss Doris Chambers captained the British and Irish team, Mrs. Vare the United States. The two teams tied again, 9–9, in their 1994 meeting at the Honors Course in Tennessee.

# May 7

## 1989: Juli Inkster Wins Crestar Classic

Juli Inkster, who was born in Santa Cruz, California, in 1960, had an outstanding amateur career before joining the LPGA Tour in 1983. She was a college all-American at San Jose State in 1979, 1980, 1981, and 1982. In 1982 she won her third U.S. Women's Amateur in a row, joining Virginia Van Wie (1934), Glenna Collett Vare (1930), Alexa Stirling (1920), and Beatrix Hoyt (1898) as the only golfers to accomplish this feat. Inkster joined the Curtis Cup team in 1982 and won both her matches 7 and 6. She won the individual title in the 1982 Women's World Amateur Team Championship by four strokes with a 290. Juli also won the 1981 California State Amateur.

Juli Inkster turned professional in 1983 and won her fifth professional start, the Safeco Classic. She set a new LPGA season record for rookie earnings ($217,424) and was voted Rookie of the Year. Inkster's win in the Crestar Classic, after firing a 54-hole total of 210, was her last LPGA win before giving birth to her daughter, Hayley, in February of 1990. Earlier in 1989, she won the Nabisco–Dinah Shore for the second time.

Juli Inkster has been regaining her golfing form since her sabbatical at the end of 1989. A fierce competitor and an excellent putter who is also long off the tee, the 5-feet-7-inch Inkster won over $170,000 in all her events in 1993.

# May 8

## 1988: Juli Inkster Wins Crestar Classic in Four-Way Play-off

Juli Inkster, Rosie Jones, Nancy Lopez, and Betsy King found themselves in a four-way play-off as they each finished with 54-hole totals of 209 at the Portsmouth Sleepy Hole Golf Club, a 6,126-yard, par-72 layout in Virginia. On the par-5 play-off hole, Inkster hit a 220-yard 4-wood to within inches of the hole to tap in for an eagle and win $45,000, her first LPGA Tour win in twenty-one months. This was the fourth consecutive LPGA Tour event that had to be decided by a play-off. Inkster finished tenth on the LPGA Money List in 1988 with $265,319 in earnings.

# May 9

## 1870: Birthday of Harry Vardon, Winner of Six British Opens

Harry Vardon, popularizer of the Vardon grip and member of the Great Triumvirate of golf along with James Braid and J. H. Taylor, was born in Grouville, Jersey, England. He raised the level of the game of golf by winning a record six British Opens (1896, 1898, 1899, 1903, 1911, 1914) at a time when most of the best players in the world were from the British Isles. Three of Vardon's six championships were won after the introduction of the rubber-cored ball (the Haskell) in 1899, but it was with the gutty that he was supreme.

Vardon popularized the overlapping grip, used an open stance when a somewhat-closed stance was the preference of most golfers, and allowed his left arm to bend, straightening it again as he began his downswing, though the effect was smooth and graceful and his rhythm superb. All accounts agree on his ability, although a modest 5 feet 9 inches tall, to call on greater length with no apparent extra effort. Bernard Darwin, the noted British golf writer, observed: "I do not think that anyone who saw him in his prime will disagree as to this, that a greater golfing genius is inconceivable."

In his own book, *The Complete Golfer,* Vardon wrote that he used ten clubs, including an extra driver and brassie because shafts tended to break and clubheads tended to fly off in those days. His arsenal included a driving cleek, a light cleek, an iron mashie, niblick, and putter. He was always a fine putter but had more difficulty putting the Haskell.

Vardon learned to play golf while a caddie at Grouville near St. Helier in the Channel Islands. His brother Tom, who had become an assistant professional at St. Annes, advised him to take a post as the first professional at the Studley Royal Golf Club in Yorkshire (1890). He moved to Burg, and then in 1896 to Ganton. Here J. H. Taylor, then the reigning British Open champion, came to play him and was trounced 8 and 6 in match play. Vardon won his first Open that year, defeating J. H. Taylor in a play-off.

In 1900 Vardon ventured to the United States, where he played a series of exhibition matches at a time when golf was just gaining popularity in the New World. Vardon had an arrangement with the A. G. Spalding Company to promote its new ball, the Vardon Flyer, during his exhibitions. The company arranged a series of matches where he often played against the better ball of two other golfers. Vardon won over fifty matches, halved two, and lost thirteen during a tour that covered over twenty thousand miles from Canada to Florida.

Vardon and Taylor also entered the U.S. Open, adding prestige to the event. The first five U.S. Opens had been won by British-born players who had settled in the United States for at least part of the year. This was the first time it had drawn the best golfers across the Atlantic just to compete in the United States' National Championship, a less-prestigious event than the U.S. Amateur.

Vardon was successful in the U.S. Open, which was held at the Chicago Golf Club in Wheaton, Illinois. His 72-hole total of 313 bettered J. H. Taylor by two strokes. He returned again to play the Open at the Country Club in 1913, but was surprised by a twenty-year-old Massachusetts amateur named Francis Ouimet, who defeated Vardon and his countryman Ted Ray in a rain-soaked 18-hole play-off. Ouimet became a national hero and foreshadowed America's move to the forefront of competitive golf. Vardon competed in his last U.S. Open in 1920, at the age of fifty. He was ahead five strokes with seven holes to go at the Inverness Country Club, but took 35 shots on the final seven holes to lose to Ted Ray by a single stroke.

From 1903 until the end of his life on March 20, 1937, Vardon was the professional at the South Herts Club in North London. In his memory, the professional golfers of Great Britain and the United States compete annually for the Harry Vardon Trophy, awarded annually to the professional of each country possessing the best playing average.

# May 10

### 1964: Mickey Wright Captures Squirt Ladies' Open Invitational, Wins Eleven Tournaments, Money Title, and Vare Trophy in 1964

Herbert Warren Wind described Mickey Wright this way: "A tall, good-looking girl who struck the ball with the same decisive hand action that the best men players use, she fused her hitting action smoothly with the rest of her swing, which was like Hogan's in that all the unfunctional moves had been pared away, and like Jones's in that its cohesive timing disguised the effort that went into it."

Wright was at the top of her game in 1964 when, at the age of twenty-nine, she won the Squirt Ladies' Open, her second consecutive tournament win. The following week she won her third straight at the Muskogee Civitan Open, on her way to a total of eleven tournament wins and $29,800 in earnings, her fourth straight LPGA winnings title. She won the Vare Trophy for the fifth consecutive time with a stroke average of 72.46 per round.

In 1964, the total LPGA Tour prize money was $350,600 for thirty-three events. By 1993, total purses amounted to $400,000 for one event, the Health South Palm Beach Classic, and almost $20 million for the entire Tour. Mickey Wright won eighty-two tournaments in her career, yet is not among the top twenty-five all-time leading money winners on the LPGA Tour because she was a bit too early for the economic boom in women's golf.

# May 11

## 1894: The American St. Andrews, Charter Member of United States Golf Association, Moves to Grey Oaks

The oldest permanent golf club in the United States is reputed to be St. Andrews, which is now located at Ardsley-on-Hudson, north of New York City. The idea for a golf club was inspired by John Reid, who asked friend Robert Lockhart of New York to bring back some golf clubs and balls when he visited Scotland in 1887. Mr. Reid and some friends played on some makeshift courses, including a six-hole layout in an apple orchard on Palisades Avenue in Yonkers established in 1888. The club then moved, on May 11, 1894, to Grey Oaks, where they built a 9-hole course. The club was among the five charter members of the United States Golf Association, which was established December 22, 1894. The St. Andrews Golf Club, now an 18-hole venue, was moved to its present site, Mount Hope, in 1897.

# May 12

## 1991: Chi Chi Rodriguez Posts Fourth Senior Tour Win of Season, Captures Murata Reunion Pro-Am

Juan "Chi Chi" Rodriguez, the 5-feet-7-inch, 132-pound golf impresario from Bayamón, Puerto Rico, shot an 8-under-par 54-hole total of 208 to win the Murata Reunion Pro-Am at the Stonebriar Country Club in Frisco, Texas. The fifty-five-year-old Rodriguez won his fourth PGA Senior Tour victory of the season and totaled $794,013 in earnings for the year. Chi Chi, who has represented Puerto Rico on twelve World Cup teams and played on the 1973 U.S. Ryder Cup team, won a total of twenty-two Senior PGA Tour victories and over $5 million through the 1994 season. Rodriguez won the 1989 Bob Jones Award, given by the USGA for distinguished sportsmanship in golf. He was the inaugural inductee into the World Sports Humanitarian Hall of Fame.

# May 13

## 1973: Judy Rankin Wins Second Tournament in a Row, the Lady Carling Open

Judy Rankin shot a 54-hole score of 215 to win the $4,500 first prize in the Lady Carling Open. The previous week, she won the America Defender–Raleigh Classic. Rankin also won the Columbus Ladies' Open and the GAC Classic in 1973, finishing second in LPGA Tour earnings with $72,989. She also won the Vare Trophy for lowest scoring average (73.08 per round), and she won it again in 1976 (72.25) and 1977 (72.16). Rankin led the LPGA Tour in earnings in 1976 ($150,734) and 1977 ($122,890).

Rankin was a bit of a golf prodigy, growing up in the St. Louis area. At the age of eight, she had won four consecutive St. Louis Pee Wee titles, and at fourteen she was the youngest to win a Missouri State Championship. At the age of fifteen, she was the low amateur in the U.S. Open (1960). She joined the professional tour in 1962 but didn't win her first tournament until 1968, when she won the Corpus Cristi Civitan Open and captured the $1,875 first prize. She won a total of twenty-eight tournaments through 1979.

Rankin was the first woman to exceed $100,000 in earnings in one season, in 1976, when she was named LPGA Player of the Year. She also was named LPGA Player of the Year in 1977. A bad back and surgery eventually forced Judy Rankin from LPGA competition, but she now provides knowledgeable golf commentary on national television and in articles in golf magazines.

# May 14

## 1978: Lee Trevino Wins the Colonial National Invitation

Lee Trevino, the 5-feet-7-inch, 180-pound fierce competitor from Dallas, won his second Colonial by shooting a then-tournament-record 268 on the 7,142-yard, par-70 Colonial Country Club layout in Fort Worth, Texas. Trevino had previously won the tournament in 1976. Trevino's second win in the Colonial was his twenty-first career win. He startled the golf world in 1968 when he won the U.S. Open, the Hawaiian Open, and $132,127 in his second year on the tour. He led the tour in winnings with $157,037 in 1970, when he won the Tucson Open and National Airlines Open.

Lee Trevino became the first Senior Tour player to earn $1 million in one year when he joined that circuit in 1990. By the end of 1993 he was the all-time money winner in regular and Senior Tour with combined earnings totaling almost $7.4 million. Trevino, who had been raised in a shack without running water or electricity and had to leave school after the eighth grade to earn money, had come a long, long way. Trevino, a Mexican American, added a new and healthy dimension to the game of professional golf: another socioeconomic underdog who had broken the old caste system of a sport formerly dominated by the country-club set.

# May 15

## 1930: Robert T. Jones Jr. Wins in Team Match, Captains United States Walker Cup Team

The Walker Cup match was first held in 1922; the United States defeated Great Britain 8 and 4 at the National Golf Links of America in Southampton, New York. This men's amateur event was held the following year at St. Andrews, then returned to the Garden City Golf Club, Garden City, New York, in 1924. The contest has been held every other year, except for the World War II period (1939–46), since then.

The 1930 event was held at the Royal St. George's Golf Club in Sandwich, England. On the U.S. side were George Von Elm, George J. Voight, Dr. V. F. Willing, Roland Mackenzie, Donald Moe, Harrison Johnston, Francis Ouimet, and the playing captain, Bobby Jones. In 1928, Jones had won his singles match by a record 13 and 12 score in the match-play event. Representing Great Britain and Ireland in 1930 were Cyril Tolley, Roger Wethered, Rex Hartley, Tony Torrance, Sir Ernest Holdeners, James Stout, William Campbell, and John N. Smith. The U.S. team won easily, 10 and 2. Jones and Willing won 8 and 7 in foursomes, then the following day Jones won 9 and 8 in singles.

Jones, who went on to win the Grand Slam in 1930, then retired from competitive golf to practice law. Francis Ouimet became the captain of the U.S. Walker Cup team in 1932, an honor that he retained until 1951, when William P. Turnesa took over. The Walker Cup matches, though dominated by the U.S. teams to date, serve primarily as a venue for international friendship and understanding. The Royal and Ancient and the United States Golf Association organize the event.

# May 16

## 1982: Kathy Whitworth Wins 82nd LPGA Tournament, Ties Mickey Wright's All-Time Record

Kathy Whitworth shot a 54-hole total of 207 in the Lady Michelob tournament to win her eighty-second LPGA tournament, tieing Mickey Wright for the all-time record. Whitworth did not break the record until 1984 when she won the Rochester International on July 22 at age forty-five. She went on to win a total of eighty-eight Tour victories and has earned more than $2 million in LPGA events.

America's golf sage, Herbert Warren Wind, described Whitworth's game in his classic, *The Story of American Golf*:

> The difficulty is that Miss Whitworth's skills are not as directly visible as were those of great champions who preceded her. From tee to green her game lacks style and her swing does not have a pervasive rhythm. Her main weakness technically is a tendency to get into a flat position at the top of her backswing, where she also lays the clubhead off a little. She is able to get away with this shut-face position, for on the downswing she moves her left hip quickly out of the way and keeps her right elbow in close to her body. Because she is a good, strong athlete, Kathy hits the ball solidly with all the clubs and she gets her tee shot out a helpfully long distance. She has a lovely touch around the greens, but it is on the greens that she really comes into her own. It can be stated categorically that there has never been a better woman putter.

The words were written when Kathy Whitworth was in her prime. Like another great golfer, Nancy Lopez, she was unable to win the Women's Open. But Whitworth, who won the LPGA Player of the Year Award seven times, remains among the best of all women golfers.

# May 17

### 1992: Mike Hill Wins Doug Sanders Kingwood
### Celebrity Classic and Collects $52,500

Mike Hill shot a 36-hole total of 2-under-par 134 at the Deerwood Club in Kingwood, Texas, to win the Senior Tour's Doug Sanders Kingwood Celebrity Classic by two strokes. Hill, who joined the Senior Tour in 1989, also won the Tour's Vintage Arco Invitational and Digital Senior Classic to finish fourth on the money list with $802,423. Hill led the Tour in earnings in 1991 with $1,065,657. In only five years on the senior circuit, Hill had won fifteen tournaments and close to $4 million by the end of 1993. His Senior Tour play-off record is a spotless 5 and 0.

Hill, a native of Jackson, Michigan, whose older brother Dave is also on the Senior tour, attended Jackson (Michigan) Junior College and Arizona State prior to turning professional in 1967. He won three PGA Tour events and earned $573,724 on golf's "golden grind" before his successful transition to the Senior Tour. Hill grew up on a dairy farm adjacent to a golf course and started out as a caddie. He and Lee Trevino have been highly successful partners in the Liberty Mutual legends-of-golf tournaments, which they won in 1991 and 1992.

# May 18

## 1958: Wiffi Smith Wins Betsy Rawls Peach Blossom Open

Margaret C. "Wiffi" Smith of St. Clair, Michigan, was one of the fine amateurs to join the LPGA Tour in the 1950s as professional women's golf began to gain national attention and economic viability. Smith won the Mexican Women's title in 1953, was a semifinalist in the U.S. Women's Amateur in 1954 and 1955, won the British Ladies' and the French Ladies' in 1956, and played on the Curtis Cup team in 1956. That same year, at the age of nineteen, she turned professional and won her first LPGA tournament, the Dallas Open, on April 14, 1957, followed by the San Francisco Open in October. It seemed that Smith had a promising professional golf career ahead of her when she won the Betsy Rawls Peach Blossom Open in 1958. However, an illness curtailed her career and she soon left the Tour. She won only three more LPGA Tournaments, the Havana Open (1959), the Royal Crown Open (1960), and the Waterloo Open (1960).

# May 19

## 1887: Birthday of Jerome Dunston Travers, Winner of Four U.S. Amateurs and the 1915 U.S. Open

Jerry Travers first learned golf on his front lawn—the rather large one on his father's estate in Oyster Bay, Long Island. As a result of his family's wealth and social position, Travers had the benefit of early golf lessons from professionals, such as Alex Smith at the Nassau Country Club, and developed into a fine golfer at an early age. At the age of seventeen he defeated Walter Travis, three-time winner of the U.S. Amateur, then America's most prestigious golf tournament, in the finals of the Nassau Invitation Tournament. It was the start of a friendly rivalry between the young Travers and Travis, then forty-two years of age.

Travers went on to win the U.S. Amateur in 1907, 1908, 1912, and 1913. He opted not to defend his Amateur title in 1909 or in 1910. Travers also won the important Metropolitan Amateur in 1906, 1907, 1911, 1912, and 1913. The Metropolitan Golf Association was formed on April 14, 1897, shortly after the United States Golf Association was organized. The first Metropolitan Amateur, a match-play event, was held in 1899 and was won by H. M. Harriman, who later was the first American-born golfer to win the U.S. Amateur. He captured that title at Owentsia in 1899 when he defeated Findlay Douglas in the final by 3 and 2.

Travers won his first Metropolitan by 3 and 1 over Eben Beyers at St. Andrews in 1906. He then defeated Douglas, 8 and 7, the following year at the Nassau Country Club. In 1911, he defeated Oswald Kirby, 4 and 3, at Garden City, defeated Kirby again the following year, 9 and 8, at Baltusrol, and outgunned August Kamer, 8 and 7, at Fox Hills for his third straight Metropolitan in 1913. After Jerry Travers won the 1915 U.S. Open, he retired from competitive golf except for some Red Cross exhibition matches during World War I.

In Herbert Warren Wind's excellent account of Travers, whom he called "the Great Young Man," in *The Story of American Golf,* he comments on Travers's competitive tenacity as he went "cold as a halibut" during a match and, like Walter Hagen, whose on-course temperament was different, could always find a way to win. Wind concluded that "like most rich men's sons who have played a sport well, Travers could afford to play the game as if his next meal depended on winning."

# May 20

## 1984: Peter Jacobsen Wins the Colonial National Invitation, His Second Career Tour Win

Peter Jacobsen is a journeyman golf raconteur who is as well known for his mimicry of other players' golf swings and his musical group, Jake Trout and the Flounders, as he is for his golf game. Jacobsen was born in Portland, Oregon, in 1954 and turned professional in 1976 after attending the University of Oregon. His first Tour victory came at the Buick-Goodwrench Open in 1980 and his second at the Colonial, when he won in a play-off over Payne Stewart. Jacobsen won the Sammy Davis Jr. Greater Hartford Open in 1984 and finished tenth in earnings ($295,025). His biggest money year was 1990, when he won the Bob Hope Chrysler Classic by one stroke over Scott Simpson and Brian Tennyson and earned $547,279 for the year. His first Tour win in five years was a two-stroke victory in the 1995 Pebble Beach Pro-Am. The following week he won the Buick Invitational at Torrey Pines in La Jolla by shooting a 19-under-par 269. He has over $3.7 million in PGA Tour earnings to date.

Peter Jacobsen is also a golf-course designer, a golf television analyst, and a contributing editor to *Golf* magazine. His book, *Buried Lies, True Tales and Tall Stories from the PGA Tour*, coauthored with Jack Sheehan, provides witty and incisive insights into the world of professional golf.

# May 21

## 1932: The United States Wins the First Curtis Cup Match

The first Curtis Cup Match, an international match-play competition held between women amateur golfers from the United States and Great Britain, was preceded by informal matches leading up to the formal event. On May 25, 1905, a team of British ladies played against a group of American women who had entered the British Ladies' Championship at Royal Cromer. The American side won just one of the seven matches, but two of the team members, Harriot and Margaret Curtis of Manchester, Massachusetts, wanted to see regular matches of this kind continue. Financial considerations prevented a regularly scheduled competition from developing until both the Ladies' Golf Union in Britain and the United States Golf Association agreed to sponsor the event. The Curtis sisters offered the cup named in their honor, a simple silver bowl inscribed "To stimulate friendly rivalry among the women golfers of many lands." The Curtis Cup is still considered the world's premier international women's amateur golf event.

The American team attending the first match at the Wentworth Golf Club in England included Mrs. Edwin H. Vare, Jr. (Glenna Collett Vare), Mrs. O. S. Hill, Miss Virginia Van Wie, Miss Helen Hicks, Miss Maureen Orcutt, and Mrs. L. O. Cheney. Miss Marian Hollins captained the team and Mrs. Harley G. Higbie was the reserve. Miss Joyce Wethered was the playing captain for the British, whose team included Miss Wanda Morgan, Miss Enid Wilson, Mrs. J. B. Watson, Miss Molly Gourlay, Miss Doris Park, Miss Diana Fishwick, and Miss Elsie Corlett. The Americans won by a score of 5½ to 3½ in three foursomes matches and five singles.

The Curtis Cup matches are held every other year at alternate sites in the United States and Great Britain. The United States has won the vast majority of the matches, but in recent years the competition has become much closer. In 1994 the teams tied, 9–9, in the twenty-eighth Curtis Cup Match, and the GBI team retained the vessel.

# May 22

## 1891: The Founding of the Royal Melbourne

Royal Melbourne, Royal Adelaide, and Royal Sidney rank among Australia's and the world's greatest golf courses. Royal Melbourne now comprises the West and East courses, which were opened in 1926 and 1932 respectively. Constructed on seaside duneland studded with oaks, tea trees, dwarf reed, heather, and bracken, the current site of Royal Melbourne is its third location since Royal Melbourne, Australia's oldest golf club in continuous existence, was founded in 1891. Dr. Alister Mackenzie, the noted British golf architect who would later design Augusta National with Robert Tyre Jones Jr. (1933), Cypress Point with Robert Hunter (1928), and many other excellent layouts, was retained along with Australian amateur Alex Russell, the 1924 Australian Open winner, to design the West Course. Russell designed the East Course. Both courses were remodeled by Dick Wilson in 1959.

Championship events are now played on a composite course of the best holes from the East and West courses. This tradition began with the 1959 Canada Cup to avoid busy roads that cross each layout. Sam Snead holds the course record, 65, on this 6,946-yard, par-72 championship layout, which measures 3,174 yards on the par-35 front side, and a hefty 3,772 yards on the back. The course is noted for its dry, fast greens, most of which are well-bunkered. A variety of slopes and undulations can lead to four putts on the greens. Sam Sarrudhin, a golfer from Indonesia, had the misfortune of shooting a 105 on the composite championship course.

Many excellent golfers have come from Australia, including Greg Norman, Bruce Crampton, Bruce Devlin, Graham Marsh, Walter Travis, Peter Thomson, Jan Stephenson, and Kel Nagle, to name a few. Since the time that the Honorable Michael Scot, a Britisher, teed it up and won his first Australian Open in 1904, Australia has had a strong impact on the international golf scene.

# May 23

## 1946: Birthday of David Graham, Winner of 1981 U.S. Open

David Graham was born in Melbourne, Australia, and left school on his fourteenth birthday, against his father's wishes, to become a professional golfer. As Robert Sommers relates in his wonderful book *The U.S. Open: Golf's Ultimate Challenge,* Graham began his career as a shopboy at a Melbourne club, but he was dismissed for allegedly calling a member by his first name. At eighteen he became the head professional at a club in Tasmania, the island state off the southern coast, but in three years he accumulated debts of $6,000. A man of great integrity, Graham set out to pay back his creditors. He took a job with Precision Golf Forgings, an Australian golf-club manufacturer, and for eighteen months he never went out, lived on baked beans and fish-and-chips, and paid off his debts.

Independent, resolute, and determined, he had the self-discipline to succeed on the golf course. He won the World Cup Team Championship with Bruce Devlin in 1970. Graham joined the PGA Tour in 1971 and won eight tournaments and over $1.8 million including a $60,000 first-prize purse in the 1979 PGA, which was played at the Oakland Hills Country Club, a 7,014-yard, par-70 layout in Birmingham, Michigan. Graham shot a 65 on the final round to tie Ben Crenshaw at 272. He then holed putts of eighteen feet and ten feet to halve the first two holes. Graham birdied the third extra hole to win the championship.

Graham staged another dramatic charge in the 1981 U.S. Open, held at the Merion Golf Club in Ardmore, Pennsylvania. He played 2 under par the last five holes and carded a final-round 67 to win the tournament by three strokes over Bill Rogers and George Burns. In his final round Graham had four birdies, all from fifteen feet or less, missed three from inside ten feet, and six more from inside twenty. Three missed putts touched the hole. Graham had missed only one fairway and putted in regulation on all eighteen holes.

# May 24

## 1910: Birthday of Jimmy Demaret, First to Win Three Masters Titles

Jimmy Demaret, among the great golfers, such as Hogan, Nelson, Trevino, Zaharias, and Whitworth, to come out of Texas, was a nightclub singer when he won six consecutive tournaments in 1940, finishing with his first Masters. He won thirty-one PGA Tour victories from 1935 through 1957, placing him thirteenth on the all-time list along with Harry Cooper. Demaret was known for his colorful wit and style of dress. He used to wear old tam-o'-shanter hats flopped on his head and loud-colored outfits that often clashed. Demaret won his second Masters in 1947 and his third in 1950, the first golfer to win three. Sam Snead and Gary Player also won three, Arnold Palmer four, and Jack Nicklaus six. Demaret commented to Byron Nelson after the decision makers at Augusta National named its three bridges after Gene Sarazen, Ben Hogan, and Nelson, "Hey, I won it three times and I never even got an outhouse!"

Jimmy Demaret was a member of three Ryder Cup teams (1947, 1949, 1951) and never lost a match. He was in the Navy during World War II, but assigned to special services or "playing golf with the generals," as Al Barkow explains in his enlightening book *Golf's Golden Grind*. According to Barkow, "Jimmy Demaret was candid enough to say that he never got out of Sherman's, which was not a tank but a favorite bar in San Diego." Jimmy Demaret was co-owner with Jack Burke of the Champions Golf Club in Houston for many years. He was elected to the PGA Hall of Fame in 1960 and died in Houston in 1983.

# May 25

### 1948: Ben Hogan Wins the PGA Championship, Wins
### 36-Hole, Match-Play Final, 7 and 6

In his definitive survey, *The Story of American Golf*, Herbert Warren Wind made these observations about the 135-pound Ben Hogan: "Ben Hogan was perhaps the best golfer pound per pound who ever lived. He was a thrilling golfer. He expected perfection from himself and was always thinking in terms of the flawless shot, not the good shot. . . . The astonishing distance he gained was the result of perfect timing, exchange of weight, and the most incredible speed at which Ben accelerated his clubhead as it entered the hitting area." By 1946, Hogan, then thirty-four years old, was beginning to come into his own. The interruption of the Tour by World War II and the belated mastery of his own game, especially a tendency to hook, cost him some good years.

Hogan led the Tour in wins in 1946 (13), 1947 (7), and again in 1948 (10), so it was unfortunate for Mike Turnesa that he had to face "Bantam" Ben in the match-play final of the 1948 PGA Championship at the Norwood Hills Country Club in St. Louis. Hogan had endured a series of grueling matches over a span of five days. He defeated Jock Hutchison Jr. 1-up at the twenty-third hole in the 18-hole first round, Johnny Palmer 1-up in the 18-hole second round, Gene Sarazen 1-up, Chick Harbert 2 and 1, and Art Bell 2 and 1 in the 36-hole rounds. Turnesa had several close matches before meeting Hogan in the 36-hole final, which Ben won easily, 7 and 6. Hogan was 35 under for the 213 holes he played.

Hogan's PGA wins in 1946 and 1948 were the only ones that he would have. He later won the U.S. Open in 1948, making him the first to win the U.S. Open and the PGA Championship in the same year since 1922, when Gene Sarazen did it.

# May 26

### 1985: Hale Irwin Wins Memorial Tournament, Seventeenth Career Tour Win

Hale Irwin, who joined the PGA Tour in 1968 after graduating from the University of Colorado with a degree in marketing, won his seventeenth Tour tournament by carding a 72-hole total of 281 in the Memorial Tournament. Irwin won the 1967 NCAA men's individual golf championship and was also a two-time all–Big Eight selection as a defensive back at Colorado.

Irwin has won the U.S. Open three times—at Winged Foot (1974), Inverness (1979), and Medinah (1990). His win at Medinah came in a grueling 19-hole play-off with Mike Donald. irwin sank a 60-foot putt on the seventy-second hole to force the play-off. He became, at age forty-five, the oldest golfer to win the U.S. Open.

Irwin, who also won the Memorial in 1983, has won over $5 million on the PGA Tour. His best year was 1990, when he won the U.S. Open and the Buick Classic to earn $838,249. Earlier in his career, from 1975 through 1978, Hale Irwin played eighty-six tournaments without missing a cut. The only golfers to surpass this achievement are Jack Nicklaus (105) and Byron Nelson (113).

The Memorial Tournament is played on the Jack Nicklaus–designed (with Desmond Muirfield), 7,027-yard, par-72 Muirfield Village Golf Course in Jack's native state of Ohio. The tournament began in 1976 and was first won by Roger Maltbie. Nicklaus won the event in 1977 and 1984.

# May 27

## 1912: Birthday of Sam Snead, Won PGA Record 81 Tour Events

Samuel Jackson Snead was born in Hot Springs, Virginia, in 1912, the same year as two of his longtime rivals, Texans Byron Nelson and Ben Hogan. Snead, who had a great natural swing, became a professional in 1933 and amassed a men's Tour record of eighty-one PGA Tour wins over a span of twenty-nine years. He recorded eleven victories in 1950, eclipsed only by Byron Nelson's eighteen victories (1945) and Ben Hogan's thirteen (1946). Snead won the Greater Greensboro Open eight times and the Miami Open six times. He had at least one Tour victory for twenty-nine straight years, from 1936 to 1965. He won the 1965 Greater Greensboro Open at the age of fifty-two years and ten months, becoming the oldest player ever to win a Tour event. He received his largest paycheck for a Tour event, $11,000, at the Greensboro. He became the youngest professional to shoot his age when at age 67 he shot a 4-under-par 66 in the 1979 Quad Cities Open. For fifteen years he was in the top ten on the money list, leading the list in 1938, 1949, and 1950.

Great golfers are measured by the number of major tournament victories they have won. Snead won the Masters (1949, 1952, 1954), the PGA Championship (1942, 1949, 1951), and the British Open (1946). Even though Snead won seven majors and holds the all-time record for tournament wins, his failure to win the U.S. Open leaves a gap in his golf résumé. On many occasions Sam had an opportunity to win that tournament, but the fates, and perhaps his own golf-course management skills, weren't with him.

When Sam arrived at the U.S. Open in 1937, the Tour was looking for a new star with charisma who could fill the vacuum left when Bobby Jones, the all-American golf folk hero, retired after his Grand Slam in 1930. The youngest of five sons of a powerhouse worker, Snead had learned to play golf while roaming barefoot through the farm fields of his native Virginia with homemade clubs hewn out of sticks. After caddying at Hot Springs, Sam eventually landed a job at the pro shop at the Greenbrier resort in White Sulphur Springs, West Virginia. Legend has it that Snead shot a 61 at the Greenbrier while playing in a foursome that included Lawson Little, winner of both American and British Amateurs, and two former U.S. Open champions, Johnny Goodman and Billy Burke. After his success at Greenbrier, he received backing from some friends at home and joined the professional winter circuit. Snead won a professional event in Oakland with a 72-hole total of 270, then won the Bing Crosby Open.

Blessed with a fluid swing and tremendous power, Snead arrived at his first U.S. Open in Oakland Hills, a long course with tabletop greens, amidst great fanfare. He didn't disappoint as he fired a 72-hole 283, which was considered enough to win. Ralph Guldahl, a husky Texan, finished with a 69 as Sam waited in the clubhouse and passed Snead with a 281 total. Unbeknownst to Sam, this was the beginning of his demise in U.S. Open competition.

Snead finished fifth, two strokes behind the leader in the 1939 Open after firing a triple-bogey 8 on the final hole. In 1947, he sank a clutch birdie on the final regulation hole to tie Lew Worsham at 282. In the 18-hole play-off, both players were dead even through seventeen and within three feet of the hole and putting for pars on the par-4 eighteenth. Snead, thinking he was away, prepared to putt, but Worsham called for a measurement. Snead was indeed away, by one and a half inches, but, his concentration broken, he missed his putt while Worsham sank his for the one-stroke win. In the 1949 Open at Medinah, Sam needed to par the last two holes to tie Carey Middlecoff, who was in the clubhouse at 286. Snead bogeyed the seventeenth and lost by a stroke. Sam came in second for the fourth time in the U.S. Open in 1953 when he could only manage a 76 on the last round to fall six shots short of the winner, Ben Hogan. In 1955, Sam opened with a 79 at the Olympic Country Club in San Francisco and could only manage a tie for third after rallying with scores of 69, 70, and 74.

The closest Snead ever again came to winning the Open was in 1959, when he finished five strokes off the pace set by Billy Casper at Winged Foot. In 1953, Sam Snead was inducted into the PGA Hall of Fame with Byron Nelson and Ben Hogan, his contemporaries. However, Nelson had won his U.S. Open and Hogan had won four.

# May 28

## 1989: Bobby Nichols Wins Southwestern Bell Classic, After Play-off With Orville Moody

Bobby Nichols was born in Louisville, Kentucky, in 1936 and graduated from Texas A&M in 1958 with a business degree. An excellent athlete, he was offered a scholarship to A&M after winning several Junior titles. The golf coach at the time was the legendary Paul "Bear" Bryant, who also coached football.

Nichols joined the PGA Tour in 1960 and won eleven tournaments, including the PGA Championship (1964) and the Canadian Open (1974). He earned just under $1 million on the Tour before joining the Senior Tour in 1986. His best year on the Senior Tour thus far is 1991, when he won $252,764 and finished twenty-ninth in earnings. Through 1993, he had won a little over $1.5 million on the Senior circuit.

Nichols's 1989 win in the Southwestern Bell Classic, the result of a 7-under-par 54-hole score of 209 at the Quail Creek Golf and Country Club in Oklahoma City, earned him $45,000. He was tied with Orville Moody at the end of regulation but won the play-off. Nichols played on the 1967 Ryder Cup team and won 4½ out of a possible 5 points for the victorious U.S. squad.

# May 29

## 1903: Birthday of Bob Hope, Staunch Supporter of Golf and Founder of the Bob Hope Classic

Bob Hope was born in Ethan, England, and did not take up golf until he was twenty-four years old while in Cleveland on a vaudeville tour. He played a round at Highland Park in 1927, couldn't hit a thing, and gave up the game until 1930, when he was on tour with the Diamond brothers and became a devoted golfer. Hope got his handicap down to 4 in 1951 and played in the British Amateur at Porthcawl in Wales. He lost in the first round, 2 and 1, to "a man smoking a pipe" by the name of Charlie Fox.

In his various roles as fund-raiser and entertainer, Hope has played, by his estimate, almost two thousand golf courses worldwide. As part of his public demeanor, he would carry a golf club to his shows. He credits Gene Sarazen as one of the early American ambassadors for golf. In a tribute to Sarazen, Hope said, "Gene and those he played with and against were just as eager as the pros of today, but they understood that winning wasn't everything and the way you conducted yourself was just as important." Bob Hope founded the Bob Hope Desert Classic in 1960. The Classic had its origins in the Old Thunderbird Invitational, a 36-hole pro-am instituted in 1952 at the Thunderbird Ranch and Country Club. The Classic has a field of 136 professionals and 408 amateurs and is a 90-hole event played over four desert courses in the Palm Springs area. Amateurs are drawn for three-man teams early in the week and stay together for four days playing with a different professional each day. On the last day, the professionals play alone for the money. The amateurs pay a sizable amount of money to participate, and Hope has selected celebrity amateurs such as Dwight Eisenhower, Johnny Cash, Jack Lemmon, Clint Eastwood, Gerald Ford, Joe Garagiola, James Garner, among others.

The Classic has raised millions of dollars for charity, most notably the Eisenhower Medical Center, which is located in Palm Springs on eighty acres of prime real estate donated by Bob Hope.

# May 30

## 1937: Denny Shute Wins His Second Straight PGA Championship

Herman Densmore Shute was noted for the peaks and valleys of his career. In 1933, for example, as a member of the U.S. Ryder Cup team, he took three putts on the last green in the decisive singles match to lose to Syd Easterbrook at Southport, Lancashire. A few weeks later, at St. Andrews, he tied fellow American Craig Wood at the end of regulation play in the British Open, then won a 36-hole play-off with rounds of 74 and 76.

Shute had won the 1936 PGA Championship over a field of sixty-three other golfers at the Pinehurst Country Club in North Carolina. Denny managed to defeat Jimmy Thomson 3 and 2 in the final, even though Thomson often outdrove him by as much as sixty yards. Shute's approach shots and short game prevailed as he eagled the par-5 thirty-fourth hole to close out the match. The 1937 PGA Championship final pitted Denny Shute against Harold McSpaden at the Pittsburgh Field Club in Aspinwall, Pennsylvania. Shute again prevailed, 1-up, in a 37-hole overtime win. He became the fifth and last player to win two consecutive PGA Championships.

# May 31

## 1942: Sam Snead Wins First PGA Championship

Sam Snead won his first major tournament by defeating Jim Turnesa 2 and 1 at the Seaview Country Club in Atlantic City, New Jersey. Turnesa, a corporal in the U.S. Army, defeated Byron Nelson 1-up in three extra holes to reach the 36-hole match-play finals. Snead, who was to report to the Navy the day after the tournament, defeated Jimmy Demaret by a score of 3 and 2 in the semifinals.

Turnesa led 3-up after eighteen holes, but Snead tied the match on the twenty-fourth hole. Snead closed out the match at the thirty-fifth hole when he holed a 60-foot chip shot for a birdie. Snead would win two more PGA titles, in 1949 and 1951.

# June 1

## 1975: Kathy Whitworth Wins Fourth LPGA Championship

The LPGA Championship, established in 1955, is one of the four majors on the Ladies' Professional golf circuit along with the U.S. Women's Open (established in 1946), the Nabisco–Dinah Shore Winners Circle (1972), and the du Maurier Classic (1973). Miss Whitworth, who turned professional in 1958, won the LPGA title for her fourth and last time by shooting a 72-hole total of 288 to collect the $8,000 first prize. Mickey Wright is the only other golfer to win the LPGA Championship four times. Miss Whitworth won the Dinah Shore in 1977 and former majors the Titleholders (1965, 1966) and the Women's Western Open (1967). Although she holds the all-time LPGA tournament victory record with eighty-eight wins, she did not win the U.S. Women's Open or the du Maurier. Her six LPGA major wins places her behind Patty Berg (15), Mickey Wright (13), Louise Suggs (11), Babe Zaharias (10), and Betsy Rawls (8) on the all-time list.

*Opposite:* Arnold Palmer making his second shot on the tenth hole at the 1963 Los Angeles Open

# June 2

## 1953: Birthday of Craig Stadler, Winner of the 1982 Masters

Craig Stadler, a portly 210 pounds at 5 feet 10 inches and known as the Walrus, had an impressive golf résumé before he joined the Tour in 1976. He won the 1971 World Junior Championship, the 1973 U.S. Amateur, played on the 1975 Walker team, and was a two-time all-American at the University of Southern California (1974, 1975).

Craig won his first professional tournament in 1980 at the Bob Hope Desert Classic. His best year was 1982, when he won the Joe Garagiola–Tucson Open, the Kemper Open, the World Series of Golf, and the Masters. His Masters win came in a play-off with Dan Pohl, and his World Series victory was in a play-off over Raymond Floyd. Stadler almost blew his Masters chances when he lost a five-stroke lead with seven holes to play. He parred the first play-off hole to defeat Pohl, who had a final round 67 to tie in regulation.

Craig Stadler has won ten PGA tournaments and over $5 million on the Tour. He was a member of the 1983 and 1985 Ryder Cup teams.

# June 3

## 1904: Walter Travis Becomes First Foreigner to Win British Amateur

Walter Travis, called the Great Old Man in golf lore, was born in Maldon, Victoria, Australia, in 1862 and did not take up the game of golf until he was in his midthirties. Although he emigrated to America in his early years, he occupied himself with tennis, cycling, and other pursuits before he started playing golf at the Oakland course on Long Island in 1896.

A determined perfectionist, Travis became a student as well as a practitioner of the game. He read the instructional theories of Horace Hutchinson, Willie Park Jr., and others, then developed his own style, which featured a compact swing, excellent shot management, and a reliable pendulum putting stroke. He sported a beard, a Rough Rider–style hat, a long cigar, and had stoic but fierce determination as he would often outduel his longer-hitting opponents with a devastating short game.

By 1904 he had won the U.S. Amateur three times (1900, 1901, 1903) and was tied for runner-up in the 1902 U.S. Open. During an earlier trip to Britain in 1901, Travis played against ranking Scottish and English players, lost most of his matches, but identified the deficiencies in his game. After working on these, he decided to enter the British Amateur to be held at Royal St. George's in Sandwich, Kent, in 1904. The links at Sandwich measured 6,135 yards swept by winds off the North Sea. He arrived in Britain three weeks before the tourney to practice at St. Andrews and North Berwick before going down to Sandwich. Travis, who was having problems with his putting, borrowed a Schenectady putter, which had a shaft inserted in the center of a mallet-shaped head. The club, unconventional at the time, had been introduced by Mr. A. W. Knight, a resident of Schenectady, New York.

Travis defeated four opponents in the match-play event before reaching Harold Hilton, who, having won two British Opens and two Amateurs, was considered one of the best golfers in the world. Travis won their match, 5 and 4, after going out in 34. In the semifinals, Travis did away with Horace Hutchinson, then in his mid-forties and past his prime, by a score of 4 and 2 to reach the final. Hutchinson, a fluent golf essayist whose books Travis had studied, had last won the British Amateur in 1887. Hutchinson did finish second in 1903, but he was no match for Travis on this day.

Travis stunned the British by defeating Edward "Ted" Blackwell in the 36-hole final, 4 and 3. Walter J. Travis had become the first "foreigner" to win the British Amateur. There had been a conflict between Travis, his contingent of American friends, and the British during his stay at Sandwich. Travis's winning putt was actually greeted by silence. At the cup presentation Travis endured the one-hour recitation by Lord Northbourne on the wonders of British golf. After Northbourne briefly acknowledged that Travis had won, Walter gave a short, graceful acceptance speech and left, never to return to the British Isles. Later the Royal and Ancient barred Schenectady putters and similar implements from British tournaments.

Travis's last notable golf triumph was in the 1915 Metropolitan Amateur, where he dropped a 30-foot putt to close out the match. In his later years, he founded and edited *The American Golfer* magazine and designed and refurbished golf courses. Travis, who died in 1927, is a charter member of the PGA Hall of Fame (1940).

# June 4

## 1927: U.S. Wins First Ryder Cup Match

The Ryder Cup, a solid-gold trophy, was donated by Samuel Ryder, a wealthy British seed merchant, to be awarded in a series of matches between professionals of the American and British Golfers' Association. This donation followed a highly successful exhibition between the British and the Americans, which was won by the British 13½ to 1½ in England in 1926.

Ryder set forth certain terms for the competition including that (1) the matches would be played every other year on a home-and-home basis; (2) while both parties had to agree on the specific dates for each match, the host team could select the site and would be responsible for such arrangements and details as are normally the function of a sponsoring group; (3) the matches would consist of two days of play with the first being devoted to foursomes and the second to singles matches; (4) each member of the competing teams had to be a member of his country's PGA, and furthermore, had to be a native-born citizen of that country. The matches have been held continuously every other year since 1927 except for 1939 through 1946.

The members of the 1927 Ryder Cup Team included Leo Diegel, Al Espinosa, Johnny Farrell, Johnny Gooden, Walter Hagen, Bill Mehlhorn, Gene Sarazen, Joe Turnesa, and Al Watrous. The match was played at the Worcester Country Club in Massachusetts. The U.S. team was captained by Walter Hagen, and Ted Ray captained the British team, which included Aubrey Boomer, Archie Compston, George Duncan, George Gadd, Arthur Havers, Herbert Jolly, Ray Robson, Charles Whitcombe, and Ted Ray. The United States won 9½ to 2½.

The British won in 1929, 7 and 5, at the Moortown Golf Club in Leeds, England. The United States then won 9 and 3 at the Scioto Country Club in Columbus, Ohio, in 1931, and the British, capitalizing on their home-course advantage, regained the Cup at the Southport and Ainsdale Golf Club in Southport, England, by a score of 6½ and 5½ in 1933. This is the last time the British won the competition until 1957, when they defeated the United States 7½ and 4½ at the Lindrick Golf Club in Yorkshire, England. The United States then won every Ryder Cup match until 1985, when the European team, including British Isles and Continental golfers, won back the cup in 1985 at the Belfry in Sutton, Coldfield, England.

Since 1983, under a format that includes morning foursomes, afternoon four-balls, and singles contests that now total 28 points worth of matches, the competition has been extremely close, featuring many of the best golfers in the world. The Ryder Cup's popularity reflects how golf has truly become an international game. It also reflects a change in the balance of power in golf. Originally, at the turn of the century and into the 1920s, the British dominated golf, but the Americans, with players like Gene Sarazen, Walter Hagen, and Bobby Jones, were quickly closing that gap. The Americans then dominated into the 1970s with Byron Nelson, Sam Snead, Ben Hogan, Jack Nicklaus, Arnold Palmer, Lee Trevino, and many others leading the way. Now there is more parity between American and European golf with Ian Woosnam, Nick Faldo, Bernhard Langer, Seve Ballesteros,

Jose Maria Olazabal, and others as well known to international golf enthusiasts as American PGA Tour players. The Ryder Cup has proved an excellent way to showcase international golf on some of the best golf courses in the world.

Samuel Ryder took up golf at the age of fifty to improve his health, which had deteriorated due to overwork. He practiced six days a week for a year and reduced his handicap to 6. His legacy, the Ryder Cup matches, is one of the last great sporting events based on prestige rather than prize money.

# June 5

## 1925: Willie MacFarlane Wins U.S. Open in Play-off With Bobby Jones

Willie MacFarlane, born in Aberdeen, England, in 1890, was an unlikely participant in one of the most exciting finishes in U.S. Open history. MacFarlane had a graceful golf swing and was considered an excellent middle and short iron player. A quiet, pleasant man, he played golf for enjoyment and really did not like tournament competition. However, he was a consistent tournament winner from the end of World War I to the mid-1930s, winning nineteen tournaments.

The 1925 U.S. Open, with a final field of ninety-two golfers, was played at the Worcester Country Club in Worcester, Massachusetts. Entering the last hole, seven golfers were in contention including Bobby Jones, who had won the 1923 Open at the age of twenty-one and was runner-up in 1924, and Willie MacFarlane. Johnny Farrell, Francis Ouimet, Gene Sarazen, Walter Hagen, and Leo Diegel were among those who faded at the end as Jones finished with a 74 to tie MacFarlane, who hung on to shoot 78 on the final day for a 72-hole total of 291. MacFarlane had been ahead of Jones by three strokes with seven holes to play, but lost them all.

A play-off round of eighteen holes was played on June 5, and both golfers shot 75 to force another round in the afternoon, the longest U.S. Open play-off to date. Jones jumped off to a four-stroke lead at the end of the front nine, but MacFarlane rallied for a 33 on the back nine to finish with a 72 while Jones shot a 38 to lose by a single stroke. MacFarlane had not played in a U.S. Open since 1920 and had played only thirteen rounds since the previous October.

Jones later described his playoff defeat:

> In the second play-off I went pretty fast on the first nine and picked up four strokes. I thought I had won, sure. But Willie started back with a 2, got another deuce at the thirteenth, where I took a distressing 4, and caught me at the fifteenth, where I made the mistake of forgetting my friend, Old Man Par, and went to playing Willie; I tried to get home with my second on an uphill hole of 555 yards and break his back with a birdie 4, instead of which he got a par 5 and I a buzzard 6.

MacFarlane never won another major tournament. Jones would win his next Open the following year.

# June 6

## 1936: Tony Manero Wins U.S. Open at Baltusrol, the Only Major Victory in His Career

Tony Manero, an obscure professional from the Sedgefield Club in Greensboro, North Carolina, shot a record 282, including a 67 on the last round at Baltusrol, to win the U.S. Open by two strokes over Henry Cooper. After shooting 73 and 69 in the first two rounds, Manero shot a 73 in the third and trailed Cooper by four shots going into the final eighteen holes. Manero, paired with Gene Sarazen, the most famous Italian American golfer of all time, was calmed by the great champion as the galleries swarmed to watch Manero play the final holes. Manero's 282 eclipsed the old Open record of 286 by Gene Sarazen (1932, at Fresh Meadow) and Chick Evans (1916, at Minikahda). Manero played on the 1937 Ryder Cup team.

# June 7

## 1980: U.S. Wins Curtis Cup in Wales

The United States team won the twenty-first Curtis Cup match 13–5 for its seventeenth victory in the series, which was inaugurated in 1932. The contest was held at the St. Pierre Golf and Country Club in Chepstow, Wales. The American side, led by nonplaying captain Mrs. Nancy Roth Syms, included Lancy Smith, Lori Castillo, Patty Sheehan, Mary Hafeman, Brenda Goldsmith, Judy Oliver, Terri Moody, and Carol Semple. Patty Sheehan was undefeated in four foursomes and singles matches. All eight American players contributed at least one point to the victory. The British and Irish contingent was captained by Carol Comboy and included Mary McKenna, Claire Nesbitt, Tegwen Thomas, Gillian Stewart, Maureen Madill, Carole Caldwell, Jane Connachan, and Lynda Moore.

The American side extended its winning streak to thirteen matches in 1982 and 1984, then lost two consecutive matches in 1986 and 1988. The United States won in 1990, 14 and 4, at the Somerset Hills Country Club in New Jersey, but Great Britain and Ireland regained the Cup with a 10-to-8 win at the Royal Liverpool Golf Club in Hoylake, England, in 1992 and retained it with a 9–9 tie in 1994.

# June 8

### 1935: Golf Unknown Sam Parks Wins U.S. Open

In 1935, Oakmont, site of the U.S. Open, played 6,981 yards, with nearly two hundred bunkers and lightning-fast greens. It was and is the ultimate penal golf course, immediately penalizing an errant shot. Sam Parks, twenty-five years of age and the son of a Pittsburgh real estate businessman, was in contention after two rounds with a score of 150, 8 over par and four strokes behind the leader, Jimmy Thomson, then the longest hitter in golf. A former captain of the University of Pittsburgh golf team and the pro at the nearby Southern Hills Country Club, Parks had never won a professional tournament. But he knew Oakmont by heart and planned to play the course conservatively, avoiding bogeys wherever possible.

Parks shot a 73 on the third round to lead with 213 with Thomson, Walter Hagen, Denny Shute, Ray Mangrum, Henry Picard, and Gene Sarazen very much in contention. A large crowd gathered to cheer the local boy home, much as they would cheer Arnold Palmer years later. Parks did not disappoint them as he carded a final-round 76 to defeat Jimmy Thomson, who three-putted sixteen and seventeen, by two strokes.

Sam Parks had pulled off one of the biggest upsets in U.S. Open history. His winning total of 299 was the highest since Tommy Armour and Harry Cooper tied at 301 in the 1927 Open at Oakmont. A U.S. Open winner has not shot more than 299 since.

# June 9

## 1940: Lawson Little Defeats Gene Sarazen in U.S. Open Play-off

Lawson Little, a twenty-nine-year-old Stanford graduate and two-time winner of the British Amateur and U.S. Amateur (1934 and 1935), mastered the winds off Lake Erie to win the U.S. Open, 70–73, in an 18-hole play-off with Gene Sarazen at the Canterbury Golf Club in Cleveland, Ohio. Horton Smith shot a final-round 69 to finish second, one stroke behind at 288, at the end of seventy-two holes of regulation play. Six players, including Ed "Porky" Oliver, who shot a 287, were disqualified for starting their final rounds ahead of schedule in order to avoid an impending storm. Sam Snead, who would never win a U.S. Open, shot a disastrous 81 on the final round to balloon to a 295 finish, eight strokes off the pace.

# June 10

## 1933: Johnny Goodman Wins U.S. Open, Last Amateur to Win Title

Johnny Goodman, the last amateur to win the U.S. Open, fired a 287 at the North Shore Golf Club in Glenview, Illinois, to win the championship. Goodman shot a tournament low 66 on the second round, which tied Gene Sarazen's single-round record, then fired a 70 on the third round to lead by six strokes with a 54-hole score of 211. After shooting 4, 3, 2—a par, eagle, and birdie—on the first three holes of the final round, the twenty-three-year-old Goodman began to falter. But he held on to shoot a 76 and edge twenty-two-year-old Ralph Guldahl by one stroke. His 72-hole total was one stroke higher than the Open record held by Gene Sarazen and Chick Evans. Guldahl, who made up a nine-stroke deficit with fifteen holes remaining, needed a par 4 on the last hole to tie, but missed a four-foot putt after hitting an excellent niblick shot out of a greenside bunker.

Goodman was the fourth amateur to win the trophy. The others were Francis Ouimet (1913, at the Country Club), Chick Evans (1916, Minikahda), Bobby Jones (1923, Inwood; 1926, Scioto; 1929, Winged Foot; 1930, Interlachen). The closest an amateur has come to winning the U.S. Open since Goodman is Jack Nicklaus's fine effort in 1960 when he came in second to Arnold Palmer at Cherry Hills. Palmer had to shoot a 65 on the final round to win as he recorded a 280 to Jack's 282. Nicklaus, who was then twenty years old, was not an ordinary amateur. At age thirteen, he shot a 69 from the back tees at Scioto, a 7,095-yard course that had been the site of Bobby Jones's victory in the 1926 Open. In the 1960 World Amateur Team Championship at Merion, Nicklaus shot 66, 67, 68, and 68 for 269 to better Ben Hogan's 1950 U.S. Open winning score (at Merion) by eighteen strokes.

# June 11

## 1950: Hogan Comes Back From Automobile Accident to Win U.S. Open at Merion

Eight months after winning the 1948 U.S. Open, Ben Hogan was seriously injured in a car accident, preventing him from defending his championship in June 1949. After returning to the tour in January 1950, he tied Sam Snead in the Los Angeles Open, but lost to him in a play-off. He entered the U.S. Open, held at the Merion Golf Club near Philadelphia, and trailed the leader, Lloyd Mangrum, by two strokes after fifty-four holes. In those days, the final two rounds of the Open were played on the same day, and it was uncertain whether Hogan's legs, severely injured in the accident, could hold up under the strain.

George Fazio and Mangrum finished the final eighteen with 72-hole scores of 287. Paired with Cary Middlecoff, the defending champion, Hogan was playing behind the two leaders and was even with them as he prepared to tee off on the difficult 448-yard, par-4 final hole at Merion. He hit an excellent drive that carried 210 yards across an old stone quarry and reached a level spot over the crest of a hill. Hogan selected a 1-iron for his approach, normally a 4-iron for him, but due to his fatigue he needed much more club to reach a slick green protected by two bunkers to its right and another two on the left and forward. The 1-iron shot sailed true to the green, landing on the left forty feet from the pin. Hogan two-putted for par and a four-round total of 287. The following day he fired a 1-under-par 69 to defeat Mangrum (73) and Fazio (75) to win his second U.S. Open.

Hogan's 1-iron, which was stolen from his bag that day and later mysteriously turned up again in 1983, now resides in the United States Golf Association Museum, next to his portrait.

# June 12

### 1939: Byron Nelson Wins His Only U.S. Open in a
### Play-off With Craig Wood

The first three-way U.S. Open play-off since Ouimet, Vardon, and Ray in 1913 came about because Sam Snead bogeyed the par-4 seventeenth and then shot an improbable 8 on the 558-yard, par-5 eighteenth during the final round at the Philadelphia Country Club. Sam bogeyed seventeen when his second putt from six feet away stopped a full foot short. Teeing off on eighteen and needing only a six to tie, Snead hooked his drive, pushed a brassie into a bunker, duffed his third shot, which stayed in the trap, hooked his fourth shot wide of the green, reached the green in five, and three-putted.

Craig Wood, a handsome thirty-seven-year-old New Yorker from the Winged Foot Club in Westchester; Byron Nelson, a twenty-seven-year-old rising star from Texas; and Denny Shute, a thirty-four-year-old former British Open champion playing out of Huntington, West Virginia, teed it up for the 18-hole play-off. Shute shot himself out of the running with a 76, leaving Nelson and Wood to duel each other to the last hole. Nelson birdied the hole to tie Wood, who parred it after felling a spectator with his second shot. Both recorded 68s and returned to the first tee the next day for a second play-off round. Nelson, a master of long irons, took command of the match on the fourth hole when he rifled his second shot, a 1-iron, 210 yards and into the cup for an eagle 2. Byron went on to win the play-off and his only U.S. Open title 70–73.

The son of a Fort Worth, Texas, feed merchant, Nelson had won a crucial play-off earlier in his career when, at age fifteen, he edged Ben Hogan by one stroke to win the caddie championship of the Glen Garden Country Club. His first-place prize was a brand-new midiron.

# June 13

## 1893: Lady Margaret Scott Wins the First British Ladies' Amateur

Lady Margaret Scott, the dominant lady golfer of her day, won her first of three straight British Ladies' Amateur titles, 7 and 6, over Issette Pearson, at Royal Lytham and St. Annes Ladies' Course (nine holes). This was the first time the event was held, and thirty-eight golfers entered. Lady Margaret won again over Issette Pearson, 3 and 2, at Littlestone in 1894 and the following year defeated Ms. Lythgoe, 5 and 4, at Portrush. Lady Margaret Scott had an old St. Andrews swing, bringing the backswing in a corkscrew motion, with both elbows bent and the club nearly bouncing off the player's neck. After her third straight British Ladies' Amateur win, she retired from golf and gave up membership in the three clubs to which she belonged—Cotswold Hills, Cheltenham, and Westward Ho! She then married and became Lady Margaret Hamilton-Russell. Only Cecil Leitch and Enid Wilson share the distinction of having won three consecutive British Ladies' Amateur titles.

The Ladies Golf Union, formed on April 19, 1893, at the Grand Hotel, Trafalgar Square, London, was responsible for organizing the British Ladies' Amateur, which lent great stature to women's golf. It would take fifteen more years after the inaugural Ladies' Amateur for women to be allowed to compete in the Olympics.

# June 14

## 1952: Julius Boros Wins First of His U.S. Opens

Julius Boros surprised the experts, who had assumed that Ben Hogan would retain his U.S. Open title. Ben had won his third Open in four years at Oakland Hills in 1951 and started out with a pair of 69s in the 1952 Open, held at the 6,782-yard, par-72 Northwood Club in Dallas, Texas. Julius Boros, who had only been on the Tour since turning professional in 1950, fired 71 and 71 on the first two rounds. Hogan then skied to final rounds of 74, both held on the same day in blistering heat, while Boros shot 68 and 71 to win by four strokes with a 281. Ed "Porky" Oliver dropped a 50-foot putt for birdie on the last green to take second place, leaving Hogan in third at 286, one stroke behind. Boros won another U.S. Open in 1963 at the Country Club and won the PGA Championship in 1968.

# June 15

## 1980: Jack Nicklaus Wins His Fourth U.S. Open

Jack Nicklaus won his fourth U.S. Open at the Baltusrol Golf Club in Springfield, New Jersey, and set a new 72-hole record of 272 over the 7,076-yard, par-70 Lower Course, which has hosted the tournament seven times (1903, 1915, 1936, 1954, 1967, 1980, 1993). Nicklaus and Tom Weiskopf opened with 63, tieing Johnny Miller's 18-hole Open record set at Oakmont in 1973. Paired with Isao Aoki for the fourth consecutive day, Nicklaus played a 275-foot drive, a 2-iron, a sand iron, and a critical twenty-two-foot putt to birdie the infamous 636-yard seventeenth. Nicklaus then birdied the par-5 eighteenth to finish with a 68, edging Aoki by two strokes.

# June 16

## 1821: Birthday of Old Tom Morris, Winner of Four British Opens

The son of a letter carrier from St. Andrews, Scotland, "Old" Tom Morris became an apprentice to the legendary golfer and maker of clubs and balls, Allan Robertson, at a young age. Morris eventually worked his handicap down to that of his mentor, and the two of them became a formidable golf team. They squared off against the famous Dunn brothers from Musselburgh and won by two holes in match play after being down four with eight to play. The match was played over courses at Musselburgh, St. Andrews, and North Berwick.

A dispute arose between Robertson and Morris over the development of the new gutta-percha ball, which was introduced in 1848. Morris opted to go with the new technology, but Robertson, a featherie ball maker as was Tom at the time, was set against it. Tom went into his own ball and club business, then, in 1851, accepted a position as custodian of the links at the newly formed club at Prestwick. The British Open was inaugurated in 1860 by the Prestwick Golf Club, one year after Robertson's death. It was open only to professionals the first year, when Willie Park shot 174 over three rounds at the 12-hole course to defeat Old Tom Morris by two strokes. The event was open to amateurs the following year, and Tom Morris won his first of four contests. He also won in 1863, 1864, and 1867.

Old Tom's son, Tom junior, won five British Opens, four straight from 1867 to 1870, and another in 1872. This prompted his father to say, "I could cope wi' Allan [Robertson] mysel' but never wi' Tommy." Old Tom returned to St. Andrews to become greenskeeper at the Royal and Ancient, holding that position until he retired in 1904. His death in 1908 was an occasion for universal mourning at St. Andrews.

# June 17

## 1973: Johnny Miller Shoots a Final-Round 63 to Win the U.S. Open at Oakmont

Johnny Miller entered the final round of the U.S. Open at the Oakmont Country Club with 216 strokes for fifty-four holes, six strokes behind the leaders—Jerry Heard, John Schlee, Julius Boros, and Arnold Palmer. Palmer, then forty-three years old and the people's choice, was born in nearby Latrobe, Pennsylvania. His army of fans thought he had a good chance to win his second Open. Miller, a Brigham Young University dropout, joined the Tour in 1969 and had won only two PGA Tour tournaments. It seemed unlikely that he would overcome Oakmont's notorious obstacle course of 187 bunkers and lightning-fast greens to win a grueling test against the seasoned and more-acclaimed competition.

But something strange happened on the way to the final round. Rains on early Saturday morning and then overnight into Sunday morning softened the greens and opened the door for an aggressive golfer who could hit precise irons. Johnny Miller obliged by opening with a birdie after hitting his 5-iron approach five feet from the cup. He birdied the next three holes to go 1 under par. Miller parred the next three, bogeyed the eighth, then birdied the ninth for a 32. He parred the tenth, then birdied the eleventh and the 603-yard twelfth after hitting a 4-iron to within fifteen feet of the cup. He birdied the thirteenth to go 4 under for the tournament and 7 under for the day. By that time he shared the lead with Arnold Palmer. Miller parred the fourteenth, then birdied the 453-yard fifteenth with a 280-yard drive, 4-iron, and a 10-foot putt. Miller had the lead with Palmer playing four holes behind him.

Palmer bogeyed himself out of the Open on twelve, thirteen, and fifteen while Miller parred the final three holes. Miller finished with a 279 with a final-round 63, the lowest round ever shot in the Open up until then. Schlee finished second, one stroke behind at 280, and Weiskopf was third at 281. Palmer, Nicklaus, and Trevino carded 282s.

Miller's 63 will long be remembered as one of the best rounds of golf ever played.

Palmer would never win another Open. He finished second in 1962 to Nicklaus in a play-off at Oakmont; third in 1963 after a three-way play-off with Julius Boros and Jackie Cupit at the Country Club; second in 1966 after a play-off with Billy Casper at the Olympic Club; and second again in 1967 at Baltusrol when he lost to Nicklaus by four strokes. Palmer played his last Open at Oakmont in 1994.

# June 18

### 1964: An Exhausted Ken Venturi Conquers
### Congressional to Win the U.S. Open

The final two rounds of the U.S. Open used to be played on Saturday, but that didn't stop Ken Venturi, then thirty-three years old and trying to regain his earlier championship form despite severe back problems. Considered one of the best iron players ever, Venturi was a teenage phenomenon who learned to play in San Francisco's Harding Park where his father was a professional and manager of the pro shop. An early indication of his promise was 10 and 9 and 12 and 11 match-play victories in the 1953 Americas Cup. Early in his career, he was tutored by Byron Nelson, who reconstructed his golf swing. Venturi almost won the 1956 Masters as an amateur. He shot 66, 69, and 75 to build a four-stroke lead, but faded to an 80 on the final round and lost to Jake Burke Jr. by one stroke.

By 1964 Venturi was in a major slump, his fluid swing shortened to a much-abbreviated stroke. He surprised everyone at Congressional by shooting 72 and 70 in the first two rounds, then carding a 66 on the first eighteen holes of the final round to come within two strokes of Tommy Jacobs, who had 206 through fifty-four holes. By the time the final round started, Venturi was suffering from heat exhaustion and dehydration in the 100-degree humid hothouse at Congressional, a 7,073-yard, par-70 layout in Bethesda, Maryland. Dr. John Everett, a Congressional Club member, kept Venturi on a diet of tea and salt tablets between rounds. Periodically being ministered to by Dr. Everett, Venturi holed a critical 18-foot birdie putt on the thirteenth hole of the final afternoon round to take a four-stroke lead, which he preserved until the end. This was one of the most emotional and sentimental finishes to an Open. Tommy Jacobs shot a final-round 76 to Venturi's 70 and finished second at 282. Arnold Palmer, a pretournament favorite, tied for fifth, finishing with a 75–74 after a strong 68–69 start.

Venturi won the American Golf Classic later that year, his golfing confidence restored. But a blood-circulation problem that affected his hands caused him another setback, forcing an early retirement in 1969.

# June 19

### 1955: Jack Fleck Upsets Ben Hogan in U.S. Open Play-off

Robert Trent Jones Sr. was retained by the Olympic Club in San Francisco to toughen up its 6,430-yard layout for the 1955 U.S. Open. Trent Jones made Olympic a more difficult test of golf by increasing the length to 6,748 yards, adding bunkers, narrowing the fairways, and raising the height of the rough. More than thirty thousand eucalyptus, pine, and cypress trees, ranging from sixty to one hundred feet tall, created narrow, parklike alleyways on the Lakeside Course, venue for the Open. Ben Hogan was the favorite to win because the tight course with its small greens and strategically placed bunkers required the kind of precision shot-making and golf-course management that Hogan was noted for. No one had heard of Jack Fleck.

Since 1952, Jack Fleck, manager of two public golf courses in Davenport, Iowa, had won almost $7,500 in forty-one tournaments. Ironically, prior to the Open, he had ordered a set of Hogan clubs and used them in his own meticulous preparations for the tournament. Fleck played forty-four holes every day prior to the tournament, but carded a 76 in the opening round and trailed Tommy Bolt (67) and several others. A second-round 69 and a 75 in the third set the stage for one of the more unlikely finishes in U.S. Open history.

Hogan started the final round three shots ahead of Fleck and carded a methodical 70 for 287. Fleck, playing behind Hogan, was one stroke off the pace as he teed it up on the 603-yard sixteenth hole. He had just birdied the 144-yard, par-3 fifteenth to pull within striking distance. His tee shot on the sixteenth carried a slight dogleg. He then hit a fairway wood to within wedge range, but pulled his approach shot into the rough. Fleck scrambled to get up and down, then barely missed a birdie putt on the short par-5 seventeenth. His last chance came on the eighteenth, a 337-yard par-4. Fleck pulled his drive slightly into the rough, one hundred yards from the green. He then hit a three-quarter 7-iron, which cleared a bunker guarding the front entrance to the green. He curled his slick 7-foot birdie putt into the hole with his Hogan putter to finish with a 67 and 287 total, tied with Ben Hogan. Only six subpar rounds were recorded in regular play, and Fleck had two of them.

In the play-off round, Fleck led Hogan by two strokes at the end of nine holes. He seemed unfazed that he was playing with one of the best golfers of all time, a four-time Open winner. Fleck was ahead by a stroke going into the final hole. Hogan hooked his tee shot into the deep rough, hit his second shot one foot, then slashed a wedge a few more feet. His fourth shot got him to within one hundred feet of the green, and his approach left him thirty feet for a double bogey. Hogan gamely sank the putt for a 6, but Fleck was on in regulation and two-putted for par and the championship. Jack Fleck had his brief shining golf moment. Hogan would never win his fifth Open.

# June 20

## 1982: Tom Watson Sinks Clutch Chip Shot on Seventeenth, Wins U.S. Open at Pebble Beach

Jack Nicklaus won his first Open at Oakmont in 1962 when he defeated the legendary Arnold Palmer 71–74 in a play-off after they tied at 283. At the age of forty-two, Nicklaus was looking for his fifth U.S. Open win as he finished with a 69 and carded a 284 at Pebble Beach. He had previously won the Open at Pebble Beach in 1972, when he fired a 290 to edge Bruce Crampton by three strokes. Critical shots in that tournament were Nicklaus's 8-foot putt to save bogey on the 205-yard, par-3 twelfth and a spectacular 1-iron tee shot on the 218-yard, par-3 seventeenth, which hit the flagstick, leaving a 1-foot birdie putt.

Nicklaus was not to win his fifth Open because Tom Watson, who had attended Stanford University and had frequently played Pebble Beach, was about to make one of the greatest clutch shots in Open history. Even with Nicklaus, who had finished, as he approached the seventeenth tee, Watson hit a 2-iron tee shot into the rough between two bunkers to the left of the green on the 209-yard, par-3 hole backed by Carmel Bay. Fortunately, the ball was not deep in the grass, and Watson, an excellent short-game player, chopped a sand wedge through the rough and popped the ball into the cup approximately eighteen feet away. A likely bogey became an amazing birdie, and a resuscitated Watson went on to birdie the final hole, a 540-yard par-5 with a 3-wood from the tee, a 7-iron, a full 9-iron, and a cautious putt to win his first Open.

Nicklaus had been outgunned by Watson before, most notably in their classic 65–66 duel in the final round of the 1967 British Open at Turnberry. But this was a tougher defeat as Nicklaus was unable to surpass Willie Anderson (1901, 1903, 1904, 1905), Bobby Jones (1923, 1926, 1929, 1930), and Ben Hogan (1948, 1950, 1951, 1953), the only other four-time U.S. Open winners.

# June 21

## 1971: Lee Trevino Defeats Jack Nicklaus in U.S. Open Play-off at Merion

The design of the 6,544-yard, par-70 Merion Golf Club (East Course) was the first effort of Hugh Wilson. Wilson went to Scotland and England to study the British linksland first-hand before creating his one masterpiece, which opened in 1912. Wilson died at the young age of forty-six before having a chance to pursue his belatedly found vocation.

When the U.S. Open was played at Merion in 1971, the course measured only twelve yards longer than the shortest course used for a championship since World War I. Approximately one-sixth of the course's length, 1,135 yards, was contained on the layout's only two par 5s, the 600-yard fourth hole and the 535-yard second. Merion, which covers only 110 acres, is a fine test of championship golf because it demands accuracy from the tee, judgment, ability to maneuver the ball, and a deft putting touch because of its slick greens. It was here that Ben Hogan fired a 69 to win a three-way play-off against Lloyd Mangrum (73) and George Fazio (75) to capture the second of his four U.S. Open titles.

In 1971, the stage was set for a classic confrontation between Lee Trevino, who had won his first Open by four strokes over Jack Nicklaus at Oak Hill in 1968, and Jack Nicklaus, who had won Opens at Oakmont (1962) and Baltusrol (1967). In 1960, Jack Nicklaus shot a phenomenal 66, 67, 68, and 68 for 269 in the World Amateur at Merion. By 1971, Nicklaus was considered the best golfer in the world, but Lee Trevino, who had honed his competitive skills on the public golf courses of his native Texas, was long accustomed to competing for money, even when he didn't have any. In a head-to-head money contest, Trevino was not an easy man to beat.

Nicklaus and Trevino were tied at 280 after regulation play at Merion. Trevino was one stroke ahead of Nicklaus going into the 458-yard, par-4 eighteenth on the final round, but bogeyed the hole after missing an 8-foot putt. Nicklaus, playing behind Trevino, missed a 14-foot putt on the final hole, forcing an 18-hole play-off. Jim Simons, a twenty-one-year-old Walker Cupper, was in the hunt until the last hole, but had a 6 to finish third. The last amateur to win the U.S. Open was Johnny Goodman, who won by one stroke over Ralph Guldahl at the North Shore Country Club in 1933.

Trevino holed a critical 25-foot putt on the 378-yard, par-4 fifteenth to card a birdie and retain a two-shot lead with the tough 430-yard, par-4 sixteenth, 224-yard, par-3 seventeenth, and the demanding eighteenth on the horizon. Trevino built a three-shot lead on seventeen as he birdied while Nicklaus parred after finding a bunker with his tee shot. Trevino outlasted Nicklaus 68 to 71, and in the span of one month he would win three national championships—the U.S. Open, the Canadian Open, and the British Open.

# June 22

## 1958: Patty Berg Wins Her Seventh Western Open

The Western Women's Open was among the eleven original tournaments scheduled on the LPGA Tour when it began in 1950. Babe Zaharias won that event and four others to dominate the Tour in its first year. By 1958, the Tour had expanded to twenty-five events, and Patty Berg, the leading LPGA money winner in 1957 ($16,272), won the Open with a 72-hole total of 293. The forty-year-old Berg also won the U.S. Women's Open that year.

Patty Berg turned professional in 1940 and was one of the pioneers of American women's golf and a great ambassador for the game. She was the first president of the LPGA, won the LPGA earnings title three times (1954, 1955, 1957), the Vare Trophy three times (1953, 1955, 1956), and was inducted into the LPGA Hall of Fame in 1951 along with three other charter members, Betty Jameson, Louise Suggs, and Babe Zaharias.

The Western Women's Open began in 1930 and was first won by Mrs. Lee Mida. Patty Berg won the tournament a record seven times (1941, 1943, 1948, 1951, 1955, 1957, 1958). It was discontinued in 1967 after Kathy Whitworth captured the title.

# June 23

### 1910: Birthday of Lawson Little, Winner of British Amateur, U.S. Amateur, and U.S. Open

Lawson Little, then a twenty-four-year-old amateur, won both the U.S. Amateur and British Amateur in 1934 and 1935. No one else has won these two events in consecutive years, and it required winning thirty-one consecutive match-play contests against some of the best golfers in the world. At the time there was no limit on the number of clubs a golfer could carry, so Little carried twenty-three clubs in his bag. Little's victory in the final round of the British Amateur in 1934, a 14 and 13 thrashing of James Wallace, was described by Bernard Darwin as "one of the most terrific exhibitions in all golfing history."

Lawson Little turned professional in 1936 and won the Canadian Open the same year. In his career he won eight titles on the PGA Tour including a 1940 U.S. Open win in a play-off with Gene Sarazen, whom he defeated 70–73 at the Canterbury Golf Club in Cleveland, Ohio. Little was inducted into the PGA Hall of Fame in 1961.

# June 24

### 1911: John McDermott Becomes First American to Win U.S. Open

John McDermott, a 130-pounder, became the first American to win the U.S. Open. All sixteen previous Open winners had been born in the British Isles. McDermott tied M. J. Brady from Wollaston in England at 307 after seventy-two holes. He then edged Brady 80–82 in an 18-hole play-off at the Chicago Golf Club in Wheaton, Illinois.

# June 25

## 1932: Gene Sarazen Wins U.S. Open at Fresh Meadow, Fires Final-Round 68

Gene Sarazen shot a 66 on the last round to win the U.S. Open by three shots at the 6,815-yard, par-70 Fresh Meadow Country Club in Flushing, New York. Sarazen, who won his first Open in 1922 at the Skokie Country Club when he carded a final-round 68 to win by one stroke, covered the final twenty-eight holes at Fresh Meadow in only 100 strokes. Earlier that year Sarazen had won the British Open, held at the Prince's, by five strokes, breaking Bobby Jones's record 285, set at St. Andrews in 1927, by two strokes.

Sarazen's natural style was that of a gambler and a showman. He played an attacking game of golf, which he modified in 1932 in order to win the Open. He also added a new club, the sand iron, which he developed to replace his niblick, which he found inadequate for bunker play. His modifications did not work at Fresh Meadow, where he had been the home professional in his early years. After two conservative rounds, Sarazen was five strokes behind the leaders with a 74-76 for 150. After carding a 38 on the front nine of the third round, Sarazen adopted an attacking style and shot a 32. After fifty-four holes Sarazen was one stroke off the pace with a 220. He continued his aggressive play into the fourth round by shooting 32-34 to win his second national championship. Bobby Cruickshank and T. Philip Perkins finished in a tie for second, three strokes behind, at 289.

# June 26

## 1914: Birthday of Mildred Didrikson "Babe" Zaharias, Pioneer in Women's Professional Golf

Babe Zaharias was born Mildred Didriksen in Port Arthur, Texas. An all-around athlete, she was the sixth of seven children born to Mr. and Mrs. Ole Didriksen, natives of Oslo who had migrated to Port Arthur. The family moved to Beaumont and she starred on the high school basketball team. After graduating, she worked for a Dallas insurance company and developed her skills in other sports including swimming and diving, softball, bowling, tennis, and track and field.

Didriksen, who changed her name to Didrikson as an adult, gained national attention in the 1932 national AAU Track and Field Championships held at Dyche Stadium in Evanston, Illinois. The Babe entered seven events and won the javelin throw, baseball throw, shot put, broad jump, and eighty-meter hurdles, tied for first in the high jump, and placed fourth in the discus. Restricted to three events in the 1932 Olympics in Los Angeles, Didrikson won the javelin throw with a new women's world record of 143 feet 4 inches. She won the high hurdles in record time and tied for first in the high jump, but had to take second because an official ruled she "dived" over the bar, an illegal maneuver at the time.

After the Olympics, she capitalized on her celebrity by turning professional and traveling in vaudeville shows as a dancer and harmonica player. She then played for the House of David, a barnstorming baseball team, but, by 1934, she had turned to golf. After touring with Gene Sarazen in 1935, she moved to southern California and refined her game. By 1938, she had met George Zaharias, an amiable wrestler, at a golf benefit in Los Angeles. They married and she seriously pursued her professional golf career.

Babe was briefly reinstated as an amateur in 1943 and won the U.S. Women's Amateur in 1946, the British Ladies' Amateur Championship in 1947, the first American to win that title since the event was established in 1893, and the U.S. Women's Open in 1948. From

1946 through 1947, Babe won seventeen straight tournaments. The Babe turned professional again in 1948 and became the biggest attraction in women's professional golf. Zaharias was named Woman Athlete of the Year by the Associated Press in 1931, 1945, 1946, 1947, 1950, and 1954. She died of cancer in 1956.

# June 27

## 1950: Chandler Harper Wins PGA Championship

An unlikely matchup between Henry Williams and Chandler Harper took place in the 36-hole match-play final of the PGA Championship at the Scioto Country Club in Columbus, Ohio. Former champions including Sam Snead, Denny Shute, Vic Ghezzi, Jim Ferrier, Bob Hamilton, and Henry Picard were eliminated, leaving the door open for Harper and Williams. Henry Williams staged a dramatic comeback to rally from six holes down with eight to play to tie Henry Picard in the regulation 36-hole semifinal. Williams won the match at the thirty-eighth hole when Picard three-putted for bogey, missing a second putt of twenty inches. Harper upset Jimmy Demaret 2 and 1 in his semifinal match. It was the third time Demaret had been eliminated in the PGA Championship semifinals.

Harper, a native of Portsmouth, won the Virginia State amateur in 1930 at the age of seventeen and again in 1933 and 1934. Williams had never won a major tournament. Williams shot 79 in the morning round and was down three holes. The thirty-seven-year-old Harper closed the match out at 4 and 3 on the thirty-third hole. He became a Ryder Cup member in 1955 and won the World Senior Championship in 1968.

# June 28

## 1916: Chick Evans Fires a 68 in the Second Round on His Way to a U.S. Open Victory

Charles "Chick" Evans became the third amateur after J. D. Travers (1915) and Francis Ouimet (1913) to win the U.S. Open. He was the first amateur to win the U.S. Amateur and U.S. Open in the same year. Evans shot a 70-69 in the first two rounds at the Minikahda Club in Minneapolis to build up a three-stroke lead over Wilfred Reid. After scoring a 74 on the third round to maintain a three-stroke lead, he hung on to withstand Jock Hutchinson's final-round 68 to win by two strokes, 286–288.

Like Francis Ouimet, Chick Evans broadened the social base of American golf. He showed great promise at an early age by winning the first of his six Chicago City Amateur championships at age seventeen. He won the Western Open, second in importance to the U.S. Open at the time, at the age of twenty. It took him until 1916, when he was twenty-six years old, to win his first U.S. Amateur after seven previous attempts. At this stage of his career he played with only seven hickory-shafted clubs—but he had three reserve putters. Putting was the weak part of his game.

Evans, like Bobby Jones, elected not to turn professional. He played in fifty consecutive U.S. Amateur Championships. A significant contribution by Evans, who had been a caddie, was to establish a caddie scholarship fund at Northwestern University. Evans won the 1920 U.S. Amateur and was a member of the Walker Cup team in 1922, 1924, and 1928.

# June 29

## 1906: Alex Smith Wins U.S. Open, First to Score Less Than 300 in a 72-Hole Tournament

Alex Smith became the first U.S. Open winner to post a 72-hole total of less than 300 when he shot a 295 to easily win the Open by seven strokes at the Owentsia Club in Lake Forest, Illinois. Smith, a Scottish professional from Carnoustie, outdistanced his own brother, Willie, who finished second. For winning, Smith received a purse of $300. He won a second U.S. Open in 1910. Smith was also noted as a golf instructor and is credited with having developed the games of Jerry Travers and Glenna Collett.

# June 30

## 1929: Bobby Jones Defeats Al Espinosa by 23 Strokes in a 36-Hole U.S. Open Play-off at Winged Foot

The 1929 U.S. Open was played on the 6,980-yard, par-70 Winged Foot West Golf Course designed by A. W. Tillinghast, who had finished twenty-fifth in the U.S. Open of 1910 and created other masterpieces including Baltusrol, Bethpage Black, Fresh Meadow, Ridgewood, Five Farms, the San Francisco Golf Club, and Quaker Ridge. The star attraction at Winged Foot was Robert Tyre Jones, who, though an amateur, was golf's superstar in an era of many sports luminaries.

Jones shot 69, 75, and 71 on the first three rounds and appeared to have the tournament won as he walked to the thirteenth tee on the final round. Al Espinosa, his nearest challenger, had just made an 8 at the twelfth and was six strokes behind with six holes to play. Relaxed because he thought he had no chance against a competitor as great as Jones, Espinosa completed the last six holes in 22 strokes to salvage a 75. Jones, playing behind the veteran professional, bogeyed the thirteenth, had a 7 at the fifteenth, and three-putted the sixteenth from twenty feet. Jones now needed a pair of fours on the last two holes to tie.

The 444-yard, par-4 seventeenth is a dogleg right guarded by a cluster of bunkers to the right of the tee-shot landing area and a pair of huge bunkers each protecting the left and right side of a deep green. Beautiful trees including ash, sycamore, Norway maple, little-leaf linden, and other varieties guard the fairway from tee to green. Jones got his four at seventeen, then proceeded to the 448-yard, par-4 eighteenth, which plays down an avenue of trees to a deep green with two bunkers to its left.

After a good drive up the middle, Jones's pitch caught the rim of a deep bunker and rolled down the embankment, stopping in the tall grass just short of the sand. Jones chopped the ball out of the heavy grass, and it rolled to within twelve feet of the flag. The crucial putt for par would have to navigate curving terrain causing the ball to break at least one foot. Jones rolled the ball over the ice-slick green, and it seemed to hesitate before the patented Jones "dying ball" putt dropped in. The next day he clobbered Espinosa by twenty-three strokes in the 36-hole play-off, 141–164.

Commentators such as the noted golf journalist Grantland Rice believe that Jones's clutch putt was critical to establishing him as one of golf's all-time greats. Rice wrote, "If Bobby had missed that great putt on Winged Foot's eighteenth in 1929, and gone down to defeat rather than getting into the play-off which he won, I do not believe he would have gone on to achieve his great victory a year later when he won the Grand Slam of Golf, the first time it had ever been done. I will always believe that the remainder of Jones's career hung on that putt."

# July 1

## 1961: Mickey Wright Wins Her Third U.S. Women's Open, Won Four in Her Distinguished Career

Mickey Wright, one of the best golfers ever to play on the LPGA Tour, won her third U.S. Women's Open in four years when she shot a 72-hole total of 293 on the 6,372-yard, par-72 Lower Course at Baltusrol. There were eighty-five entries, eighty-two starters, and forty-one contestants who completed the 72-hole event. Ms. Wright won $1,800 out of a purse of $8,000. Among the top finishing amateurs were Mrs. Marlene Stewart Streit, who shot 306 and tied for seventh, and Mrs. Philip J. Cudone, who shot 308 and tied for ninth.

The first Women's Open, held in 1946, was conducted by the Women's Professional Golf Association, precursor of the LPGA. That event was the first and last match-play Women's Open and was won by Patty Berg 5 and 4 over Betty Jameson. The total purse was $19,700 and Miss Berg collected $5,600 in first-prize money. The newly formed LPGA conducted the event beginning in 1949; the USGA began administering it in 1953. It took until 1972 for the first-prize money to again reach the level of the inaugural 1946 Open.

Mickey Wright won her last U.S. Women's Open in 1964 and collected $2,200. Ken Venturi, the winner of the Men's Open, collected $17,000. The only other golfer to win four U.S. Women's Opens is Betsy Rawls.

*Opposite:* Patty Berg, Betty Mims Danoff, Babe Zaharias, and Louis Sluggs

# July 2

## 1967: Catherine Lacoste Becomes First Amateur to Win U.S. Women's Open Championship

Catherine Lacoste is the daughter of the famous French tennis player René Lacoste and Simone Thion de la Chaume, winner of the British Ladies' Golf Championship (1946). She became the first amateur player to win the Women's Open when, at age twenty-two, she shot a 71, 70, 74, and 79 for 294 at the 6,191-yard, par-71 Cascades Course in Hot Springs, Virginia. Susie Maxwell and Beth Stone tied for second place with scores of 296. Miss Lacoste had built up a seven-stroke lead in the final round, but had to hang on to win when she began to play poorly.

Catherine Lacoste learned her golf at Chantao, the course at the foot of the Pyrenees that belonged to the Lacoste family. She won the Ladies' Open of France in 1967, and in 1969, her mother with her, she won the British Ladies' Amateur at Portrush, on the same golf course where her mother had won twenty-three years previously. In 1969, she won the French Close, French Open, and Spanish Open. Lacoste then went to Texas, where she won the U.S. Women's Amateur. She bested Shelley Hamlin of California, 3 and 2, in the 36-hole final at the 6,022-yard, par-72 Las Colinas Country Club in Irving. She won the French Open again in 1970 and 1972, then retired.

Catherine Lacoste was noted for her natural golf swing, excellent long-iron play, and her ability off the tee. She was one of the few women in golf to regularly play a 1-iron. She was fiercely independent and a fiery competitor. Lacoste traveled alone to the United States at the age of twenty-two to win her Women's Open. When she returned to the United States again in 1969 to compete in the U.S. Amateur, she reportedly turned to a USGA official when she was 3-up in the final round and asked, "When I win, how are we going to ship the trophy to France?"

# July 3

## 1954: Mildred Didrikson Zaharias Wins Her Third Women's Open Championship by 12 Shots

"Babe" Zaharias, fighting cancer diagnosed in a physical examination in 1953, won her third U.S. Women's Open by twelve strokes, 291 to 303, at the 6,393-yard, par-72 Salem Country Club in Peabody, Massachusetts. She had won the Open in 1948 and 1950 and won a total of thirty-one LPGA events from 1948 through 1955. She was elected to the LPGA Hall of Fame in 1951, a charter member along with Patty Berg, Louise Suggs, and Betty Jameson.

Mrs. Zaharias, a renowned all-round athlete and 1932 Olympic gold medal winner in track and field, was a tomboy from Beaumont, Texas, who was named the woman athlete of the first half-century in a 1950 Associated Press poll. She mastered virtually every sport and game ranging from basketball and baseball to billiards and fencing. She was also an excellent ballroom dancer and could type one hundred words a minute. At the 1932 Olympics, sportswriter Paul Gallico asked Babe if there was anything that she didn't play. "Yeah, dolls," she replied.

Although she felt rejuvenated after her 1954 Open win, she slowly succumbed to cancer. She won her last tournament in 1955, the Peach Blossom Classic in Spartanburg, South Carolina. She died September 27, 1956, at the age of forty-two.

# July 4

## 1965: Carol Mann Wins U.S. Women's Open, Open Telecast Nationally for the First Time

Carol Mann shot rounds of 78, 70, 70, and 72 to post a 2-over-par 290 on the 6,220-yard, par-72 Atlantic City Country Club in Northfield, New Jersey, to win her first U.S. Open. The 6-feet-3-inch Ms. Mann made two pars and a birdie on the final three holes to hold off Kathy Cornelius, the 1956 champion, who shot a final-round 69 to finish two strokes back at 292. The final two rounds were played on two separate days for the first time, and the Open was telecast nationally for the first time.

Ms. Mann won 38 tournaments in her twenty-one years on the Tour and was elected to the LPGA Hall of Fame in 1977. She manages her own consulting firm and is active in golf instruction and business development and is on several advisory boards.

# July 5

## 1970: Donna Caponi Wins Her Second Consecutive U.S. Women's Open

Donna Caponi, a twenty-five-year-old native of Detroit, Michigan, won her second U.S. Women's Open by shooting a 287 to win by one stroke on the 6,210-yard, par-71 Muskogee Country Club in Oklahoma. Caponi had opening rounds of 69, 70, and 71 but then soared to 77 as she held on to win her second straight Open over Sandra Haynie and Sandra Spuzich, who tied at 288. Caponi had also won the Open by one stroke in 1969 as she fired a final-round 69 to edge Peggy Wilson at the 6,308-yard, par-73 Scenic Hills Country Club in Pensacola, Florida. Donna Caponi's 72-hole total of 287 at Muskogee tied Mickey Wright's scoring record for a U.S. Women's Open.

Miss Caponi took up golf at the age of eight under the tutelage of her father, Harry Caponi, a professional. She turned professional in 1965, won twenty-four LPGA tournaments, and finished among the top ten money winners ten times while earning over $1.3 million on the Tour. Caponi retired in 1989 but is still among the top twenty-five all-time money winners on the Tour. In addition to her back-to-back Open wins, she won the LPGA Championship in 1979 and 1981.

# July 6

## 1931: Burke Defeats Von Elm in Longest U.S. Open Play-off

The 1931 U.S. Open was played at the Inverness Club in Toledo, Ohio. Total prize money for the tournament was $5,000, and there were 1,141 entries as compared to the eleven golfers who competed in the inaugural Open at the Newport Golf Club in Newport, Rhode Island, in 1895. Golf boomed through the 1920s. The number of courses grew from the original St. Andrews built in a cow pasture in Yonkers, New York, in 1889 to an estimated 5,700 courses across the nation.

By 1931, the economic gloom of the Depression began to catch up with golf, and the retirement of Bobby Jones, at the age of twenty-eight, after his Grand Slam victories in 1930, reduced the public's interest in the game. Golf fans were waiting for a successor to "Emperor" Jones, and it would take Hogan, Snead, Nelson, Palmer, Nicklaus, and the post–World War II economic and communications boom to restore the growth of golf to its earlier pace.

Although established stars such as Gene Sarazen and Walter Hagen finished in the money at the 1931 Open, this event is remembered for its record 72-hole play-off between George Von Elm, a young Californian who had recently turned professional after a distinguished amateur career, and Billy Burke, a club pro at Round Hill in Greenwich, Connecticut, in his fifth year of an undistinguished professional career. Burke and Von Elm finished the regulation seventy-two holes tied at 292 after Von Elm dropped a 10-foot putt for a birdie on the seventy-second green. This was the last year of the U.S. Open's 36-hole play-off format. They tied again, at 149. Once more Von Elm had birdied the final hole to earn a tie. Another thirty-six holes were required to settle the championship. During the morning round of the final 36 holes, Von Elm shot a 76 to lead by a stroke. In the afternoon, Burke caught Von Elm on the tenth hole, passed him, and won by a single stroke, 148 to 149.

# July 7

### 1953: Walter Burkemo Wins the PGA Championship

Walter Burkemo, a journeyman golf professional from Detroit, Michigan, won his first and only major tournament by defeating Felice Torza, 2 and 1, at the Birmingham Country Club in Birmingham, Michigan. A field of 136 golfers entered the tournament and 64 qualified. Burkemo never relinquished the lead to Torza after building a 1-up advantage after the first eighteen holes of the 36-hole match-play final. Over ten thousand fans came out to see their local hero clinch a victory with a par on the thirty-fifth hole. Burkemo earned a spot on the victorious 1953 Ryder Cup team, but did not play.

# July 8

### 1899: H. M. Harriman Wins His First U.S. Amateur

The U.S. Amateur was established by the newly formed United States Golf Association in 1895. Thirty-two golfers played in the first event, a match-play contest at the Newport (Rhode Island) Country Club. Charles B. Macdonald of the Chicago Golf Club won that event by defeating Charles E. Sands of the St. Andrews Club in New York, 12 and 11. The fifth U.S. Amateur was held at the Onwentsia Club in Lake Forest, Illinois, in 1899. There were 112 entries and 32 golfers qualified with scores ranging from a low of 168 (the medalist, Charles B. Macdonald) to 187 for thirty-six holes. H. M. Harriman of the Knollwood Country Club in White Plains, New York, defeated Findlay S. Douglas, 3 and 2, in the final.

    At this stage in the history of American golf, the U.S. Amateur was the most prestigious tournament in the United States. The U.S. Open, held at the Baltimore Country Club's Roland Park Course in 1899, had 81 entries and only 28 contestants who finished seventy-two holes of medal play. Willie Smith of the Midlothian Club shot 315 to win by eleven strokes.

# July 9

## 1904: Willie Anderson Wins Second Straight U.S. Open

Willie Anderson, professional at the Apawanis Club in Rye, New York, fired a 303, including a final-round 72, to win his second straight U.S. Open title at Glen View Golf Club in Golf, Illinois. Glen View, a 6,574-yard, par-72, heavily treed layout, was the site of the first Western Open and Western Amateur in 1899. Designed by Britisher Herbert James Tweedie, architect of the Midlothian Country Club, Glen View opened in 1904. H. J. and his brother L. P. were friends of golf architect C. B. Macdonald and members of his original Chicago Golf Club, site of the U.S. Open in 1897, 1900, and 1911.

# July 10

## 1926: Bobby Jones Wins His Second U.S. Open by One Stroke

Bobby Jones shot a final-round 73 at the Scioto Country Club in Columbus, Ohio, recording a 72-hole total of 293 to win by a stroke over Joe Turnesa. Jones had shot a 79 on the second round, partly as a result of a penalty that he called on himself when his ball turned over as he was addressing his putt. Jones's birdie 4 on the final hole gave him a come-from-behind victory. Earlier in the year Jones had won the British Open; thus he became the first golfer to hold the U.S. Open and British Open title in the same year.

Jones started his trip abroad by entering the British Amateur at Muirfield in Scotland. He lost in the fifth round to Andrew Jamieson, 4 and 3. Jess Sweetser then became the first American-born golfer to win the Amateur when he defeated A. F. Simpson, 6 and 5, in the match-play final. Jones, Sweetser, Francis Ouimet, George Von Elm, Jesse Guilford, Watts Gunn, Roland Mackenzie, and Capt. Robert Gardner then went to St. Andrews in early June and won the Walker Cup, 6 to 5, from a strong team from Great Britain and Ireland. Jones put on a devastating display of golf as he eliminated Cyril Tolley, 12 and 11, in the singles. Jones never lost a Walker Cup singles contest in his five competitions before he retired in 1930.

At the last minute, Bobby Jones decided to stay in England to compete in the British Open. He played what some consider to be a "perfect round of golf" at Sunningdale during the qualifying rounds. Jones shot record rounds of 66 and 68 to lead all qualifiers with a 134. His symmetrical 66 consisted of 33 strokes per side, 33 shots from tee to green, and 33 putts. He scored either 3 or 4 on every hole of the estimated 6,500-yard layout. Jones's card:

|       | Front 9 | | | Back 9 | | | Total |
|-------|-----|-----|----------|-----|-----|----------|-------|
| Par   | 544 | 344 | 434 = 36 | 544 | 353 | 444 = 36 | 72 |
| Jones | 444 | 334 | 434 = 33 | 434 | 343 | 444 = 33 | 66 |

The only time Jones missed a green in regulation was on the 175-yard, par-3 thirteenth, where he put a mashie (4-iron) into the bunker. He chipped to within six feet and parred.

Jones went to the British Open at Royal Lytham and St. Annes and found himself in a struggle with six other Americans. After opening with a pair of 72s, Jones held a two-stroke lead over Al Watrous, a young professional from Grand Rapids who had come over with the U.S. Ryder Cup team. Watrous and Jones were paired on the final day, and after Watrous shot a fine 33-36 for 69, Jones was two strokes behind after the morning round. After sixteen holes on the final round, the match was all even. Jones then hooked his drive on the 411-yard, par-4 seventeenth, a dogleg left, and landed in the sand guarding the dogleg. Watrous had hit a straight tee shot, and his approach was on the front edge of the green. Jones was left with a blind shot of 175 yards that had to clear dunes along the left fairway. He took a mashie and hit a clean shot to the green, well inside Watrous's approach. A rattled Watrous three-putted while Jones parred.

The contest between Jones and Watrous was over. Watrous lost another stroke on the eighteenth and finished with a 78 and 293. Jones totaled 74 and 291. Walter Hagen, still out on the course, needed an eagle on the par-4 eighteenth to tie, but parred. Jones had won his first British Open. Today a bronze plaque stands near the spot where he played his magnificent approach shot. When he returned by passenger ship to the United States, he was given a hero's welcome in a ticker-tape parade down Broadway hosted by Mayor Jimmy Walker.

Jones, who had played in eleven national championships between 1916 and 1922 without winning, played in ten national championships in the four years including 1923 and 1926, winning five and finishing second three times. He attributed his change of fortune to his change in attitude, most notably patience: "So maybe that is the answer—the stolid and negative and altogether unromantic attribute of patience. It is nothing new or original to say that golf is played one stroke at a time. But it took the many years to realize it. And it is easy to forget, now. And it won't do to forget, in tournament golf."

# July 11

## 1919: Walter Hagen Wins His Second U.S. Open

Walter Hagen won his second U.S. Open in an 18-hole play-off with Mike Brady at the Brae-Burn Country Club in West Newton, Massachusetts. Brady led Hagen by five strokes going into the final round, but ballooned to an 80 as Hagen worked his way into position to win the championship by reaching the two-tiered green on the par-4 finishing hole with a strong midiron shot to within eight feet of the cup. Hagen, ever the showman, summoned Brady, who had already finished and was waiting in the clubhouse, to the green so he could witness Hagen's birdie putt, which, if holed, would give him a one-stroke victory.

Hagen missed the putt but won the play-off by one stroke, 77–78. The twelve lowest-scoring professionals shared in the $1,745 purse with $500 going to Hagen. For the first time, play was scheduled on three days with eighteen holes to be played on each of the first two days and thirty-six holes on the third day. At the age of twenty-six, Hagen had won his second U.S. Open. This would be his last Open victory even though he continued to compete in the Open through 1937.

# July 12

## 1930: Bobby Jones Wins U.S. Open on His Way to Grand Slam

Since 1926 Bobby Jones had privately contemplated the possibility of the Amateur and Open championships of both Britain and the United States. At twenty-eight years of age, he was at the top of his game. He was a golf prodigy much the way Jack Nicklaus would later be. He won the Junior Championship Cup at the Atlanta Athletic Club at age nine, shot his first 80 at age eleven on his home course at East Lake in Georgia, and won the East Lake Club Championship in 1915, at age thirteen. He won his first U.S. Open at Inwood at the age of twenty-one after a play-off with Bobby Cruickshank. Jones won the U.S. Open in 1923, 1926, 1929, and 1930. He also won the U.S. Amateur in 1924, 1925, 1927, 1928, and 1930, won the British Amateur in 1930, and won the British Open in 1926, 1927, and 1930. Jones was a renaissance man and a national hero in the Golden Age of Sport, which produced heroes such as Jack Dempsey, Babe Ruth, Red Grange, and Jim Thorpe. During his championship years he was a part-time golfer, having earned his degrees from Georgia Tech and Harvard by 1924. He later attended the Law School of Emory University preparatory to his admission to the bar in 1928.

In 1930, Jones had just returned from a British Open victory and a ticker-tape parade down Broadway in New York City when he teed up for the U.S. Open at the Interlachen Country Club in Minneapolis. He had time for only a few practice rounds but managed to shoot 71, 73, and 68 on the first three rounds to take a commanding five-stroke lead. Jones double-bogeyed three par-3 holes on the final round to record a 75 to win the tournament by two strokes. Bobby Jones had now won three of the Grand Slam titles in the same year. He later won the U.S. Amateur at the Merion Cricket Club.

Jones, an amateur, retired from competitive golf in 1930. His life's plan was clearly simple: "My wife and children come first, then my profession. Finally, and never in a life by itself, comes golf."

# July 13

## 1937: Birthday of Charles Coody, Winner of 1971 Masters

Charles Coody, born in Stamford, Texas, secured his place in golf history by winning the 1971 Masters. After starting out with a sizzling 66, Coody shot workmanlike rounds of 73, 70, and 70 for a 72-hole total of 279, two shots ahead of Johnny Miller, who finished with a pair of 68s, and Jack Nicklaus. Charles Coody had been ahead by three strokes with three holes to go in the 1969 Masters but bogeyed them all to finally lose by two strokes to George Archer.

Johnny Miller almost won the 1971 Masters on the final round by recording six birdies through fourteen holes to lead the field by two strokes. But Miller bogeyed sixteen and eighteen while Coody, playing behind Miller, birdied fifteen and sixteen to take the lead. Coody later played on the 1971 Ryder Cup team and joined the Senior Tour in 1987.

# July 14

## 1962: Richard Sikes Wins His Second Consecutive U.S. Amateur Public Links

The Amateur Public Links Championship involves two competitions. The Standish Cup, presented in June 1922 by James D. Standish Jr., the chairman of the USGA Public and Municipal Golf Courses Committee, is awarded to the individual winner of the match-play event. It was Standish who persuaded the USGA Executive Committee to establish this event. In 1923 Warren G. Harding, then the president of the United States and a member of the USGA Executive Committee, donated a trophy for a team competition. That competition was a medal-play event.

Richard Sikes, twenty-two years old, defended his title by defeating thirty-two-year-old Hung Soo Ahn from Honolulu, by 2 and 1, in the 36-hole final match at the 6,697-yard, par-70 Sheridan Park Golf Course in Tonawanda, New York. The Seattle, Washington, team won the Harding Trophy by defeating the Honolulu team by one stroke. George Archer, the future PGA Tour player, was medalist in this event with a 73-72 for 145.

# July 15

## 1923: Bobby Jones Won His First U.S. Open in a Play-off

Bobby Jones won his first U.S. Open at the Inwood Country Club in Inwood, New York, by defeating Bobby Cruickshank in an 18-hole play-off (76–78) after tieing at 296 after seventy-two holes. A total of 360 entries qualified on-site before the field was narrowed to 77 when the tournament began. By the end of the 1922 season, Jones, then twenty years of age, had appeared in, and failed to win, no less than eleven British and American national tournaments. Within a span of eight years, Jones, an amateur and part-time golfer, would win thirteen major tournaments, including four U.S. Opens.

The 1923 Open is considered a major tournament in the exceptional playing career of Robert Tyre Jones, who had played in his first national championship in 1916 as a fourteen-year-old prodigy. He had entered his first U.S. Open in 1920, when he was eighteen, and finished fifth. Jones was ahead by three strokes going into the final round of the 1923 Open, but bogeyed the sixteenth and seventeenth holes and found himself in trouble on the par-4 eighteenth when he hooked his second shot, leaving a delicate pitch to the green. He mishit his chip into a bunker and took a six. Later in the day, Bobby Cruickshank birdied the last hole to force a play-off.

More than eight thousand fans came out the next day to watch the 18-hole showdown. Jones and Cruickshank were dead even after seventeen holes. Cruickshank, who had the honor, hit a weak 150-yard drive, forcing him to lay up on his second shot. Jones outdrove Cruickshank by 100 yards, leaving him about 195 yards from the pin. His ball lay on a patch of bare ground, and if he didn't hit a perfect shot to the green, he ran the risk of dropping his approach into a water hazard that protected it. His second shot was perfectly struck to within six feet of the cup. Jones then nursed two putts to a par while Cruickshank struggled to make six. Later, Jones recalled that Stewart Maiden, his golf instructor, said about that critical approach "that I never played a shot more promptly or decisively.

He says I picked up a number-two iron from the bag and banged it. . . . I saw the ball on the green near the pin. Next thing I knew somebody was propping me up by the arm. . . . I won the hole with a four to Bobby's six. And the championship." Jones's seven lean years had ended. He had won a national title.

# July 16

## 1960: U.S. Amateur Public Links Held Outside Continental United States for the First Time

The U.S. Amateur Public Links Championship was held at the 6,677-yard Ala Wai Golf Course in Honolulu, Hawaii, the first time a USGA event was held outside the continental United States. Verne Callison, forty-one, a tavern owner from Sacramento, California, easily won the 36-hole match-play final, 7 and 6, after winning five 18-hole match-play contests. Of the 2,718 total entries, 150 qualified for the tournament, which was played over six days. The team championship went to the three-man Pasadena contingent, which had a score of 453 for thirty-six holes, four better than second-place Honolulu.

# July 17

## 1988: Seve Ballesteros Wins Third British Open, Fires 65 on the Final Round to Beat Price by Two

Seve Ballesteros learned golf on the shores of his native Spain with a 3-iron made from a rusty clubhead and a "shaft" whittled from a stick. He improvised shots by hitting round stones found on the beaches near Pedrena, where he was born in 1957. Ballesteros has been improvising shots ever since, in the scrambling fashion that made Arnold Palmer so popular with golf fans. Seve turned professional in 1974 and won the Spanish Young Pro Open. At the age of nineteen, he led by two shots going into the final round of the 1976 British Open at Royal Birkdale, but finished tied for second, six strokes behind Johnny Miller. That same year he became the youngest golfer to win the European Order of Merit. His first victory in the United States was the 1978 Greater Greensboro Open, which came after he led Spain to the World Cup title in 1976 and 1977. When he won the Masters in 1980 at the age of twenty-three, he was the youngest golfer to win that title. Ballesteros won another Masters title in 1983.

As the last round of the 1979 British Open began, Hale Irwin, the U.S. Open champion, led by two strokes over Ballesteros, but seven golfers were in a position to win. By the time Seve had reached the sixteenth tee at Royal Lytham and St. Annes, on the western coast of England, about a mile inland from the Irish Sea, he was two strokes ahead. After hitting his tee shot on the 356-yard, par-4 hole, he hit a great 9-iron into the wind and to within ten feet of the hole. He then made the critical birdie and went on to shoot 70 for the round and 283 for the tournament, three strokes ahead of Jack Nicklaus and Ben Crenshaw.

By 1988, Ballesteros had established himself as one of the world's best golfers. He had won two Masters and two British Opens when he returned to Lytham and St. Annes for the British Open. Trailing by two going into the final round, he was teamed with Nick Price, who led, and Nick Faldo, who was also two strokes behind. After playing the front nine in 31, Ballesteros drew even with Price by the sixteenth, both 10 under par. Ballesteros hit a 1-iron to within 135 yards of the flag on the par-4 sixteenth, then hit a windswept 8-iron to within inches of the hole. Price hit his 125-yard approach shot to within twenty feet but could not make the putt. Seve was one stroke ahead with one hole to play after both golfers parred the seventeenth. On the 412-yard, par-4 finishing hole, Ballesteros drove into the right rough, then pulled a 6-iron to the left and over the green. Price was on the green in two but far from the hole. Seve's ball was sixty feet from the hole and he feathered a delicate sand wedge that almost went in the hole. He had his par and Price could not make his birdie. Ballesteros had finished with 65 on the final round, 273 for the tournament, and had won his third British Open.

Ballesteros continues to prefer the European Tour and seldom plays elsewhere. By 1994 he had passed $10 million in career earnings, placing him in an elite with Norman, Langer, Kite, Couples, Faldo, Trevino, Ozaki, Woosnam, and Frost. At the end of 1993, players from eight different countries were among the top ten career money winners. Golf had truly become an international game.

# July 18

## 1898: James Foulis Wins the Second U.S. Open

James Foulis, a native of Scotland who emigrated to the United States with his brother in the 1890s, won the second U.S. Open, held at the Shinnecock Hills Golf Club, Long Island, New York, with a 78-74 for 152. A field of twenty-eight golfers entered the event, which had total prize money of $355. Foulis's 74 stood as a record for seven years, but at that time the Shinnecock course measured only 4,423 yards.

# July 19

## 1980: Jodie Mudd Wins U.S. Amateur Public Links Title

Jodie Mudd, twenty, of Louisville, Kentucky, won the 55th Amateur Public Links Championship, 9 and 8, over Richard Gordon, of Santa Clara, California, at the 7,127-yard, par-72 Edgewood Tahoe Golf Course in Stateline, Nevada. Mudd, a junior at Georgia Southern College, is the brother of Eddie Mudd, the 1976 champion. There were 4,416 total entries in the qualifying rounds, and 64 qualifiers started in 18-hole match-play contests that continued through five elimination rounds to the 36-hole final. Mudd's victory margin of 9 and 8 was the second largest in the history of the event. In 1965, Arne Dokka defeated Leo Zampedro 10 and 9 in the final.

Jodie Mudd was a three-time all-American at Georgia Southern. He won the Public Links again in 1981, then turned professional in 1982. His best year on the Tour to date was 1990, when he won the Players Championship and the Nabisco Championship and earned $911,756.

# July 20

### 1958: Dow Finsterwald Wins First Stroke-Play PGA Championship

Dow Finsterwald, a journeyman professional on the PGA Tour, won his only major PGA title with a historic win in the first PGA stroke-play event, held at the 6,710-yard, par-70 Llanerch Country Club in Havertown, Pennsylvania. The twenty-eight-year-old Finsterwald fired a final-round 67, including a 31 on the front nine, to edge Billy Casper by two strokes with a 72-hole score of 276. A total of 167 entered the event, including Arnold Palmer, then in his fourth year on the Tour, who finished tied for fortieth place at 298. First-place finisher Finsterwald received $5,500 from the total purse of $39,388 for his efforts. George Griffin, who finished sixty-fourth and last in the money, earned $100. Finsterwald earned $572,025 on the Tour before joining the Senior Tour in 1980. He was a member of the 1957, 1959, 1961, and 1963 Ryder Cup teams and had an overall record of nine wins and three losses in singles and foursomes play.

# July 21

### 1974: Sandra Haynie Wins U.S. Women's Open by One Stroke

Sandra Haynie birdied the final two holes and shot 73, 73, 74, and 75 for 295 at the 6,266-yard, par-72 La Grange Country Club in La Grange, Illinois. Haynie was a successful amateur, winning the Texas State Women's Public Links (1957, 1958), the Texas Women's Amateur (1958, 1959), and other events before joining the LPGA Tour in 1961. She played during the peak years of Mickey Wright, Kathy Whitworth, Carol Mann, and other excellent LPGA competitors but managed to win at least one tournament every year from 1962 through 1975. Haynie was named LPGA Player of the Year in 1970. She won forty-two LPGA Tour victories and over $1 million before retiring in 1989. In 1977 she was inducted into the LPGA Hall of Fame.

# July 22

## 1962: Gary Player Wins His First PGA Championship

Gary Player, who turned professional in 1953 at the age of eighteen, won his first PGA Championship at the 7,045-yard, par-70 Aronimink Golf Club in Newtown Square, Pennsylvania. Player, who would win over $2.8 million as a professional and 128 tournaments worldwide before joining the Senior Tour in 1985, staved off a late charge by Bob Goalby to win by a single stroke. Player shot 278 to win the $13,000 first prize in a field of 170. Player won his second PGA title in 1972 at the Oakland Hills Country Club. He was elected a charter member of the PGA World Golf Hall of Fame in 1974.

# July 23

## 1967: Don January and Don Massengale Tie in PGA Championship, January Wins 18-Hole Play-off

Don January, a thirty-seven-year-old professional from Plainview, Texas, tied Don Massengale, thirty, out of Jacksboro, Texas, after seventy-two holes at the PGA Championship at the 7,436-yard, par-72 Columbine Country Club in Denver, Colorado. Both golfers finished at 281, forcing an 18-hole play-off won by January, 69 to 71. Jack Nicklaus and Don Sikes finished tied for third at 282. January's victory was his sixth since joining the Tour in 1956 after graduating from North Texas State University in 1953. Before joining the Senior Tour in 1980, he had won ten Tour events and over $1.1 million. January has had tremendous success in his second professional golf life on the Senior Tour. He has won over $2.7 million and twenty-two Tour events (through 1993). January was a member of the Ryder Cup team (1965, 1977) and won the Vardon Trophy in 1976, at the age of forty-six.

# July 24

## 1960: Jay Hebert Wins the PGA Championship

Jay Hebert, brother of 1957 PGA champion Lionel Hebert, won the tournament by one stroke at the 7,165-yard, par-70 Firestone Country Club in Akron, Ohio. Firestone's South Course was originally designed by Bert Way, a noted golf-course architect who was born in Devonshire, England, and later emigrated to the United States. The original Firestone South Course opened in 1929 but was toughened by Robert Trent Jones, who redesigned the course in 1959. Jones added fifty bunkers, two ponds, and two greens. The remaining sixteen greens were enlarged to two to three times their original size, so that an eighty-foot putt over a sharply undulating surface was a possibility. As a result, only thirteen subpar rounds were shot by the 185 golfers who entered the 1960 PGA Championship.

Jay Hebert shot a second-round 67 and finished with a 72-hole total of 281 to prevail by one stroke over Jim Ferrier, who carded a 66 on the third round. Hebert never reached the upper echelons of golf because of his poor short game. He won seven times on the PGA Tour, which he joined in 1948 after graduating from Louisiana State University. Before completing his degree, he enlisted in the U.S. Marines in World War II, rose to the rank of lieutenant, and was wounded at Iwo Jima. He worked primarily as a club professional until 1956, when he became a full-time tournament player. Hebert was a member of the 1959 and 1961 Ryder Cup teams and was nonplaying captain of the 1971 contingent, all winners.

# July 25

## 1993: Bob Charles, the Best Left-Handed Golfer Ever, Wins the British Senior Open

Bob Charles, the fifty-seven-year-old veteran from New Zealand, put together rounds of 73, 73, 71, and 74 to win the Senior British Open by one stroke over Gary Player and Tommy Horton at the 6,673-yard, par-71 Royal Lytham and St. Annes Golf Club. Charles collected $36,650 in prize money, which was not included in his $1,046,823 U.S. PGA Senior Tour earnings for the year. Through 1993, Charles had won twenty-one Senior Tour events and almost $4.7 million since joining the circuit in 1986. He has won numerous "worldwide" senior events in Japan, South Africa, Australia, Great Britain, and elsewhere.

Charles, a 6-feet-1-inch, 170-pound, smooth-swinging southpaw, was the first left-hander to win on the PGA Tour when he won the 1963 Houston Classic. That same year he won the British Open, also at Royal Lytham and St. Annes, when he defeated Phil Rogers, 140 to 148 in a 36-hole play-off. Charles had shot a 68, 72, 66, and 71 for 277 in regulation. This achievement and his subsequent successes have established Bob Charles as the best left-handed and New Zealand golfer of all time.

Charles's continued success is due to his even temper, beautiful swing rhythm, and excellent short game. He has won the Byron Nelson Trophy for best Senior Tour scoring average three times. He was the first player to win $4 million on the Senior Tour when he won the Quicksilver Classic in 1993. Before joining the Senior Tour, Charles won five PGA Tour events and less than $550,000, although he won many international events such as the British Open, New Zealand Open, and Swiss Open.

# July 26

## 1987: Laura Davies Wins U.S. Women's Open in a
## Three-Way Play-off, Defeats Okamoto and Carner

Laura Davies, a twenty-three-year-old, long-hitting, 5-feet-10-inch native of Coventry, England, won her first U.S. Open by defeating Ayako Okamoto and JoAnne Carner in a play-off at the Plainfield Country Club in Edison, New Jersey. After the three contestants tied at 285 in regulation, Miss Davies won the 18-hole play-off with a 3-under-par 71. Miss Akamoto had a 73 and Mrs. Carner a 74 in the extra round. Miss Davies, who had won the British Ladies' Open as an amateur in 1986, won $55,000 in first-prize money. In 1993 she was thirteenth on the Women's World Money List with $418,825 in earnings. In 1994 Ms. Davies led the LPGA Tour in earnings with $687,201. She won her first LPGA major tournament, the McDonald's LPGA Championship, and two other Tour events in 1994.

# July 27

### 1958: Art Wall Jr. Wins the Eastern Open, Named
### Player of the Year in 1959

Art Wall Jr. won his first of fourteen career Tour victories in 1953 when he captured the Fort Wayne Open, worth $2,400. Wall's biggest win on the Tour was his come-from-behind victory in the 1959 Masters, when he started the final round six shots behind Arnold Palmer and Stan Leonard. He shot a 66, including five birdies on the last six holes, to win by one stroke with a total of 284 (73, 74, 71, 66). In 1959, Wall was the leading money winner ($53,167), Vardon Trophy winner (70.35), and was selected PGA Player of the Year. Art Wall was a member of the 1957, 1959, and 1961 Ryder Cup teams. He joined the Senior Tour in 1980.

# July 28

### 1985: Lee Elder Wins Merrill Lynch–Golf Digest
### Commemorative Pro-Am

Lee Elder opened with an 11-under-par 61, then posted a 72 in a rain-shortened event at the 6,566-yard, par-72 Newport Country Club in Rhode Island. Elder was tied at 133 with Peter Thomson but won the play-off on the first extra hole to win $27,000 in this Senior Tour contest. On his record first round, Elder hit every fairway, every green, and took only twenty-six putts. Elder won the tournament on the 468-yard, par-5 play-off hole by hitting his second shot, a 4-wood, to within fifteen feet and sinking the eagle putt. Lee Elder won three other Tour events in 1985.

# July 29

## 1957: Betsy Rawls Wins Women's Open, Mrs. Pung Is Disqualified

Betsy Rawls of the Spartanburg Country Club in South Carolina shot a 299 to win her third Women's Open Championship by six strokes at the 6,246-yard, par-73 Winged Foot Golf Club in Mamaroneck, New York. Mrs. Jacqueline Pung, playing out of San Francisco, had an actual score of 78, 75, 73, and 72 for 298, but the card she signed and returned, as kept by her marker and fellow competitor, Betty Jameson, showed a 5 at the fourth hole where Mrs. Pung actually had 6. The penalty for Mrs. Pung's failure to catch this error was disqualification, even though Mrs. Pung's total had been correctly stated, under the rule that makes the competitor solely responsible for the correctness of the score recorded for each hole. Spontaneously, Winged Foot members contributed to an unofficial purse exceeding $3,000 to recompense Mrs. Pung for the $1,800 first prize she had lost.

Betsy Rawls won her fourth Women's Open Championship in 1960 when she defeated Joyce Ziske, of Waterford, Wisconsin, 292 to 293 at the 6,137-yard, par-72 Worcester Country Club in Massachusetts. Miss Rawls, a member of the LPGA Hall of Fame, was thirty-two years of age when she won this, her last Open. She turned professional in 1951 and won fifty-five LPGA events including ten in 1959. Betsy Rawls is the only golfer other than Mickey Wright to win four Women's Open Championships.

Betsy Rawls, whose golf teacher was Harvey Penick, was the leading money winner in 1952 and 1959. She was appointed president of the LPGA in 1961 and 1962. After Miss Rawls retired in 1975 she was hired as the LPGA's tournament director. As a pioneer on the LPGA Tour, a world-class golfer, and an excellent golf executive, Betsy Rawls has made a significant contribution to the game.

# July 30

## 1993: Nick Price Fires Second-Round 65, Goes On to Win St. Jude Classic

Nick Price shot a second-round 65 on the 7,006-yard, par-71 TPC at Southwind in Germantown, Tennessee, and went on to win the Federal Express St. Jude Classic with a 69, 65, 66, and 66 for 266, three strokes better than Rick Fehr and Jeff Maggert. Price collected $198,000. In 1993, Price won four Tour events and $1,478,557, first on the earnings list. Price won the Vardon Trophy (69.11 adjusted scoring average) and was voted PGA Player of the Year. A regular winner on the international golf circuit, Price was at the top of the World Money List with $2,825,691 in earnings in 1993. He was fourth in the final SONY rankings behind Nick Faldo, Greg Norman, and Bernhard Langer. In 1994 Price led the Sony rankings and was second on the World Money List behind Ernie Els.

# July 31

## 1983: Jan Stephenson Wins U.S. Women's Open, Wins Four Tournaments in 1983

Jan Stephenson, a thirty-one-year-old from Sydney, Australia, won the Women's Open at the Cedar Ridge Country Club in Tulsa, Oklahoma. Ms. Stephenson edged JoAnne Carner and Patty Sheehan by one stroke when she fired a 6-over-par 290. Jan Stephenson, one of the more glamorous golfers on the Ladies' Tour, also won the Tucson Conquistadores PGA, the Lady Keystone, and the J C Penney Classic (with Fred Couples) and won a total of $193,364 in 1983.

Stephenson turned professional in 1973 and won the Australian Open and three other events and was named Rookie of the Year in 1974. In addition to her major win in the Open, Stephenson won the 1981 Peter Jackson (now the du Maurier) with rounds of 69, 66, 72, and 73 to win by a stroke over Nancy Lopez and Pat Bradley. In 1982, she won the LPGA Championship at the Jack Nicklaus Sports Center north of Cincinnati by shooting 69, 69, 70, and 71 to win by two strokes over JoAnne Carner.

Jan Stephenson has won over $2 million on the LPGA Tour despite recurring back problems, an automobile accident in 1987, and a broken ring finger suffered in an attempted mugging in Miami in 1990.

# August 1

## 1964: Johnny Miller Wins U.S. Junior Amateur, 2 and 1 at the Eugene, Oregon, Country Club

Johnny Miller, seventeen, of San Francisco showed his early promise as he won both the qualifying medal and the Junior Amateur Championship at the 6,627-yard, par-71 Eugene Country Club. It was the first time that the championship included stroke-play qualifying at the site. From a field of 150 who qualified from 1,583 regional entries, the low 64 scorers survived for match play. Miller's qualifying scores were 71-68 for 139, three under par. Miller won five 18-hole matches to reach the final against Enrique Sterling Jr. of Mexico City, the first foreign player ever to reach the final. Miller won 2 and 1 in the 18-hole championship.

Johnny Miller turned professional in 1969 and won twenty-four tournaments, including a surprise 1994 win in the AT&T Pebble Beach National Pro-Am after leaving regular Tour play in 1990. He is best remembered for his dramatic final-round 63 and come-from-behind win in the 1973 U.S. Open at Oakmont and his brilliant iron play, which put him on every green in regulation. He won the British Open in 1976 at Royal Birkdale. Miller was named PGA Player of the Year in 1974 when he led the Tour with eight wins.

*Opposite:* Gleanna Collett at Pebble Beach, 1928

# August 2

## 1959: Bob Rosburg Wins the PGA Championship by One Stroke

Bob Rosburg, a 1948 graduate of Stanford University and later a distinguished television golf commentator, won the PGA Championship, his only major tournament win, at the 6,850-yard Minneapolis Golf Club in St. Louis Park, Minnesota in 1959. The thirty-three-year-old fired a 66 on the final round to defeat Jerry Barber and Doug Sanders by a single stroke.

Rosburg's steady short game, especially his putting, made him a competitor on the professional circuit. At the age of forty-two, he was a contender for the 1969 U.S. Open at the Champions Golf Club in Houston, but missed a short putt on the seventy-second hole to finish tied for second at 282, one stroke behind Orville Moody.

Rosburg was a member of the victorious 1959 Ryder Cup team, winning both his singles and foursomes matches at the Eldorado Country Club in Palm Desert, California. He won the Vardon Trophy in 1958 and a total of six tournaments after joining the Tour in 1953. Rosburg has played occasionally on the Senior Tour since 1981, but has primarily been a golf commentator for ABC Television.

# August 3

## 1978: John Mahaffey Shoots a 75 on the First Round, Then Comes Back to Win the PGA Championship

John Mahaffey, a native of Kerrville, Texas, and a member of the 1970 University of Houston NCAA Championship golf team, won his only major title in a play-off with Jerry Pate and Tom Watson at the Oakmont Country Club, a 6,989-yard, par-71 layout. Mahaffey, who overcame a debilitating injury to his left elbow that severely reduced his play during the 1977 season, trailed third-round leader Watson by seven strokes, but fired a final-round 66 to force a three-way sudden-death play-off. Mahaffey then birdied the par-4 second extra hole to win the $50,000 first prize. His regulation 72-hole total of 75, 67, 68, and 66 for 276 was 8 under par.

Al Barkow, in his book *The History of the PGA Tour*, relates how Mahaffey revealed his competitiveness in his description of a recurring dream where he had a crucial shot but the gallery was right up behind his ball and wouldn't move. Mahaffey's solution: "I started whacking at the gallery with my club, trying to get it to back off." Mahaffey was a member of the 1979 Ryder Cup and the 1978 and 1979 World Cup teams. He has won over $3.6 million on the PGA Tour.

# August 4

## 1904: Birthday of Harry Cooper, Member of PGA Hall of Fame

Harry Cooper, nicknamed Light Horse Harry because he quickly played and pursued his shots, won many professional tournaments in the 1920s and 1930s, but was never able to win a national championship. Born in Leatherhead, England, but raised in Texas, Harry was an excellent scorer and shotmaker. He burst on the national scene by winning the Los Angeles Open in 1926, the first time that tournament was held. He was in position to win the 1927 U.S. Open, but three-putted the seventy-first green from eight feet at Oakmont to allow Tommy Armour to catch him in regulation, necessitating an 18-hole play-off. Armour won the play-off 76–79 and Cooper never recovered. Though he had the tools and dedication to win, he would never break into the highest echelons of competitive golf.

In the 1936 Open on the Upper Course at Baltusrol, Harry made some clutch shots on the third round to finish with a 70 and 211 for fifty-four holes, a new record. On the sixteenth he had avoided a collapse by holing a sand wedge for par after chunking his third shot from difficult rough into a bunker. Cooper then dropped a 45-foot putt for birdie on the seventeenth, and it looked as if the tournament belonged to Harry. But this was not to be, even though he shot a respectable 73 on the final round to total 284, two strokes lower than the previous Open record of 286. Out on the golf course, Tony Manero, who had grown up on Westchester County's golf courses at the same time Gene Sarazen and the Turnesa brothers were developing their games, closed with a 67 to better Cooper by two strokes with a 282. It was the only major Manero would win.

In 1937 Cooper was the leading money winner ($14,138.69), took the first Vardon Trophy (then called the Radix), and won the most events (eight). He won a total of thirty-one Tour tournaments and finished second in the Masters (1936) and U.S. Open (1927, 1936). He ranks thirteenth on the all-time tournament winners list tied with Jimmy Demaret. The last significant tournament that Cooper won was the Atlantic City Senior Open in 1962.

# August 5

## 1990: Tom Kite, the PGA Tour's All-Time Money Winner, Wins Federal Express–St. Jude Classic

Tom Kite shot a 269 to win the St. Jude Classic at the 7,006-yard, par-71 TPC at Southwind in Germantown, Tennessee. Kite defeated John Cook in a play-off to win the $180,000 first prize. This tournament win was Kite's fifteenth on the Tour. By the end of 1993, Kite, who joined the Tour in 1972, would have nineteen wins and lead the all-time PGA money list with total career earnings in excess of $8.5 million.

Tom's best year monetarily was 1989, when he won the Nestlé Invitational, the Players Championship, and the Nabisco Championship and led the Tour in earnings with $1,395,278. However, he didn't get the full credit he deserved from the golfing world and the general public until he won his first major, the U.S. Open, at Pebble Beach in 1992. Herbert Warren Wind, the great chronicler of American golf, classifies the game into golf, tournament golf, and major-tournament golf. Describing the gut-wrenching competition at the highest level, the majors, he writes:

> The men who are used to playing under fire have long ago learned how to harness their nervousness. They seldom lose because of a jumpy feeling in their stomach, and contradictory as it seems at first, they worry about not being worried, about becoming phlegmatic and missing that little tingle that keeps a player sharp and dangerous. But put the seasoned campaigner of tournament golf into a major championship—say the United States or British Open—and he begins to sweat like a novice, that welcome little tingle becomes a nauseating thump, and the golfer finds himself playing his shots by some cloudy memory of his formula and praying that his trained reflexes will see him through.

Kite was not up to the task in the 1989 Open at Oak Hill when, after leading at the end of the third round, he shot a 78 and dropped into a tie for ninth place. Kite redeemed himself in blustery conditions at Pebble Beach when he shot a steady final-round 72 to win by two strokes.

# August 6

## 1972: Gary Player Wins His Second PGA Championship, Two-Stroke Victory at Oakland Hills

Gary Player pushed his tee shot to the right on the sixteenth hole at Oakland Hills in the final round of the 1972 PGA Championship, and it looked as if his chances to win had faded. He had bogeyed the fourteenth and fifteenth holes and was on the verge of a collapse. His ball was behind a willow tree, which obstructed his view to the green. Somehow Player lofted a 9-iron over the tree to within four feet of the hole, then dropped in his putt for a birdie. He went on to score a two-stroke victory over Tommy Aaron and Jim Jamieson.

Player proved to be the most successful foreign national to play the PGA Tour. He won twenty-one PGA Tour victories including the 1961, 1974, and 1978 Masters, the 1965 U.S. Open, and the 1962 and 1972 PGA titles. He won the British Open in 1959, 1968, and 1974. Only 5 feet 7 inches and 147 pounds, Player has always been in great physical shape and able to keep pace with the big hitters. Especially noted for his excellent sand play and driving accuracy, he has continued his excellent performance on the Senior Tour, where he has won over $3 million and has posted victories in the 1986, 1988, and 1990 PGA Seniors' Championship.

Player has designed a number of golf courses in the United States and abroad in association with Karl Litten, Ron Kirby, Arthur Davis, and others.

216

# August 7

## 1972: Amy Alcott Wins Medal in Girls' Junior, but Nancy Lopez Wins the Tournament

Amy Alcott from Los Angeles, California, shot the low medal round on this date at the U.S. Girls' Junior Championship, but was eliminated, 2 and 1, by Barbara Barrow in an 18-hole semifinal match-play contest. Miss Nancy Lopez, fifteen years old, reached the finals and defeated Catherine Morse, 1-up, to win her first Girls' Junior title. The event was played on the 6,125-yard, par-72 Jefferson City Country Club in Missouri. Nancy Lopez won the U.S. Girls' Junior again in 1974 after Miss Alcott won the 1973 championship.

Nancy Lopez had a phenomenal career as an amateur, foreshadowing her success on the LPGA Tour. Born in Torrance, California, she took up golf at the age of eight under the guidance of her father, Domingo, who owned an auto repair shop and played golf to a 3 handicap. She won the New Mexico Women's Amateur at age twelve and later won three Western Juniors (1972, 1973, 1974) and the 1975 Mexican Amateur. In 1975, still an amateur, she shot 299 in the Women's Open to tie for second, four strokes behind Sandra Palmer. Nancy Lopez attended Tulsa University on a Colgate Palmolive scholarship for two years and won the AIAW National Collegiate Championship, the Western Amateur, the Trans-National, and four other collegiate titles. She was a member of the 1976 Curtis Cup and World Amateur teams. She turned professional in 1977 after finishing third in LPGA Qualifying School.

# August 8

## 1977: Beth Daniel Wins First Match, Goes On to Win Her Second Women's Amateur

Beth Daniel, a twenty-year-old from Charleston, South Carolina, defeated Barbara Riedl of Sidney, Ohio, 1-up in the 18-hole first-round match-play contest, then won her next five matches to win her second U.S. Women's Amateur. The tournament took place on the 5,978-yard, par-73 Cincinnati Country Club course. Among the 162 entries were future LPGA professionals Patty Sheehan and Lori Garbacz. Miss Daniel won the Women's Amateur in 1975 on her first attempt. In 1994 Beth Daniel won LPGA Rolex Player of the Year honors and captured her third Vare Trophy for low stroke average (70.90) on the Tour. She has now earned over $4 million on the LPGA Tour.

# August 9

## 1953: Lew Worsham's Eagle Wedge on the Final Hole
## Captures the World Championship of Golf by a Stroke

George May, a former Bible salesman who became the president of his own business consulting company, was one of golf's most colorful entrepreneurs. May enriched the professional Tour by sponsoring the World Championship of Golf at the Tam O'Shanter Club in Chicago, which he owned. The tournament began in 1941 as the Tam O'Shanter Open and was first won by Byron Nelson. In 1943 a professional women's event was added, and amateur events were also held at the friendly confines of Tam O'Shanter.

May was rather like Bill Veeck, the baseball impresario who was always thinking of ways to improve and promote his sport. May used numbers on the backs of golfers for identification purposes, door prizes, clowns, bleacher seats beside greens, permanent grandstands, and other tactics, such as televising the event to put his tournament on the map.

One of the earlier golf telecasts was the local coverage of the eighteenth hole by a mounted camera on a flatbed truck at the 1947 U.S. Open. Lew Worsham won that tournament in a play-off with Sam Snead. At the 1953 Tam O'Shanter, he needed to finish with two birdies to tie when he stepped onto the seventeenth tee on the final round. Worsham got his birdie on the seventeenth, then teed it up on the eighteenth, the only hole being covered for a national television audience. Worsham's drive left him 110 yards to the green on the 410-yard, par-4 finishing hole. Worsham lofted a wedge toward the pin, hoping for his birdie. Miraculously, the ball hit in front of the green then rolled up and in for an eagle and the $25,000 first prize, the richest purse in golf.

Like Bill Veeck, George May was eventually spurned by the PGA professionals, who considered him too much of a showman and a distraction from the dignity of the game and, of course, them. May finally withdrew from supporting the World Championship. It was last held in 1957, and the winner-take-all first prize was $50,000, compared to the

$10,000 first prize and $40,000 total purse in the Tournament of Champions, the second-richest event on the Tour. George May then posted a sign, NO PGA PROS ALLOWED, at Tam O'Shanter.

# August 10

## 1975: Jack Nicklaus Wins His Fourth PGA Title, Shoots a 276 at Firestone to Win by Two Strokes

Jack Nicklaus put another notch in his championship belt as he shot a 72-hole score of 276 to win the PGA Championship at the 7,180-yard, par-72 Firestone Country Club in Akron, Ohio. Bruce Crampton finished second with a score of 278. Of the 139 players entered, 71 made the final cut, and Nicklaus, whose career Tour earnings would eventually total more than $5.3 million, won $45,000 for his first-place finish. Nicklaus was golf's leading money winner in 1975 with $298,149 in Tour earnings. He also won the most money in 1964, 1965, 1967, 1971, 1972, 1973, and 1976. He was the PGA Player of the Year in 1967, 1972, 1973, 1975, and 1976.

In Nicklaus's book, *My Most Memorable Shots in the Majors*, he describes how he recovered in the third round from a poor drive on the 625-yard, par-5 sixteenth hole at Firestone:

> The ball [drive] finishes in the water hazard way left. I drop out under penalty of one stroke, into a flyer lie, and whale a 6-iron 230 yards into the right rough smack behind a large tree. . . . The pin is 137 yards away. . . . The pitching wedge won't give me enough distance and the 8-iron won't climb quickly enough, so it's a 9-iron. I open the face and set the ball well forward in my stance to insure fast height, tell myself, "Stay still," and swing as hard as I can. The ball clears the tree by a few inches and the pond by a few feet and stops thirty feet past the hole. I make the putt, finish with a 67, and cruise to a comfortable victory the next day.

Nicklaus reasoned that, with a five-stroke lead in the tournament and twenty more holes to play, it was worth it to risk an 8 with the possibility of making a 5. At the peak of his game, one of golf's greatest players succeeded.

# August 11

### 1974: Lee Trevino Wins His First PGA Championship, Outdueling Jack Nicklaus to Win by One Stroke

Lee Trevino matched Jack Nicklaus stroke for stroke on the final round and won the 1974 PGA at the 7,050-yard, par-70 Tanglewood Golf Club in Clemmons, North Carolina. Trevino had built a one-stroke lead after three rounds, then matched Nicklaus's 69 on the final round to win by one stroke with a 72-hole score of 276. Trevino had come a long way since he dropped out of school to hustle for money at municipal golf courses in Dallas, Texas.

Trevino also won the New Orleans Open and the World Series of Golf in 1974. Since joining the regular Tour in 1967, Lee has won twenty-seven tournaments, placing him in eighteenth place all-time. Trevino was the PGA Player of the Year in 1971 and won the Vardon Trophy for best scoring average on the PGA Tour in 1970, 1971, 1972, 1974, and 1980. Trevino has earned more money on the PGA Senior Tour, which he joined in 1989, than he did in all his years on the regular Tour. In 1990, his first full year on the Senior Tour, he earned over $1.1 million and placed first in winnings. He did the same in 1992. Lee Trevino was inducted into the PGA World Golf Hall of Fame in 1981.

# August 12

## 1973: Jack Nicklaus Wins PGA at Canterbury, His 14th Major Championship

Jack Nicklaus won his third PGA Championship by shooting a 72-hole total of 277 to defeat Bruce Crampton by four strokes at the 6,852-yard, par-71 Canterbury Golf Club in Cleveland, Ohio. The Canterbury course was designed by New Yorker Herbert Leeds and modified a few years later by the club's professional, Jack Way. Its variety of well-treed dogleg holes and variable winds that blow off nearby Lake Erie add to the course's difficulty. The 1940 and 1946 U.S. Opens were played at Canterbury.

Nicklaus won his fourteenth major at age thirty-three to eclipse Bobby Jones's record of thirteen major tournament wins, a record that had stood for forty-three years. Jones, a part-time amateur golfer, retired in 1930 at age twenty-eight after winning the Grand Slam—British Open, British Amateur, U.S. Amateur, and U.S. Open—a feat that has never been equaled.

Nicklaus was named PGA Player of the Year in 1973 and also won that honor in 1967, 1972, 1975, and 1976. He joined the Senior Tour in 1990 and promptly won the 1991 PGA Seniors' Championship by six strokes over, coincidentally, Bruce Crampton.

# August 13

## 1920: Ted Ray Wins the U.S. Open in the Rain at Inverness

A cathedral chime clock with the following inscription sits in the clubhouse foyer of the Inverness Country Club in Toledo, Ohio:

> God measures men by what they are,
> Not what in wealth possess.
> This vibrant message chimes afar,
> The voice of Inverness.

This clock, which stands over six feet tall, was donated to the club by a delegation of professionals led by Walter Hagen because, for the first time at a U.S. Open, professional golfers were allowed to use the locker rooms, dining areas, and other club facilities. Professional golfers were often looked down upon by the country-club set, both in the United States and abroad. They won a significant social victory at Inverness in 1920.

The Open championship was won by one stroke by Englishman Edward "Ted" Ray in a hotly contested competition that left five golfers tied for second at 296: Harry Vardon, Jack Burke, Leo Diegel, and Jock Hutchinson. Ray was a notch below golf's then-fading British triumvirate of James Braid, Harry Vardon, and J. H. Taylor, who dominated golf for three decades prior to World War II. Noted for his long game, a pronounced sway that led to errant shots, a great recovery game, and a deft touch around the greens, Ray won the 1912 British Open with a 295 at Muirfield. In the 1913 U.S. Open he lost in the famous three-way play-off with Harry Vardon and Francis Ouimet at the Country Club in Brookline. Ray was the last Britisher to win the U.S. Open until Tony Jacklin won the title in 1970. At forty-three, Ray became the oldest man ever to win the U.S. Open. Hale Irwin, who was forty-five years of age when he won the Open in 1990, is now the oldest to win the national championship.

# August 14

## 1948: Dean Lind Defeats Ken Venturi in Match Play to Win First U.S. Junior Amateur

Dean Lind, seventeen, of Rockford, Illinois, defeated Ken Venturi of San Francisco to win the first annual U.S. Junior Amateur held at the University of Michigan Golf Course in Ann Arbor. A field of 495 entered the tournament; 128 qualified through a sectional round held at forty-one locations. The youngest qualifier was Mason Rudolph, fourteen, of Tennessee, who was defeated in the quarterfinals by Dean Lind. Rudolph, who later played on the PGA Tour, was defeated in the finals in 1949 by Gay Brewer, who also had a distinguished professional career. In 1950, Mason Rudolph, at age sixteen, became the youngest winner of the championship when he defeated Charles Beville, 2 and 1, in the final round.

Ken Venturi didn't win a U.S. Junior Amateur, but he did win the U.S. Open at the Congressional Country Club in 1964.

# August 15

## 1952: The United States Team Wins First Americas Cup Match, Outduels Canada and Mexico

The first Americas Cup match was contested by the United States, Canada, and Mexico at the Seattle Golf Club in Washington in 1952. The format included three 36-hole three-ball "sixsomes" on the first day and six 36-hole three-ball matches on the second day. In each contest, golfers from one country played simultaneously against the other two, one point being awarded for each victory and all matches being played to a conclusion. The United States won the competition 12, 10 (Canada), and 5 (Mexico). Representing the United States were William C. Campbell, Charles Coe, Joseph Gagliardi, Frank Stranahan, Sam Urzetta, Ken Venturi, and Harvie Ward. Canada's team included Percy Clogg, Phil Farley, Peter Kelly, Jerry Kesselring, Walter McElroy, and Nick Weslock. Reynaldo Avila, Carlos Belmont, Percy Clifford, Alejandro Cumming, Fernando Gonzales, and Roberto Morris represented Mexico. The United States won every Americas Cup contest except the 1965 match, won by Canada. This amateur event was held every other year at rotating sites in each country through 1967, when it was discontinued.

# August 16

## 1992: Nick Price Wins His First PGA Championship

Nick Price, a native of Durban, South Africa, but now a resident of Florida, shot a 6-under-par 278 on the 7,148-yard, par-71 Bellerive Country Club course in St. Louis to win the PGA Championship by three strokes over John Cook, Nick Faldo, Jim Gallagher Jr., and Gene Sauers. Price played the front nine of the final round in par, but birdied the sixteenth and seventeenth holes to seize the tournament.

By late 1994, Price had won eleven tournaments since his first PGA victory, including a British Open, Canadian Open, and another PGA win in 1994. Price's 72-hole total of 269 at Southern Hills in 1994 was a record for the PGA since it adopted medal play in 1958. Ben Crenshaw commented, "Nick's a man in full flight. I'd say that, striking the ball, he's been as good as anyone since Ben Hogan and Bryon Nelson."

Price was born in 1957 in South Africa but moved to Rhodesia (now Zimbabwe) at an early age. He served two years in the Rhodesian Air Force and carries a British passport since his parents were British citizens. He won the Junior World Golf Championship at age seventeen at Torrey Pines in La Jolla, California, and after winning several tournaments on the international circuit, joined the PGA Tour in 1983. He won over $1 million on the Tour in 1992, 1993, and 1994 and is considered one of the best golfers in the world.

In an interview with Frederick C. Klein of the *Wall Street Journal,* Price attributed his 1994 PGA success to continuing efforts to improve his swing: "I'm controlling the ball in flight better, which is very important." He believes that his short game, once erratic, is now a major strength, thanks to a number of recent changes in his putting style that include a squarer stance and slower stroke. He has also improved his mental game: "I don't let my mind wander ahead much anymore—I focus better on the shot at hand. Also, you can't place too much value on winning regularly. It does a lot for a person's self-confidence."

# August 17

## 1968: JoAnne Carner Wins Her Fifth U.S. Women's Amateur Championship

Mrs. JoAnne Gunderson Carner had an outstanding amateur career, joined the LPGA Tour in 1970, and became one of the best women's professionals. She was inducted into the LPGA Hall of Fame in 1982.

JoAnne Carner won her fifth U.S. Women's Amateur title at the 6,170-yard, par-72 Birmingham Country Club in Michigan, defeating Anne Quast Welts of Bellingham, Washington, 5 and 4. Mrs. Carner's four other Women's Amateur titles were won in 1957, 1960, 1962, and 1966.

Born in Kirkland, Washington, the 5-feet-7-inch Carner was able to hit the ball well over 250 yards off the tee in her early years, inspiring others to call her the Great Gundy. She won the 1956 Girls' Junior, the 1960 Women's NCAA title while at Arizona State University on a golf scholarship, and had earlier won her first Women's Amateur in 1957 at age eighteen. Her five victories in the U.S. Women's Amateur are second only to Glenna Collett Vare, who won six in an earlier era when there was no women's professional tour.

JoAnne Carner, who has gained the inevitable weight of middle age, is now called Big Mama. A good-natured extrovert who loves to compete in a relaxed but often lethal fashion, she has been a force in her second golf life, the LPGA Tour, for over twenty-five years. By the end of 1994 Mrs. Carner had 42 LPGA victories including two U.S. Women's Open titles. She has over $2.8 million in career earnings, placing her seventh on the all-time LPGA list. Carner has won five Vare Trophies for low stroke average and was inducted into the LPGA Hall of Fame in 1982.

# August 18

### 1990: Sandrine Mendiburn of France Defeats Vicki Goetze of Georgia in Girls' Junior, First Foreign National to Win the Championship

Vicki Goetze, winner of the U.S. Women's Amateur in 1989, was unable to win the Girls' Junior as seventeen-year-old Sandrine Mendiburn, winner of three French Junior titles, became the first foreign national to win the U.S. Girls' Junior since it began in 1949. Miss Goetze, seventeen, who has played in the Girls' Junior since she was thirteen, has lost to the eventual winner in each of her five attempts. In 1990, Goetze had been the qualifying medalist with 73-74 for 147, but could not make the big putts in the final, as Mademoiselle Sandrine dropped critical birdie putts on the eleventh, twelfth, and thirteenth to go 3-up. She eventually won 4 and 2 with a par on sixteen.

Vicki Goetze joined the LPGA Tour in late 1993. Prior to joining the Tour she won the 1992 U.S. Amateur, was the 1992 NCAA champion, and played on both the 1992 Curtis Cup and 1992 World Cup teams.

# August 19

### 1949: Marlene Bauer Wins First USGA Girls' Junior Championship

Marlene Bauer, age fifteen, from the California Country Club in Los Angeles, won the first USGA Girls' Junior Championship, held at the Philadelphia Country Club's Bala Course in Pennsylvania. Miss Bauer, who stood 5 feet 3 inches tall, defeated Barbara Bruning 2-up in the 18-hole match-play final. Other future LPGA professionals in the inaugural under-eighteen-years-old Girls' Junior event were Barbara McIntire and Barbara Romack. This was the first national title won by Miss Bauer, who also won the Western Junior Championship in 1949. She was voted Athlete of the Year by the Associated Press, Teenager of the Year, Golfer of the Year, and won the 1949 Helms Athletic Award.

The Girls' Junior champion receives the Vare Trophy, named for Glenna Collett Vare, six-time winner of the U.S. Women's Amateur. Other distinguished winners of the event include Mickey Wright (1952), JoAnne Gunderson Carner (1956), Nancy Lopez (1972, 1974), Amy Alcott (1973), and Hollis Stacy (1969, 1970, 1971).

# August 20

## 1976: The First PGA Junior Championship Is Held

The PGA Junior Championship is open to boys and girls age seventeen and under. Competitors may qualify through their local PGA sections. The field for the finals comprises one girl and one boy champion from each of the forty-one sections. Winners of selected national Junior tournaments earlier in the year and past PGA Junior Championship winners who have not reached their eighteenth birthdays round out the field. More than 9,450 Juniors competed in 1993. The format is stroke play, eighteen holes daily, and in the event of a tie after seventy-two holes, there is a sudden-death play-off.

The inaugural PGA Junior Championship, held in 1976 on the Magnolia Course at the Walt Disney World Resort in Orlando, Florida, had a field of seventy-eight boys and girls. Nancy Rubin of New Kensington, Pennsylvania, won the girls' division by one stroke with an 83, 77, 82, and 78 for 320. Larry Field of Oklahoma City, Oklahoma, won the boys' division with a 76, 72, 78, and 71 for 297 to also win by a single stroke.

Among the past championship competitors who have gone on to successful professional careers are Billy Andrade, Kathy Baker, Brandie Burton, Rick Fehr, Jim Gallagher Jr., John Inman, Michelle McGann, Billy Mayfair, Scott Verplank, and Willie Wood. Vicki Goetze, now on the LPGA Tour, won a record three PGA Junior Championships (1987, 1989, 1990).

# August 21

## 1952: Mickey Wright Wins Girls' Junior in 1-Up Final at the Monterey Peninsula Golf Club

Future LPGA professionals Mickey Wright and Barbara McIntire squared off against each other in the 18-hole match-play final of the Girls' Junior Championship, held at the 6,053-yard, par-74 Monterey Peninsula Golf Club in Pebble Beach. A field of forty-nine entries and forty-three starters began the event, which was won by Miss Wright, 1-up. Miss Wright attributed much of her success to Harry Pressler, a pro at the San Gabriel Country Club who helped perfect her technique. She later took lessons from such teachers as Lee Bolstad, Stan Kertes, and Earl Stewart to perfect what Ben Hogan called "the finest golf swing I ever saw, man or woman." Miss Wright was inducted into the LPGA Hall of Fame in 1964 and the World Golf Hall of Fame in 1976.

# August 22

## 1964: Barbara McIntire Wins Her Second U.S. Women's Amateur Championship

Barbara McIntire, of Colorado Springs, won her second Women's Amateur title 3 and 2 in a 36-hole match-play final with Miss JoAnne Gunderson. The tournament was played at the 6,001-yard, par-73 Prairie Dunes Country Club in Hutchinson, Kansas. This was Miss McIntire's third major championship. She won the 1959 Women's Amateur and the British Women's Amateur in 1960. Barbara McIntire, along with JoAnne Gunderson (now JoAnne Carner) and Anne Quast (now Anne Sander) dominated American amateur golf in the 1950s and 1960s.

Miss McIntire, who was born in 1935 in Toledo, Ohio, was a member of the Curtis Cup team in 1958, 1960, 1962, 1964, 1966, and 1972. Only Anne Quast Sander (8), Carol Semple Thompson (7), and Polly Riley (6) have matched or bettered this record.

In the 1956 Women's Open, Barbara McIntire tied Cathy Cornelius at 302 after seventy-two holes of regulation play. Mrs. Cornelius won the 18-hole play-off 75 to 82. The tournament was held at the Northland Country Club in Duluth, which had a yardage of 6,419 (par 73) for the opening round and 6,456 (par 74) for the others. Of the top fourteen finishers in the field of forty-six, only Barbara McIntire was an amateur.

# August 23

## 1958: Anne Quast Wins Her First U.S. Women's Amateur Championship

Anne Quast, a twenty-year-old Stanford University senior from Marysville, Washington, won her first Women's Amateur, 3 and 2, over Barbara Romack. Miss Quast played the last seven holes of the 36-hole final in 4 under par at the 6,467-yard, par-75 Wee Burn Country Club in Darien, Connecticut. Miss Quast, who in later years became consecutively Mrs. Decker, Mrs. Welts, and Mrs. Sander, also won the Women's Amateur in 1961 and 1963. She played on a record eight Curtis Cup teams (1958, 1960, 1962, 1966, 1968, 1974, 1984, 1990). She won the British Amateur in 1980 at the age of forty-three, a tribute to her competitive longevity.

After receiving instruction from Ed Oldfield in 1986, Sander changed her swing and won the U.S. Senior Women's Amateur in 1987, 1989, and 1990. She finished second in that tournament in 1991 and 1992. Anne Quast Sander has played more competitive rounds in USGA championships than any other player.

# August 24

## 1990: Vicki Goetze Wins Record Third PGA Junior Championship

Vicki Goetze of Hull, Georgia, won her third straight PGA Junior Championship by shooting a record 72-hole score of 71, 65, 67, and 75 for 278 at PGA National's Champion Course in Palm Beach Garden, Florida. Goetze, who joined the LPGA Tour in 1993 after attending the University of Georgia, held a fourteen-shot lead over Estafania Knuth going into the final round. Goetze finished nine shots ahead of Knuth and eighteen shots ahead of Barbara Paul, who finished third.

# August 25

## 1946: Ben Hogan Wins His First PGA Championship, Defeats "Porky" Oliver 6 and 4 in Match-Play Final

Ben Hogan bested a field of sixty-four golfers as he defeated Ed "Porky" Oliver 6 and 4 at the Portland Golf Club in Portland, Oregon, to win his first PGA Championship. The 135-pound Hogan bettered fellow Texan Jimmy Demaret 10 and 9 in the semifinal round. Hogan came from three holes down after eighteen holes to easily win the match against Oliver. Hogan, who was 7 under par for the thirty-two holes played, covered the afternoon fourteen holes in 8 under par.

The 1946 PGA Championship was Byron Nelson's last major event. He had thirty-seven wins in forty-five career PGA Championship matches. Nelson then retired to his Texas ranch at the end of the season. He occasionally played events afterward, but for all intents and purposes his professional career ended at age thirty-four. He had won fifty-four PGA Tour events including "postretirement" wins in the 1948 Texas PGA Open, the 1951 Crosby Invitational, and the Crosby Pro-Am and French Open in 1955.

Ben Hogan, Byron Nelson's contemporary whom he had defeated in 1928 in the Glen Garden Country Club Caddie Championship, ground on. Hogan again won the PGA Championship in 1948 with a resounding 7-and-6 win over Mike Turnesa at the Norwood Hills Country Club in St. Louis, Missouri. Ben would not enter another PGA Championship until 1960, when he was past his prime. The match-play grind of ten rounds in five days was too much even before his near-fatal 1949 car accident. Ben did not make the cut in the 1960 stroke-play event.

# August 26

## 1990: Phil Mickelson Wins U.S. Amateur at Cherry Hills, 5 and 4

The previous four winners of the U.S. Amateur were college players, and twenty-year-old Phil Mickelson, the 6-feet-2-inch NCAA champion and all-American from Arizona State, carried on the tradition. He defeated Manny Zerman, another twenty-year-old from South Africa, who had been his high school classmate in San Diego. Zerman was an undergraduate at the University of Arizona in Tucson. The event was played at Cherry Hills, site of three U.S. Opens (1938, 1960, 1978). Mickelson was the second left-hander to win a USGA championship, southpaw Ralph Howe having won the Public Links in 1988.

Mickelson was the qualifying medalist with a score of 135, one stroke behind the record shared by Bob Clampett (1979) and Sam Randolph (1985). Three of Mickelson's six matches were settled in one hole. He defeated David Eger, 5 and 3, to reach the final. In his 36-hole contest with Zerman, Mickelson was 3-up after the first round. Zerman cut the lead to 1-up with nine to play in the afternoon round, but Mickelson went 2-up with a par at the tenth, 3-up with a birdie at the eleventh, and after they halved the twelfth, Mickelson closed out the match with a birdie and a par.

Mickelson joined the PGA Tour in June 1992 after winning his third NCAA individual championship. He won $748,316 on the Tour in 1994 and finished twenty-second in the SONY rankings. We might still hear from Manny Zerman.

# August 27

## 1927: Bobby Jones Wins His Third U.S. Amateur, 8 and 7, at Minikahda

Bobby Jones won his third U.S. Amateur title by defeating "Chick" Evans 8 and 7 at the Minikahda Club in Minneapolis. Jones won his first two 18-hole matches 2-up and 3 and 2, but then dominated his next three 36-hole format contests 10 and 9, 11 and 10, and 8 and 7. Among the notable golfers in the field, in addition to Evans and Jones, were George Von Elm, Francis Ouimet, Densmore Shute, and Maurice J. McCarthy. Jones still holds records for most U.S. Amateur wins, five (1924, 1925, 1927, 1928, and 1930); most times in the final, seven (1919, 1924, 1925, 1926, 1927, 1928, 1930); best match-play winning percentage, .843, forty-three wins and eight losses; and youngest competitor, fourteen years and five months (1916).

# August 28

### 1994: Eldrick "Tiger" Woods, at 18 Years of Age, Becomes Youngest to Win U.S. Amateur

Eldrick "Tiger" Woods, an eighteen-year-old golf phenomenon from Cypress, California, became the youngest golfer and the first African American to win the U.S. Amateur in its ninety-nine-year history. Woods, an incoming freshman at Stanford, paired against twenty-two-year-old Trip Kuehne in the match-play final, came from six holes down to stage the greatest comeback in U.S. Amateur history.

The most highly touted amateur since Jack Nicklaus, Woods built early expectations by becoming the youngest player, at age fifteen, to win the United States Junior Amateur. He is the only player to have won three Junior Amateur titles, a championship never won by the great Jack Nicklaus.

The ninety-ninth U.S. Amateur was played at the TPC Championship Course at Sawgrass in Ponte Vedra Beach, Florida, one of the most difficult on the professional Tour. Woods played the last twelve holes of his 36-hole match in 4 under par, often scrambling with difficult recovery shots to unnerve his opponents. Kuehne, a junior psychology major at Oklahoma State, birdied seven of the first thirteen holes in the morning round to post a 66. He was three holes up going into the final nine holes. After tieing the match at the sixteenth hole, Woods hit a pitching wedge shot to the left edge of the windswept 139-yard, par-3 island-green seventeenth, two feet from the water. He then dropped a 14-foot birdie putt to go up one hole. He held on to win a permanent place in golf history. Shortly after the tournament Woods entered Stanford University and joined the school golf team.

# August 29

## 1922: The United States Wins the First Walker Cup Competition

George Herbert Walker, the grandfather of former U.S. president George Walker Bush, was a member of the National Golf Links of America Club and president of the USGA in 1920 when a group from the Executive Committee of the USGA traveled to Britain to confer with members of the Royal and Ancient Golf Club to discuss the rules of golf, which were administered by the two groups internationally. As a result of that meeting and other developments in golf at the time, including the growing parity between British and American golf, Walker offered to sponsor a trophy for an international championship among amateur golfers.

Invitations were issued by the USGA in early 1921 to all countries interested in golf to send teams to compete for the trophy. No one accepted. However, William C. Fownes Jr., who had, in 1919 and 1920, assembled U.S. teams to compete against amateur teams representing the Royal Canadian Golf Association, assembled a third team to take part in an informal match against the British prior to the 1921 British Amateur. The American team defeated the British team 9 and 3 in four morning foursomes matches and eight afternoon singles.

The following spring, the Royal and Ancient Golf Club of St. Andrews, Scotland, announced that it would send a team to compete in the United States in 1922 for what became known as the Walker Cup. The match was played at the National Golf Links of America, George Herbert Walker's club, in Southampton, New York. William C. Fownes Jr. was the playing captain of the U.S. team, which also included Jesse P. Guilford, Francis C. Ouimet, Charles Evans Jr., Robert A. Gardner, Robert T. Jones Jr., Jess W. Sweetser, and Max R. Marston. Rudolph E. Knepper was a reserve.

The British team was captained by Robert Harris, who fell ill and was replaced by Bernard Darwin, the noted golf journalist and writer of several excellent books on golf.

The British team featured Cyril J. H. Tolley, Bernard Darwin, Roger H. Wethered, Colin C. Aylmer, W. B. Torrance, C. V. L. Hooman, John Caven, and W. Willis Mackenzie.

The U.S. team won 8 and 4. The Americans won consecutive matches through 1936 and have largely dominated the competition ever since. The Walker Cup is held every other year, alternating between sites in the United States and Great Britain.

# August 30

### 1952: Jackie Pung Wins U.S. Women's Amateur Championship

Mrs. Jacqueline Pung, from the Moanalua Golf Club, became the first Hawaiian to win the U.S. Amateur when she defeated Shirley McFedters, a student at UCLA, 2 and 1, at the 6,323-yard, par-73 Waverly Country Club in Portland, Oregon. Mrs. Pung, whose maiden name was Jacqueline Liwai, learned to play golf on a public golf course and was noted for her power off the tee. She joined the LPGA Tour in 1953.

# August 31

## 1935: Glenna Collett Vare Wins Her Sixth U.S. Women's Amateur

Glenna Collett Vare won her sixth U.S. Women's Amateur, 4 and 3, over Patty Berg at Miss Berg's home course, the Interlachen Country Club in Minnesota. Mrs. Vare, one of the greatest women amateur golfers of all time, was then thirty-two years of age. Miss Berg, then seventeen, would become a pioneer in developing the women's professional tour. Only JoAnne Gunderson Carner, who won U.S. Women's Amateur titles in 1957, 1960, 1962, 1966, and 1968, rivaled Mrs. Vare's Amateur record. No doubt Mrs. Carner would have at least tied Vare's record, but she elected to turn professional in 1970 at the age of thirty. Now she's a member of the LPGA Hall of Fame.

Glenna Collett Vare was an excellent all-round athlete, but had to work hard to develop her golf game. She later wrote books on golf including *Ladies in the Rough.* A long hitter (she once hit a drive 307 yards), Glenna took a while to get control of her game. She had her problems when she tried to defeat Joyce Wethered, one of Britain's greatest golfers, who was her contemporary. In 1925 she lost to Wethered, 4 and 3, at Troon in the British Ladies' Amateur. She again lost to Wethered in the final of the Ladies' Amateur by a score of 3 and 1 at St. Andrews.

In 1932, Glenna Collett Vare played on the first Curtis Cup team, which defeated Great Britain and Ireland, led by Joyce Wethered, 5½ to 3½. Vare won in foursomes, but lost her singles match to Wethered, 6 and 4, at Wentworth in England. Mrs. Vare played on the 1934, 1936, 1938, and 1948 teams and was the captain in 1934, 1936, 1948, and 1950 (non-playing). The Glenna Vare Trophy is annually awarded by the LPGA to the player with the lowest playing average on the Tour. A Vare trophy is also presented to the winner of the USGA Girls' Junior Championship.

# September 1

### 1954: Richard Nixon Defends His Boss

Richard Nixon gave the following defense when asked whether his boss, President Eisenhower, was playing too much golf: "If the president spent as much time playing golf as [Harry] Truman spent playing poker, then the president would be able to beat Ben Hogan." President Eisenhower helped popularize the sport in America in the 1950s.

# September 2

### 1940: Byron Nelson Wins His First PGA Championship, Outduels Sam Snead at the 18th Hole

Two golf legends, Byron Nelson and Sam Snead, met in the 36-hole final round of the PGA Championship at the Hershey Country Club in Pennsylvania. Sixty-four players qualified for the match-play event, but former champions Leo Diegel (1928, 1929), Jim Barnes (1916, 1919), and Tom Creavy (1931) did not. Walter Hagen, then thirty-seven years old, won his fortieth and last PGA match against Vic Ghezzi before being eliminated by Harold McSpaden, 1-up, in the third round.

Snead and Nelson were the final-round losers in the previous two PGA Championships. Nelson took the morning lead, 1-up, after shooting 71 on the first eighteen holes. The match was tied going into the final two holes as Snead came roaring back. Nelson

*Opposite:* Joyce Wethered

made a 2-foot putt after hitting a beautiful wedge on the thirty-fifth hole, a short par-4, but Snead could not sink his 6-footer and went 1-down with one to play. Nelson later recalled the final hole: "Then we came to the eighteenth, a long par 3, and it was my honor. I'll never forget it. I took my 3-iron, almost hit the flag, and went about ten feet past the hole; I'd be putting downhill. Sam put his tee shot about twenty-five feet to the left of the hole and putted up close, so he had 3. . . . I coasted that putt down the hill very gently and made my 3 to beat Snead and win the PGA Championship."

# September 3

### 1978: John Cook Defeats Scott Hoch in U.S. Amateur Final, Both Advance to PGA Tour

John Cook, twenty, of Upper Arlington, Ohio, defeated Scott Hoch, twenty, of Raleigh, North Carolina, 5 and 4 in the scheduled 36-hole final of the seventy-eighth U.S. Amateur. The event, which attracted over 3,000 entries and had 201 starters, was held at the 6,865-yard, par-72 Plainfield Country Club in New Jersey. For the first time in Amateur history, both 18-hole semifinal matches were decided in extra holes. Cook won his semifinal over Michael Peck by birdieing the second extra hole, a long par-4. Hoch defeated Bob Clampett with a par 4, also at the twentieth hole. In the final match, Cook's 32 and five birdies on the back nine of the morning round gave him a 5-up lead at the lunch break. He then opened the afternoon with par-birdie-birdie to take an 8-up lead and was never headed.

Cook, a native Californian, was a three-time all-American at Ohio State (1977, 1978, 1979) and played on the 1979 NCAA Championship team before joining the Tour in 1980. He has won over $4 million on the Tour and was a member of the winning 1993 Ryder Cup team. Hoch, a native of Raleigh, graduated from Wake Forest where he was an all-American in 1977 and 1978 and was a member of the 1975 NCAA Championship team. He has also won over $4 million on the Tour.

# September 4

## 1994: Simon Hobday Defeats Jim Albus in a Play-off, Wins GTE Northwest Classic

Simon Hobday, who had won the U.S. Senior Open at Pinehurst in July, won his second tournament of the season to run his earnings to $528,352. The fifty-four-year-old South African, who won six tournaments in eighteen years on the European and African Tours, tied Jim Albus at 209 on the 6,440-yard, par-72 Inglewood Country Club layout in Kenmore, Washington. Then he made a 12-foot birdie putt on the third extra hole to win $82,500. After the match, Albus commented, "Simon is tough. He's a Damon Runyon character. If you let him, he'll keep you entertained all afternoon with stories."

Albus pursued Hobday at Pinehurst No. 2 at the USGA Senior Open earlier in the year. It looked as if Hobday was ready to fold when he shanked his tee shot on the 175-yard, par-3 seventeenth and carded a double-bogey 5. He recovered for a birdie on eighteen to finish the third round with a two-stroke lead. Graham Marsh, Hobday, and Albus played in a threesome the final round. Going into the seventeenth, Hobday, at 11 under, was one ahead of Marsh and two ahead of Albus. Marsh and Albus parred the seventeenth while Hobday hooked into a bunker and bogeyed. All three were within putting distance after two shots on the par-4 eighteenth. Albus putted for a birdie and missed. Marsh approached to within nine feet but missed his putt for bogey. Albus holed out for par, even with Marsh. Hobday lagged a 40-footer to within two feet and holed out to become, after Ernie Els's play-off U.S. Open win in June, the second South African within a month to win a U.S. national championship.

# September 5

## 1925: Bobby Jones Defeats Fellow East Lake Country Club Member Watts Gun in Final of U.S. Amateur

For the first, and to this date, the last time in the U.S. Amateur Championship, two members from the same golf club reached the final. Bobby Jones, of the East Lake Country Club in Atlanta, defeated Watts Gun 8 and 7 in the 36-hole final at the Oakmont Country Club. Jones won five U.S. Amateur titles (1924, 1925, 1927, 1928, 1930) and finished second twice (1919, 1926). He was a semifinalist in 1920 and 1922. He was eliminated in his first Amateur by Robert Gardner, 5 and 3, after two wins in 1916 at age fourteen; lost to William Humer, 2 and 1, after two wins in 1921; and lost to Max Marston, 2 and 1, after winning his first-round match in 1923. The Amateur was not held in the World War I years, 1917–18, and Jones retired at age twenty-eight after his 1930 win.

Watts Gunn was an excellent golfer and a friend of Bobby Jones. Jones, three years his senior, urged Gunn's parents to let him play in the 1925 Amateur when he was twenty years of age. Gunn had won the Georgia Amateur at age eighteen and won the NCAA title in 1927 while at Georgia Tech. He won the Georgia Amateur again in 1927 and was twice a member of the Walker Cup team (1926, 1928). Gunn also largely retired from national competitive golf after 1930.

# September 6

## 1924: Dorothy Campbell Hurd Wins Her Third U.S. Women's Amateur Title

Dorothy Campbell Hurd won eleven major championships, ten of them between 1905 and 1912, and six of them in the United States and Canada. The Scottish-born Hurd won the Scottish Ladies' (1905, 1906, 1908), the British Ladies' (1909, 1911), the U.S. Women's Amateur (1909, 1910, 1924), and the Canadian Ladies' Open (1910, 1911, 1912). She was the first Scottish player to win the U.S. Women's Amateur Championship, and the first to achieve the coveted double of the British and American titles in the same year—1909, when the venues were Birkdale and Merion. The 1924 U.S. Women's Amateur was held at the Rhode Island Country Club, Glenna Collett Vare's home club, in Nyatt, Rhode Island. Mrs. Hurd, representing the Merion Cricket Club, defeated Mary K. Browne, a former American national singles tennis champion, 7 and 6, in the 36-hole final match.

Dorothy Campbell Hurd was among the pioneers in women's golf. She participated in the 1908 British Ladies' Amateur, which was held at the Royal and Ancient Golf Club in St. Andrews, the first time a significant women's event was played on that venerable layout. She was also among the leading international competitors of her day. Mrs. Hurd, then Dorothy Campbell, married J. B. Hurd of Pittsburgh in 1913 and then went into semiretirement. She returned to tournament play in the 1920s, adjusted her swing, and adopted the Vardon grip. Her last major victory in 1924 came when she was forty-three years of age.

# September 7

### 1986: Ayako Okamoto Wins Cellular One–Ping
### Championship by Six Shots with Final Round 66

Ayako Okamoto sank birdie putts of sixty and twelve feet on the first two holes of the final round, then went on to shoot a 6-under-par 66 to win the Cellular One–Ping Championship by six shots over Nancy Lopez and Colleen Walker. Okamoto, a former Japanese women's softball star, shot a 54-hole total of 207 on the Columbia-Edgewater Country Club layout in Portland, Oregon. The well-treed venue with tight fairways and fast greens reminded Ms. Okamoto of some of her favorite courses in Japan. Okamoto had previously won the LPGA Elizabeth Arden Classic in 1986.

# September 8

### 1994: Nick Price Opens With a 67, Goes On to Win His
### Second Canadian Open

Nick Price shot a first-round 67 at the 7,112-yard, par-72 Glen Abbey Course in Ontario, then went on to fire a 275 (67, 72, 68, 68) to win the Canadian Open. Mark Calcavecchia challenged Price at the end with a final-round 67, including an eagle on eighteen to tie Price, who was still out on the course. Price responded with "the best 2-iron of my life," a 229-yard approach to within two feet on sixteen for an eagle. Price's 275 edged Calcavecchia by a stroke. By the end of September, Price, who had already won seven worldwide tournaments including the PGA Championship and the British Open, had earned almost $1.5 million on the U.S. Tour alone.

# September 9

## 1990: Patty Sheehan Wins Ping–Cellular One LPGA Golf Championship, Wins Four Tournaments in 1990

Patty Sheehan shot a 54-hole total of 208 to win the Ping–Cellular One title at the Columbia Edgewater Country Club in Portland, Oregon, and $52,500 in prize money. Sheehan won four tournaments in 1990, and $732,618 in purses to finish second on the Tour, and by 1993 she was among the all-time leaders in Tour earnings. She was inducted into the LPGA Hall of Fame in 1993.

Sheehan continued her winning ways in 1994 by winning her second U.S. Women's Open in a come-from-behind victory at the Indianwood Golf and Country Club in Lake Orion, Michigan. Helen Alfredsson dominated the first half of the tournament as she became, along with Patty Sheehan (1984 LPGA Championship), the only woman ever to shoot a 63 in a major. She did that on the first round, then set an open record for women or men with a total of 132 after two rounds. Sheehan, at that point, trailed Alfredsson by five shots and after forty-three holes trailed by eight. Then the wheels came off for Alfredsson as she went 6 over on the back nine on her way to a 76. After being 13 under par she had dropped to 5 under and would eventually end up in a three-way tie for ninth, eight shots off the lead.

The following day it came down to a contest between Tammie Green, a thirty-four-year-old Ohioan, and Patty Sheehan, who played in the same twosome. They were dead even after the fifteenth hole on the final round. Sheehan then hit a 7-iron to within four feet of the cup for a birdie 3 to pick up a stroke on seventeen. Green needed a 12-foot putt on the last hole to force a play-off, but couldn't make it. Sheehan, the 5-feet-3-inch dynamo, had won her second U.S. Open in three years. Her total of 287 tied the Open record set by Liselotte Neumann when she won the Open in 1988.

Sheehan's first U.S. Women's Open win came in 1992, when she won in an 18-hole play-off over Juli Inkster at Oakmont. Sheehan, then playing in her eighteenth Open, knows something about patience and fortitude. She suffered a devastating defeat in the 1990 Women's Open at the Atlanta Athletic Club when she had an 11-shot lead early in the final round but lost to Betsy King by one stroke. As Sheehan said, "I don't hit it a mile. I have to be patient. I have to hit it straight. I have to rely on getting it up-and-down and making a few birdies here and there."

# September 10

### 1947: Birthday of Larry Nelson, Winner of Two PGA Championships

Larry Nelson, born in Fort Payne, Alabama, played his first round of golf at age twenty-one, learning the basics of the golf swing by reading Ben Hogan's classic instructional book, *The Modern Fundamentals of Golf,* written with Herbert Warren Wind. Within a year he broke par, and after developing his compact, uncomplicated swing, he turned professional in 1971 and qualified for the Tour in the fall of 1973. Since then he has won over $3.2 million and ten Tour tournaments, including two PGA Championships and a U.S. Open. He was a member of the 1979, 1981, and 1987 Ryder Cup teams.

Nelson's first PGA Championship was a four-stroke win over Fuzzy Zoeller at the 7,070-yard, par-70 Atlanta Athletic Club in 1981. In the 1987 PGA, Nelson finished at 287 in a tie with Lanny Wadkins at PGA National, a 7,002-yard, par-72 layout in Palm Beach Gardens, Florida. Nelson won the tournament with a par on the first extra hole, the par-4 tenth on the Championship course. This victory earned Nelson a $150,000 payday. Nelson's 1983 U.S. Open victory was achieved at Oakmont, where he dropped a dramatic 60-foot birdie putt on the sixteenth hole during the last round, then parred and bogeyed the final holes to finish with 280, one stroke better than Tom Watson.

Nelson had shot 65 and 67 on the last thirty-six holes to break the old record for the last two rounds of an Open, held by Gene Sarazen since 1932. Nelson broke that record under tremendous pressure on one of the most difficult golf courses in the United States.

# September 11

## 1994: Nick Price Wins Canadian Open

Nick Price won his seventh victory of the year and his fifth PGA tournament by winning the Canadian Open by a single stroke over Mark Calcavecchia 275 to 276 at the 7,112-yard, par-72 Glen Abbey Golf Club in Oakville, Ontario. Price, of Zimbabwe, won both the British Open and Canadian Open in 1994, the first golfer to win both these tournaments in the same year since Tom Weiskopf did it in 1973. Price's six PGA Tour victories in 1994 are the most in a season since Tom Watson won six times in 1986.

At thirty-seven, Price, who also won the 1994 PGA Championship, was being touted by many as the next dominating golfer. His reply: "I'm not thinking about breaking any records or anything else. I know it can't go on forever. But I'm having a hell of a time right now." Price, the 1994 PGA Player of the Year, led the PGA in tournament earnings and was first in the Sony rankings. He also led the PGA Tour in wins in 1993 with four and 1994 with five. Byron Nelson still holds the PGA Tour record for wins in a year, eighteen in 1945, and consecutive wins, eleven, in 1945.

Canadian golf has a long and rich tradition. The game was formally established in Montreal in 1873, when the Royal Montreal Golf Club was founded, although there are indications that the game was played in Canada much earlier. The Royal Canadian Golf Association was founded in 1896 to promote interest in the game of golf; establish and enforce uniformity in the rules of the game; and to administer matches and competitions. The first Amateur Championship was played at Royal Ottawa in 1895, and the first Canadian Open was played at Royal Montreal in 1904. J. H. Oke won the first Canadian Open with a 36-hole score of 156. The format was changed to 72 holes in 1907, and since then notable golfers including Leo Diegel (1924, 1925), Tommy Armour (1927, 1930, 1934), Walter Hagen (1931), Sam Snead (1938, 1940, 1941), Byron Nelson (1945), Arnold Palmer (1955), Lee Trevino (1971, 1977, 1979), Greg Norman (1984, 1992), Curtis Strange (1985, 1987), and Tom Weiskopf (1973, 1975) have won the tournament, which is the only PGA Tour event held outside the United States.

Since 1977 (with the exception of 1980), the Canadian Open has been held at Glen Abbey, a Jack Nicklaus–designed course and home of the Canadian PGA. Although Nicklaus has won seventy PGA Tour events and many other tournaments, he has never won the Canadian Open, although he has finished second seven times.

# September 12

## 1968: Tommy Armour Dead at Age 71, Winner of 1927 U.S. Open and Acclaimed Golf Instructor

Tommy Armour, known as the Silver Scot, was a seasoned professional when he arrived at the Oakmont Country Club to compete with 148 qualifiers in the 1927 U.S. Open. Armour had seen heavy duty as a tank machine-gunner in the British Army in World War I and had come out of the war a wounded hero. He lost the sight in one eye and carried eight pieces of shrapnel in his left shoulder. In 1921 he had come to the United States as a member of the British Walker Cup team. He joined the professional ranks shortly thereafter. Armour's main competition in the Open proved to be Harry Cooper, an English-born professional who became a naturalized American and was raised in Texas. His father was a professional at a municipal course in Dallas.

At the end of seventy-two holes of regulation play, Armour and Cooper were tied at 301 after Armour played the final six holes in 2 under par. This was the last time the best regulation scores exceeded 300 in the U.S. Open. Gene Sarazen, who soared to a third-round score of 80, finished one stroke back after finishing with a strong 74. He had also carded 74s on the first two rounds. Bobby Jones, the defending champion, played one of his worst Opens and finished eleventh.

Armour defeated Cooper by three strokes, 76–79, in an 18-hole play-off. He later won the 1930 PGA Championship and the 1931 British Open. He also became a highly respected golf instructor after his tournament career came to an end. His instruction book *How to Play Your Best Golf All the Time* is considered a classic.

# September 13

## 1930: Tommy Armour Wins the PGA Championship,
## Also Won British and U.S. Opens

Tommy Armour, a native of Edinburgh, Scotland, but a naturalized U.S. citizen, turned professional in 1924 and within seven years had won every major championship—the U.S. Open (1927), the British Open (1931), and the PGA Championship (1930). In 1926, he played with the American team in the Ryder Cup, the first international professional match with Great Britain—the first and only golfer to represent both countries. He played on the British Walker Cup team in 1922.

After defeating Johnny Farrell, 2 and 1, in the quarterfinals and Charles Lacey, 1-up, in the semifinals of the 1930 PGA Championship, Armour had to face Gene Sarazen, a two-time PGA champion, in the 36-hole final at Fresh Meadow Country Club in Flushing, New York, Gene Sarazen's home course. Armour had a 1-up edge after the morning round, but the match was tied when they reached the final hole, a par-4. Both golfers reached the green in three after recovering from a greenside bunker. Armour made his 12-foot putt but Sarazen missed a 10-footer to lose by a single hole.

Tommy Armour was a great competitor and was especially noted for his iron play. An excellent teacher, he gained an international reputation as an instructor at Boca Raton in Florida and Winged Foot in Mamaroneck, New York.

# September 14

### 1928: Golf in the Kingdom, Prince of Wales Tees Off
### From the Great Pyramids

The Prince of Wales, who later abdicated the throne for the woman he loved, teed it up on the Great Pyramid and hit his golf ball into the desert while a caddie and an entourage watched. The prince was on a tour of the kingdom, including the Suez Canal.

# September 15

### 1994: Sarah Lebrun Ingram Wins Third U.S. Women's
### Mid-Amateur in Four Years

Sarah Lebrun Ingram, twenty-eight, of Nashville, Tennessee, defeated Marla Jemsek of Oviedo, Florida, 2 and 1, in the 18-hole final of the U.S. Women's Mid-Amateur at the 5,975-yard, par-72 Tacoma Country and Golf Club in Washington. The Women's Mid-Amateur, an event for amateur golfers at least twenty-five years old and who have a USGA Handicap Index not exceeding 9.4, was inaugurated by the USGA in 1987. The format begins with two 18-hole rounds of stroke play to narrow the field to sixty-four low scorers who move on to 18-hole match play. The winner receives a gold medal and custody of the Mildred Gardiner Prunaret Trophy for the ensuing year.

Cindy Scholefield was the first winner of the event, held in 1987 at the Southern Hills Country Club in Tulsa. Ms. Ingram has won the event a record three times (1991, 1993, 1994).

# September 16

## 1979: European Team Plays the United States in the Ryder Cup for the First Time

The British and Irish Ryder Cup team was redefined to include continental European golfers. Ireland was added to the traditional British contingent in 1973, but the United States, featuring golfers such as Arnold Palmer, Jack Nicklaus, Lee Trevino, Billy Casper, and Tom Weiskopf, continued to dominate. The first European team, which included Seve Ballesteros, Ken Brown, Brian Burnes, Nick Faldo, Bernard Gallacher, Antonio Garrido, Tony Jacklin, Mark James, Michael King, Sandy Lyle, Peter Oosterhuis, and Des Smyth, lost 17 and 11 at the Greenbrier in White Sulphur Springs, West Virginia. John Jacobs captained the European contingent.

The American team included Andy Bean, Lee Elder, Hubert Green, Mark Hayes, Hale Irwin, Tom Kite, John Mahaffey, Gil Morgan, Larry Nelson, Lee Trevino, Lanny Wadkins, and Fuzzy Zoeller. Billy Casper was the nonplaying captain for the U.S. squad. Larry Nelson won five matches in four-balls, foursomes, and singles.

The European team was selected from the top ten money winners in the Order of Merit, and two were selected by invitation. Since 1979, the European team has won three Ryder Cup contests (1985, 1987, 1989), and the United States has won four (1981, 1983, 1991, 1993).

# September 17

### 1956: Ann Gregory Becomes the First African-American Woman to Play in a National Championship

The fifty-sixth Women's Amateur Championship was held at the 6,340-yard, par-74 Meridian Hills Country Club in Indianapolis. There were 116 entries and 105 started in the match-play event beginning with 18-hole contests leading up to a 36-hole final. When Mrs. Ann Gregory teed off in her match against Mrs. Philip J. Cudone, she became the first African-American woman to play in a national championship sponsored by the United States Golf Association. Mrs. Gregory lost to Mrs. Cudone, 2 and 1, in the first round. She competed in national Amateur events until 1988, when she played in her last U.S. Seniors' Open at age seventy-six.

Raised in Mississippi by a white family after her parents died when she was a child, Mrs. Gregory, then Ann Moore, later moved north and married. She lived in Gary, Indiana, took up golf, became a member of the all-black Chicago Women's Golf Association, which joined the USGA in 1956 so its members could play in USGA tournaments. Ann Gregory almost won the U.S. Women's Senior Amateur in 1971 at the Sea Island Golf Club, but she lost to her old rival, Mrs. Cudone, by one stroke on the last hole of the final round. Mrs. Gregory died in 1990.

# September 18

## 1926: George Von Elm Defeats Bobby Jones in U.S. Amateur, 2 and 1, at Baltusrol

George Von Elm survived a field of 144 starters to win the thirtieth U.S. Amateur at the Baltusrol Golf Club in Springfield, New Jersey. Von Elm won his 18-hole matches 1-up (19 holes) and 3 and 2, before meeting the formidable Mr. Jones, who had won the previous two Amateurs. Jones had won the medal with a 36-hole score of 143 and was heavily favored to win the event. Von Elm avenged his 9 and 8 loss to Jones in the final of the 1924 Amateur, and a 1925 loss, to win this semifinal match. A Californian playing out of the Rancho Golf Club in Los Angeles, Von Elm played underpar golf to win the final and a national-championship trophy, in this case the Havemeyer, named after the first president of the USGA.

George Von Elm, who was born in Salt Lake City, Utah, was one of the finest amateur golfers of his day. Von Elm played on the Walker Cup team in 1926, 1928, and 1930. He won the French Amateur in 1930.

# September 19

## 1954: Barbara Romack Defeats Mickey Wright in U.S. Women's Amateur

Barbara Romack, twenty-two, defeated nineteen-year-old Mickey Wright 4 and 2 in the rain-delayed 36-hole match-play final of the U.S. Women's Amateur. Romack, a native of Sacramento, California, won six 18-hole matches 8 and 7, 6 and 5, 3 and 2, 3 and 2, 7 and 5, and 7 and 6 on the 6,034-yard, par-73 Allegheny Country Club Course in Sewickley, Pennsylvania, to reach the final. The field of 144 starters included all members of the British and U.S. Curtis Cup teams, and the champions of Belgium, Canada, Cuba, Mexico, and a former champion of Argentina. Miss Romack had won the 1953 Canadian Ladies' Open and was a member of the 1954, 1956, and 1958 Curtis Cup teams.

In late 1958, Barbara Romack joined the LPGA Tour, then in its early formative years. Her first LPGA victory came in the Leesburg Pro-Am in 1960 where she won a total of $350. She soon left the Tour due to ill health and injuries. Miss Romack described the camaraderie of the early Tour to golf journalist Rhonda Glenn: "It was a team effort in many ways. There were times when we knew one of our group was hard-pressed for money, yet too proud to say anything. There would be a silent collection among the players to help her get to the next stop. Sometimes the club members would chip in. The money would mysteriously appear, sealed in a nondescript envelope, in the player's incoming mail."

# September 20

## 1924: Walter Hagen Wins His First of Four Straight PGA Championships

Jim Barnes, who barely won his semifinal match, 1-up, against twenty-four-year-old Larry Nabholtz, could not overcome four three-putt greens on the morning round and a weak final hole as Walter Hagen won his second PGA Championship, 2-up. A 36-hole qualifying round was held the Monday before the tournament at the French Springs Golf Club, a Donald Ross layout in French Lick, Indiana. Johnny Farrell was the low qualifier of thirty-two players with a 36-hole score of 140.

Barnes, a native of Lelant, Cornwall, England, came to the United States in 1906 as a professional. He won the first PGA Championship in 1916 by defeating Jock Hutchinson in the finals by 1-up. In the following year, he won his second Western Open (he had won his first in 1914), where he finished three strokes in front of Walter Hagon. In 1919 he won his second PGA Championship, his third Western Open, and the North and South Open and was runnerup in the Canadian Open. He won the 1921 U.S. Open by nine strokes, then won his last major, the 1925 British Open with an even score of 300.

Barnes stood 6 feet 3 inches tall and was nicknamed "Long Jim." As Barnes and Hagen dueled down the stretch at the 1924 PGA Championship, Barnes fought back to 1-down as they approached the final tee. He was unable to send the match into overtime because of a bad drive, followed by a shanked mashie niblick (similar to a 6-iron).

Barnes was one of the first professional golfers to write instruction books. He wrote *Picture Analysis of Golf Strokes* in 1919 and *A Guide to Good Golf* in 1925.

# September 21

## 1986: Corey Pavin Wins Play-off to Take Greater
## Milwaukee Open, Fourth Career Tour Win

Corey Pavin, a 5-feet-9-inch, 150-pound, fierce competitor, won his fourth career Tour event and $72,000 in first-prize money. After tieing Dave Barr at 272 in regulation, Pavin won the play-off, the first in his career. By the end of 1993 he was 5-2 in play-off competition and had won ten tournaments and almost $5 million. In 1991, Pavin won the earnings title and was PGA Player of the Year when he won the Bob Hope Chrysler Classic, the Bell South America Classic, and $979,430. When he shot a 21-under-par 259 to win the 1988 Texas Open, he became the fifth player in Tour history to better 260. Before turning professional in 1982, he won the Junior World title at age seventeen, played on the UCLA golf team, and was a member of the 1981 Walker Cup team. He was a member of the 1991 and 1993 Ryder Cup teams. Pavin ranked tenth in the 1994 Sony rankings. Fred Couples was the only other American in the top ten.

# September 22

## 1905: Willie Anderson Wins Record Third Straight U.S. Open

Willie Anderson won his third straight U.S. Open by scoring a 314 at the Myopia Hunt Club in Hamilton, Massachusetts. Anderson shot rounds of 81, 80, 76, and 77 to win by two over Alex Smith. Anderson won a total of four Opens, a feat equaled only by Bobby Jones, Ben Hogan, and Jack Nicklaus. On the third round, Anderson's 76 included five 3s, and at one point, after dropping a long putt on the fourth, he supposedly commented to the crowd, "That's the championship." Anderson played the front nine of the final round in 37 and finally passed Alex Smith, who had been leading since the first round.

At the time of this, his fourth, Open victory, Anderson was only twenty-five years old. His health began to fail soon after the Open and he died of arteriosclerosis at the young age of thirty-two. Smith also won four Western Opens, then considered a major tournament, second only in importance to the U.S. Open.

# September 23

### 1930: Maurice McCarthy Jr. Defeats George Von Elm
### on Tenth Extra Hole in Second Round of U.S. Amateur

Maurice McCarthy Jr. and George Von Elm played the longest 18-hole match-play contest in U.S. Amateur history when they had to go ten extra holes to decide their match in the second round on the Merion Cricket Club East Course. McCarthy had made a hole in one in the medalist qualifying round to make the match-play competition. He went into overtime in his first match with Watts Gunn and prevailed on the first extra (nineteenth) hole. Bobby Jones, the medalist, won this event 8 and 7 over Eugene Homans in the final to achieve the fourth leg of his historic Grand Slam. Homans had defeated Charles H. Seaver, father of Baseball Hall of Fame pitcher Tom Seaver, 1-up, to reach the final.

Maurice McCarthy Jr. was the 1928 NCAA champion. His father, Maurice McCarthy Sr., was a golf instructor and golf course designer. One of his most highly regarded creations is the Hershey Country Club Course in Pennsylvania.

# September 24

## 1929: Mlle. Genevieve le Derff, Professional Golfer, Becomes First Woman to Compete in the French Open

Genevieve le Derff, woman professional at Fourgheux and Paris, competed in the French Open Championship at Fourgheux. This was the first occasion a woman had competed in a French Open.

France, which now has an estimated 150 golf courses and 70,000 golfers, was one of the first countries outside Britain to have a golf club. Pau, laid out in the foothills of the Pyrenees in 1854, was the first golf course in France. France's most notable golfers have been Arnaud Massy, winner of the 1907 British Open, and Catherine Lacoste, who won the U.S. Women's Open as an amateur in 1967.

# September 25

## 1933: Ring Lardner, Sometime Golf Writer, Dies

Ring Lardner, who contributed golf articles to *The American Golfer, Colliers,* and other publications, died at age forty-eight in East Hampton, Long Island, New York. While golfing with President Harding in 1921, Lardner remarked when the president's errant shot hit a tree, "I did all I could to make Coolidge president."

# September 26

## 1955: First USGA Senior Amateur Championship,
## J. Wood Platt Wins Match-Play Event

The USGA Senior Amateur is open to amateur golfers who have reached their fifty-fifth birthday by the date set for national qualifying and who have a USGA Handicap Index not exceeding 8.4. The first two days feature 18-hole medal play to cut the field to sixty-four golfers, who compete in 18-hole match-play events. The first Senior Amateur Champion was Woodie Platt, eight times the Philadelphia Amateur champion and was a member of the informal American team that traveled to Hoylake, England, in 1921 to play a British team. This informal competition led to the first Walker Cup match the following year.

The first Senior Amateur was held at the 6,470-yard, par-72 Belle Meade Country Club in Nashville. The Championship attracted 370 entrants from thirty states and the District of Columbia. J. Wood Platt, fifty-six, of the Saucon Valley Country Club in Bethlehem, Pennsylvania, defeated George Stadinger, of San Francisco, California, 5 and 4. Platt was 2 under par when he closed out Mr. Stadinger at the fourteenth.

The oldest Seniors champion was Lewis Oehmig of Lookout Mountain, Tennessee, who won the 1985 competition at age sixty-nine. He holds the record for most championships won, three (1972, 1976, 1985). He was runner-up a record three times (1974, 1975, and 1979). In recent years an average of more than two thousand golfers have entered the amateur. Carts have been allowed at this event since 1969.

# September 27

## 1939: Birthday of Kathy Whitworth, Winner of a Record 88 LPGA Tournaments

Kathy Whitworth, one of the greatest golfers, was born in Monahans, Texas, and soon moved to Jal, New Mexico, a border town where her father owned a hardware store. At 5 feet 9 inches tall, she was an excellent athlete as a youth but became enamored of golf at an early age and became one of Harvey Penrick's prize pupils as a teenager. After winning a few amateur events and winning a golf scholarship to Odessa Junior College in Texas, she left school and joined the fledgling LPGA Tour in 1958. She won less than $1,250 in her first full year on the Tour, but she was determined. Miss Whitworth worked on her game, got her weight down from 215 pounds to 140 over a few years, and won her first tournament in 1962 (the Kelley Girl, in Baltimore, Maryland).

Kathy Whitworth led the Tour in money winnings in 1965, 1966, 1967, 1968, 1970, 1971, 1972, and 1973. She had ten wins in 1968 and was named LPGA Player of the Year seven times. She competed regularly against LPGA Hall of Famers Louise Suggs, Mickey Wright, Betsy Rawls, Sandra Haynie, and Carol Mann. The Associated Press named her Woman Athlete of the Year in 1965 and 1967. She won the Vare Trophy for best LPGA Tour scoring average seven times. She won over $1.7 million in LPGA Tour earnings, the first female golfer to reach the $1 million mark (1981). She was inducted into the LPGA Hall of Fame in 1975. Among the LPGA majors that she won are the Titleholders (1965, 1966), Western Open (1967), and LPGA Championship (1967, 1971). She never won a U.S. Women's Open, just as Sam Snead, second to her all-time with eighty-one Tour wins, never won a U.S. Open. She has been elected president of the LPGA three times.

# September 28

## 1946: Mildred Didrikson Zaharias Wins U.S. Women's Amateur

Mrs. Mildred Didrikson "Babe" Zaharias was one of the greatest women athletes of all time. She won three gold medals in the 1932 Olympics, setting world records in the low hurdles, the javelin, and the high jump. Her high-jump record was disallowed because of her unorthodox, and then illegal, jumping technique.

She took up golf seriously in 1933 when she was twenty-six years of age and, after winning the Texas Open in 1935, was banned from amateur events until she was reinstated to amateur status in 1943. The Women's Amateur was not held from 1942 through 1945 due to World War II. The 1946 Amateur was held at the 6,232-yard, par-75 Southern Hills Country Club, and Babe Zaharias easily won 11 and 9 over Mrs. Clara C. Sherman in the 36-hole match-play final. She then won the British Ladies' Amateur Championship in the spring of 1947, the first American since the tournament began in 1893 to do so.

She joined the women's professional golf circuit in 1947 after accepting a $300,000 offer from a film producer to make a series of ten golf films. Soon, after retaining sports agent Fred Corcoran, Babe was earning more than $100,000 a year. In 1949, Babe, her husband George, Fred Corcoran, Patty Berg, and the Wilson Sporting Goods Company helped develop the LPGA Tour. During her years on the fledgling LPGA Tour, Babe won less than $50,000 in official earnings although she won thirty-one professional tournaments.

# September 29

## 1923: Sarazen Defeats Hagen, 1-Up in Match Play, to Win His Second Straight PGA Title

In the first play-off in PGA Championship history—at the Pelham Golf Club in Pelham Manor, New York, a par-72 layout designed by Devereaux Emmett—Gene Sarazen edged Walter Hagen 1-up in thirty-eight holes. The 36-hole match was even after the morning round, but Sarazen then went 3-up through nine during the afternoon round. Hagen birdied the twenty-ninth hole to cut the lead to two, then won the thirty-fourth and thirty-fifth to square the match. On the thirty-sixth hole, Sarazen hit his tee shot into heavy rough but hit a brilliant recovery shot to within two feet of the pin. Hagen almost birdied the hole from a greenside bunker after missing his approach shot.

Hagen and Sarazen had a relatively easy time reaching the finals in a field of sixty-four golfers, who qualified in local districts. Sarazen's toughest match was a 1-up fourth-round win over Jim Barnes, while Hagen was taken to 4 and 3 by George Griffen in the first round and John Golden on the third. Hagen had not defended his 1921 PGA title in 1922, the year of Sarazen's first win, due to lucrative exhibition commitments. He would rebound to win four straight championships from 1924 through 1927 before being eliminated by Leo Diegel, the eventual winner, 2 and 1, in the third round in 1928. Sarazen would have to wait until 1933 to win his third, and last, PGA Championship.

# September 30

## 1978: Alice Dye Wins U.S. Senior Women's Amateur in an 18-Hole Play-off at Rancho Bernardo

Alice Dye, fifty-one, playing in the 50-through-54-year-old "A" group, tied at the end of regulation with Mrs. Robert H. MacLaurin, but won the 18-hole play-off, 76–79, to win the seventeenth Senior Women's Amateur Championship. The event took place at the 5,853-yard, par-73 Rancho Bernardo Golf Club in San Diego. Mrs. Dye scored 74, 75, and 83 for 232 in regulation, and Mrs. MacLaurin had rounds of 76, 81, and 75. A separate competition was held for age groups in ranges of 55 through 59 years, 60 through 64 years, and 65 and over. There were 120 starters in 1978. In 1979, Alice Dye again won the title as she scored a decisive 7-stroke win over Mrs. MacLaurin with a 70, 77, and 76 for 223 at the 5,712-yard, par-71 Hardscrabble Country Club in Fort Smith, Arkansas.

The U.S. Senior Women's Amateur was first won by Miss Maureen Orcutt in 1962. Mrs. Glenna Collett Vare was runner-up. Miss Orcutt won again in 1966. Maureen Orcutt was runner-up in the U.S. Women's Amateur in 1927 and 1936. She won two Canadian Women's (1930, 1931) and was a member of the first Curtis Cup team in 1932 and again in 1934, 1936, and 1938. She won numerous amateur events including the North and South Women's (three times), the Eastern (seven times), the Women's Metropolitan (eight times), and the New Jersey State Match Play Championship (eight times). Miss Orcutt covered the leading golf championships and women's events as a writer for the *New York Times.*

Alice Dye has had a formidable career as a player, administrator, golf-course designer, and parent. Mrs. Dye was born Alice O'Neal in Indianapolis, became a golf protégé of her father, Perry, a prominent attorney, then went off to Rollins College in Winter Park, Florida, to study premed and compete on the golf team. She met Pete Dye, who captained the Rollins men's team, married, and settled down in Indianapolis, where they both sold insurance and played competitive amateur golf. They had two children, Paul and Perry, who would later become golf-course designers, and started their own golf-course design business. One of their early courses, the Crooked Stick Golf Club, Carmel, Indiana, which opened in 1966, is rated by *Golf Digest* among the top one hundred golf courses in America, as are Dye-designed courses such as the Honors Course, Ooltewah, Tennessee (with P. B. Dye, 1983); the Golf Club, New Albany, Ohio (1967); the Long Cove Club, Hilton Head, South Carolina (1981); the TPC Stadium Course at Sawgrass (1981); and the Old Marsh Golf Club, Palm Beach Gardens, Florida (1987). Alice Dye, who directly or indirectly collaborates with Pete on his various projects, is the first woman member of the American Society of Golf Course Architects.

Alice Dye was a member of the 1970 Curtis Cup team and has served on numerous USGA and LPGA committees. She was the captain of the 1992 Women's World Amateur team, which included Vicki Goetze, Sarah L. Ingram, and Carol Semple Thompson.

# October 1

## 1921: Walter Hagen Wins His First PGA Championship

For the first time, the field for match play in the U.S. Open was composed of the top thirty-two finishers in the U.S. Open, plus the previous year's winner, Jock Hutchison. The 36-hole matches were held at the Inwood Country Club in Far Rockaway, New York. Walter Hagen defeated Jack Forrester (6 and 4), Tim Boyd (6 and 5), Jack Golden (8 and 7), and Emmett French (5 and 3) to reach the final. An early tournament surprise was nineteen-year-old Gene Sarazen's easy 8-and-6 victory over the defending champion, Jock Hutchison.

Jim Barnes, who shot four sub-70 rounds to reach the final, provided an excellent matchup for Hagen, who was one of the toughest competitors in the game. The British golf writer Bernard Darwin wrote of him: "His demeanor towards his opponents, though entirely correct, had yet a certain suppressed truculence; he exhibited so supreme a confidence that they could not get it out of their minds and could not live against it." Barnes, considered one of the best golfers of his era, had won the PGA Championship in 1916 and 1919, its first two years, and later won the U.S. Open (1921) and the British Open (1925).

Hagen shot a 69 during the 18-hole morning round to go 1-up in the final. He built a four-hole margin by shooting 4-under 33 on the front nine of the afternoon round. Hagen, one of the PGA's original founders, closed out the match, 3 and 2, at the thirty-fourth hole, winning the first of his five PGA titles.

*Opposite:* Walter Hagen

# October 2

### 1968: Mrs. Philip Cudone Shoots 80 in First Round, Goes On to Win First of Five Consecutive Senior Women's Amateur Championships

Mrs. Philip Cudone shot the first-round low score of 80 at the 5,935-yard, par-75 Monterey Peninsula Country Club in Pebble Beach, California, and followed with rounds of 79 and 77 to total 236 and win her first of a record five consecutive Senior Women's Amateur Championships by ten strokes. She shot an identical score the following year at the 5,650-yard, par-73 Ridglea Country Club in Fort Worth to tie Mrs. Lowell D. Brown. Mrs. Cudone then outdueled Mrs. Brown 76–84 in an 18-hole play-off. In 1970, Mrs. Cudone shot 231 at the 5,856-yard, par-74 Coral Ridge Country Club in Fort Lauderdale to win by eight strokes. Then she totaled 236 at the 5,711-yard, par-75 Sea Island Golf Club in Georgia to win by a single stroke over Ann Gregory. Her fifty consecutive win came on the 5,832-yard, par-74 Manufacturers Golf and Country Club in Oreland, Pennsylvania, in 1972. Mrs. Cudone shot a 231 to win by six shots.

Her streak was stopped by Mrs. David L. Hibbs, who shot a 229 at the 5,891-yard, par-74 San Marcos Country Club in Chandler, Arizona, in 1973. Mrs. Cudone shot 237 to finish fourth. She finished second in 1974 and 1975, but has been unable to win again. Her five straight victories are the most consecutive tournaments any golfer has won in any USGA event. Her ten-stroke margin of victory at Monterey is still the largest ever recorded in the Senior Women's Amateur.

# October 3

## 1895: Charles Blair Macdonald Wins First "Official" U.S. Amateur, 12 and 11, at Newport

The first U.S. Amateur was held at the 9-hole Newport Golf Club in Rhode Island. The first contest had thirty-two golfers in match-play competition; no qualifying rounds were held. Charles B. Macdonald of the Chicago Golf Club won his matches 7 and 6, 8 and 6, 5 and 3, 8 and 7, and 12 and 11 to decisively win the event, then the most important golf tournament in America. Macdonald had lost an "unofficial" amateur tournament at Newport the previous year. That tournament was a 36-hole medal-play contest. After shooting 84 on the first day, Macdonald had skied to 100 the following day and lost by a stroke to W. G. Lawrence, a member of the Newport Club. Only eight golfers finished out of a field of twenty.

Macdonald would not accept his loss gracefully. He claimed the 1894 event was not official because it was not a match-play tournament as any respectable national amateur championship should be (e.g., the British Amateur) and only one club sponsored the event. At this time there was no national governing body for golf in America. After heavy lobbying by Macdonald and others, a national golf association, initially called the Amateur Golf Association of the United States, was formed in December of 1894. The charter members were the Chicago Golf Club, Newport, The Country Club, St. Andrews, and Shinnecock Hills. Theodore Havemeyer, who made his fortune in the sugar trade and was a Newport member, was elected president. He promptly donated a thousand-dollar trophy, named in his honor, for the amateur championship.

The Amateur Golf Association quickly became the United States Golf Association, which coordinates the formulation and administration of international golf rules with the Royal and Ancient in Great Britain. It also organizes a variety of competitions ranging from junior events to national opens and international events such as the Curtis Cup. The USGA is now located in Far Hills, New Jersey, having moved out of New York

City some years ago. It has proved itself a valuable asset to the game of golf in various ways.

Charles Macdonald, though not the best model for sportsmanship, proved to be a major catalyst in establishing the USGA.

# October 4

## 1895: Horace Rawlins Wins First U.S. Open at Newport

Horace Rawlins defeated a field of eleven entries to win the first U.S. Open, held at the Newport Golf Club in Newport, Rhode Island. Rawlins, a nineteen-year-old British professional, is still the youngest person ever to win the Open. In four rounds over the 9-hole Newport Course, Rawlins shot 45, 46, 41, and 41 for 173. Willie Dunn of Shinnecock Hills finished second with a 175. Newport, long the resort of affluent society, also hosted the first U.S. Amateur, which preceded the Open. The Amateur was match play and the Open was medal play. At the time, the U.S. Amateur was considered a more prestigious tournament. The Amateur was won by Charles Blair Macdonald, who bested a field of thirty-two golfers.

Macdonald later established himself as a golf writer and golf course designer. His book *Scotland's Gift: Golf*, published in 1928, is a classic. He designed some of the best golf courses in the United States, including the Chicago Golf Club (1895), the National Golf Links of America (1911), Piping Rock Club, with Seth Raynor (1913), Sleepy Hollow Golf Club, with Seth Raynor (1914), and Yale University Golf Club, with Seth Raynor, Charles Banks, and Ralph Barton (1926). Macdonald, a successful stock broker, never accepted fees for his services. He is also credited with conceiving the Walker Cup series, which officially began in 1922 at his National Golf Links of America.

# October 5

## 1900: Harry Vardon Wins U.S. Open

Harry Vardon, a member of the great British golf triumvirate that included James Braid and J. H. Taylor, was at the top of his game at the turn of the century. Vardon won a record six British Opens, and Braid and Taylor won five each. They were later equaled by Peter Thomson and Tom Watson, who also won five. Vardon had an upright swing and popularized the overlapping grip, which is generally known by his name, though J. E. Laidlay, a Scotsman who was two-time winner of the British Amateur (1889, 1891) also used the grip.

The golfers in the 1900 Open had to contend with the wind off Lake Michigan and coarse, bumpy putting greens, which were made more tricky by a machine used to brush the grass to eliminate the grain. As a result, the field, which included such notable golfers as Vardon, Taylor, Laurence Aucterlonie, Willie Smith, and Stewart Gardner, had trouble scoring. Vardon and Taylor, however, were considered the favorites.

Taylor jumped off to a three-stroke lead by shooting a 76 in the first round, but lost the lead to Vardon, 157–158, after thirty-six holes. Vardon increased his lead to four strokes after fifty-four holes and extended it to six strokes with a birdie after a wind-assisted 270-yard drive on the par-4 seventh hole during the final round. Taylor came back to cut Vardon's lead to two strokes by the seventeenth, but Vardon closed out the match with a par on the par-5 closing hole to win by two, 313–315. The next nearest finisher was David Bell, a pro from the Midlothian Club, who shot a 323.

Then thirty years of age, Vardon never won another U.S. Open. Jerry Travers, one of the best American amateurs of his day, said Vardon's golf style was easy to identify: "If you run across one man who is making the game so easy a child could play it, whose form is the last word in poetry, and who from one hundred and eighty to two hundred and twenty yards is putting a full shot closer to the hole than most others can put a mashie, your quest for Vardon will be over."

# October 6

## 1934: Virginia Van Wie Wins Her Third Consecutive
## U.S. Women's Amateur Championship

Virginia Van Wie grew up in Chicago and, though tall and frail in her younger years, became an excellent competitive golfer with strong wrists and hands who could hit a ball more than two hundred yards off the tee. After spending time in Florida in the mid-1920s honing her game, she suffered a resounding 13 and 12 defeat to Glenna Collett in the final of the 1928 Women's Amateur at Virginia Hot Springs. She regrouped to win the medal in the 1929 Amateur, but was eliminated in the second round. She lost again in the final, 6 and 5, to Glenna Collett in the 1930 Amateur, and then lost again to Glenna Collett Vare (Glenna Collett married Edwin Vare Sr. in 1931), 2-up, in the 1931 Championship. Virginia finally broke through and trounced Mrs. Vare, 10 and 8, in the final at the Salem Country Club in 1932. The following year she defeated Helen Hicks, 4 and 3, for her second title at the Exmoor Country Club in Highland Park, Illinois.

Van Wie was a member of the first Curtis Cup team in 1932 and again in 1934. Following her 1934 Women's Amateur win at the Whitemarsh Valley Country Club in Chestnut Hill, Pennsylvania, 2 and 1 over Dorothy Traung, she retired from national competitive golf.

276

# October 7

## 1962: Judy Kimball Wins LPGA Championship, an LPGA Major, at the Stardust Country Club in Las Vegas

Judy Kimball, whose only previous LPGA Tour win was in the American Women's Open in 1961, surprised the field, headed by the defending champion, Mickey Wright, and won the LPGA Championship by shooting 282 to win by four strokes over Shirley Spork at the Stardust Country Club in Las Vegas. Kimball won $2,300, the largest purse on the LPGA Tour. It would be her last win on a Tour dominated by Mickey Wright and Kathy Whitworth in particular. Wright won the LPGA in 1958, 1960, 1961, and 1963. Whitworth won it in 1967, 1971, and 1975. The event was first held in 1955 at the Orchard Ridge Country Club in Fort Wayne, Indiana, where, at the end of fifty-four holes, the two low scorers played a 36-hole match to determine the winner. Beverly Hanson defeated Louise Suggs, 4 and 3, in that match-play final.

# October 8

## 1993: Dave Stockton Opens With a 68, Goes On to Win the Transamerican by One Stroke

Dave Stockton opened with a 68, then fired rounds of 71 and 64 on the 6,632-yard, par-72 Silverado Country Club layout to win the Transamerica by one stroke over Simon Hobday and Lee Trevino. Stockton won five tournaments in 1993 and led the Senior World Money List with $1,220,944. The only other Senior golfers to earn over $1 million in 1993 were Bob Charles, George Archer, Lee Trevino, and Raymond Floyd. Stockton continued his winning ways in 1994 by leading the Senior Tour with $1,402,519 in official winnings. The other million-dollar men were Ray Floyd, Jim Albus, Lee Trevino, Jim Colbert, and Tom Wargo.

Stockton, who won eleven tournaments on the regular PGA Tour beginning with the 1967 Colonial National Invitation, has now won over $4.5 million on the Senior Tour which he joined in 1991. Dave was a member of the 1993 Dupont Cup team that defeated Japan, 26–6, on the 6,719-yard Sawara Springs Country Club in Sawara City, Japan. Dave continues to selectively play in tournaments on the PGA Tour.

# October 9

## 1920: Alexa Stirling Wins Her Third Consecutive U.S. Women's Amateur Championship

Alexa Stirling defeated Mrs. Dorothy Hurd, 5 and 4, in the 36-hole match-play final at the Mayfield Country Club in Cleveland to win her third Women's Amateur. Ms. Stirling also won in 1915 and 1919. The event was not held during World War I (1916–18). Alexa Stirling reached the finals of the 1921 Women's Amateur, but was denied her fourth title by Marion Hollins, 5 and 4, at the Hollywood Golf Club in Deal, New Jersey. She lost again in the finals in 1923 and 1925.

Alexa Stirling toured the eastern United States with Elaine Rosenthal, Perry Adair, and Bobby Jones, raising over $150,000 for the Red Cross and the war effort. With her smooth Carnoustie golf swing taught to her by her coach, Scottish professional Stuart Maiden, Stirling was noted for her golfing grace and calmness in tournament situations. She once wrote, "The player who is going to win most often is not the one who is superior in strength of distance, but the one who can make the fewest mistakes and keep out of as much trouble as possible, but when once in trouble can cope with any situation."

Alexa Stirling, an American of Scottish parentage who later became Mrs. W. G. Fraser, played golf with a neighbor, Bobby Jones, six years her junior. She was the only female to defeat him in serious competition. Alexa won a six-hole match from Jones when he was six years old.

# October 10

## 1937: Birthday of Bruce Devlin, Tour Player and Prolific Golf-Course Architect

Bruce Devlin was born in Armidale, Australia, attended St. Patrick's College, then started out as a plumber before turning professional in 1961. As an amateur he had won the Australian Open (1960) and the Australian Amateur (1959), and he was a member of the victorious Australian team that defeated the United States in a play-off in the first World Amateur Team Championship, held at St. Andrews in 1958.

Devlin joined the PGA Tour in 1962 and won ten events and over $900,000 before joining the Senior Tour in 1987. In addition to his playing career he has built an excellent reputation as a golf-course architect along with his partner, Robert von Hagge. He has designed and built more than 140 golf courses since 1966, including Tour courses such as the Links at Key Biscayne (Florida), the TPC at the Woodlands (Texas), and Quail Hollow Resort (New Hampshire). Devlin has also provided golf commentary on national and cable television networks.

# October 11

## 1902: Laurie Auchterlonie Becomes First Golfer to Shoot Four Rounds Under 80 in U.S. Open

Laurie Auchterlonie shot rounds of 78, 78, 74, and 77 for 307 to become the first golfer to break 80 four times at the U.S. Open. Auchterlonie's 307 enabled him to win by six strokes over Stewart Gardner and Walter Travis at the Garden City Golf Club on Long Island. The introduction of the Haskell rubber-core ball, which traveled considerably farther than the traditional gutta-percha, was partly responsible for the lower scores. Herbert Warren Wind also sagely noted how this new golf ball technology broadened the appeal of the game: "The 'Bounding Billies,' as the new balls were called, were harder to control around the green than the old gutties, but a golfer did not have to strike them perfectly to get a reasonably straight shot, and far more important, the average golfer found his drive a full twenty yards farther down the fairway. Now the game was really enjoyable for the weekend player."

# October 12

## 1905: First Annual Seniors' Tournament Held

James D. Foot of Apawamis won the first annual Seniors' Tournament, held for golfers fifty-five years of age or older, at the Apawamis Club in Rye, New York. Foot scored 176 in the 36-hole tournament, still held every year at Apawamis. Foot also won the event in 1906, 1908, 1909, and 1911. The only golfer to win six titles is John Ellis Knowles, who won the Tournament every year from 1942 through 1946 and again in 1954. The Apawamis Club, designed by Willie Dunn Jr. and Maturin Ballou, opened in 1898. National championships including the USGA Girls' Junior (1970) and the U.S. Amateur (1911) have been played at Apawamis.

# October 13

## 1958: Australia Defeats U.S. Team in a Play-off to Win First World Amateur Team Championship

A plan for a World Amateur Team Championship was conceived by the United States Golf Association and presented to the Royal and Ancient Golf Club of St. Andrews, Scotland, in March 1958. The two governing bodies agreed to organize the event. The conference to organize the event was held in Washington, D.C., and the World Amateur Golf Council, with thirty-two member organizations, was formed to conduct the Championship. Friends of American Golf presented a silver trophy, called the Eisenhower Trophy (with the president's approval), to be awarded to the team winner. The trophy inscription reads: "To foster friendship and sportsmanship among the Peoples of the World."

The first Championship was held at the Old Course at St. Andrews, Scotland. Four-man teams representing twenty-nine countries gathered to compete in four rounds of medal play. The lowest three scores from each team were totaled each day for the competition. At the end of four rounds Australia and the United States were tied at 918, just one stroke ahead of Great Britain and Ireland. Representing Australia were Douglas W. Bachli, Peter A. Toogood, Bruce Devlin, and Robert F. Stevens. Charles R. Coe, William Hyndman III, William J. Patton, and Dr. Frank M. Taylor Jr. made up the U.S. team, captained by Robert Tyre Jones Jr. Australia won the 18-hole play-off 222 to 224.

The Championship is held biennially on a rotation basis among three geographic zones: European-African, American, and Australasian. Players must be amateur golfers and must be citizens of the country represented, with some exceptions. The highest participation to date has been forty-nine teams, who competed at the Capilano Golf and Country Club in Vancouver, Canada, in 1992. The first Championship in 1958 was the only time a play-off has been necessary.

# October 14

## 1916: Jim Barnes Wins the First PGA Championship

"Big" Jim Barnes, a 6-feet-3-inch naturalized American citizen from Lelant, Cornwall, England, won four match-play confrontations, including a 6-and-5 semifinal win over Willie MacFarlane, to meet Jock Hutchison, who had defeated Walter Hagen 2-up in the semis of the first annual PGA Championship, held at the Siwanoy Country Club in Bronxville, New York. Barnes and Hutchison were tied going into the last hole of the 36-hole final, and both needed short putts on the last green to par. Hutchison missed his putt, but Barnes made his to win the $500 first prize and a diamond medal. Hutchison won $250 and a gold medal.

Prior to the final at Siwanoy, qualification rounds were held in different sections of the country before the championship. Thirty-one qualifiers teed it up at Siwanoy, and five rounds of 36-hole match-play events were held. Barnes advanced to the final by defeating George Fotheringham, 8 and 7, Alex Smith, 8 and 7, Tom Kerrigan, 3 and 1, and Willie MacFarlane, 6 and 5. Lionel Hebert won the last match-play PGA Championship in 1957, 3 and 1, over Dow Finsterwald, and Finsterwald then won the first medal play event in 1958.

Nick Price won the 76th PGA Championship and $310,000 when he shot a 67, 65, 70, and 67 to total 269 on the 6,834-yard par-70 course at the Southern Hills Country Club in Tulsa, Oklahoma. In 1982, Ray Floyd, who opened with a 63, fired a four-round total of 272 to win $65,000.

# October 15

## 1976: U.S. Club Professionals Win Fourth Consecutive PGA Cup

The U.S. team defeated the Great Britain and Ireland squad 9½ to 6½ to record the fourth consecutive victory for the United States in the PGA Cup Matches, which were inaugurated at Pinehurst in 1973. The event was held at the Moortown Golf Club in Leeds, England, site of the 1929 Ryder Cup matches. The format of the event in 1976 was four foursomes matches on day one, four four-ball matches on day two, and eight singles matches the final day. The format is now identical to the Ryder Cup: match play, including foursomes (two-man teams in alternate shot), four-ball (two-man teams in better ball), and singles (18 holes at match play) for a total of 26 possible points. In 1990 the British and Irish team was expanded to a European team. The event is now held every other year at alternating sites.

The Llandudno ("La-lon-dro") International Trophy, the award of the PGA Cup Matches, was first given in England in 1939, after its club professionals won the first Home Tournament series against teams from Ireland, Scotland, and Wales. The trophy was packed away and the series was abolished with the outbreak of World War II. Peter Alliss, son of Percy Alliss, donated the trophy to be awarded to the winner of the PGA Cup Matches. Both Allisses played on a combined total of thirteen Ryder Cup teams. The United States team won the 1994 PGA Cup, held at PGA National. The series now stands 11-4-2 in favor of the United States.

# October 16

## 1983: United States Retains Ryder Cup in Tight Contest Against Europe, 14½ to 13½

The U.S. team secured its closest victory since 1953 to win 14½ to 13½ over the Europeans at the PGA National. The Americans, captained by Jack Nicklaus, were tied 8–8 after two days of foursomes and four-ball matches. The team consisted of Ben Crenshaw, Ray Floyd, Bob Gilder, Jay Haas, Tom Kite, Gil Morgan, Calvin Peete, Craig Stadler, Curtis Strange, Lanny Wadkins, Tom Watson, and Fuzzy Zoeller. The teams were still deadlocked after the first ten singles matches. Lanny Wadkins, 1-down against Jose Maria Canizares, birdied the par-5 final hole by hitting a 60-yard pitching wedge to within inches of the pin to gain a half. Tom Watson won his final match and the cup by winning the seventeenth to close out Bernard Gallacher. The European team, captained by Tony Jacklin, included Gallacher, Seve Ballesteros, Gordon Brand Sr., Ken Brown, Jose Maria Canizares, Nick Faldo, Bernhard Langer, Sandy Lyle, Sam Torrance, Brian Waites, Paul Way, and Ian Woosnam.

# October 17

## 1907: Margaret Curtis Defeats Her Sister, Harriot, to Win the U.S. Women's Amateur

Both Margaret and Harriot Curtis of the Essex Country Club in Manchester, Massachusetts, were excellent amateur golfers. The daughters of businessman Greely S. Curtis, both women would win national championships. Harriot, who was two years older than Margaret, won the Women's Amateur at the Brae Burn Country Club in West Newton, Massachusetts, in 1906 when she defeated Mary Adams, 2 and 1. The following year at the Midlothian Country Club in Illinois, Margaret Curtis won the medal with a 95 and then reached the match-play final against Harriot. Margaret, then twenty-seven, won 7 and 6 to capture the first of her three Women's Amateur titles. She won again in 1911 at Baltusrol and in 1912 at her home course in Manchester. The Curtis Cup, which was named for the Curtis sisters, who helped to establish the event and donated the cup, was played on the Essex Country Club course in 1938. The U.S. team, which was captained by Frances E. Stebbins and included Estelle Lawson Page, Maureen Orcutt, Glenna Collett Vare, Patty Berg, Marion Miley, Kathryn Hemphill, and Charlotte Glutting, defeated Great Britain and Ireland, 5½ to 3½.

Margaret Curtis teamed with Evelyn Sears in 1908 to win the women's doubles championship in lawn tennis. Miss Curtis competed twenty-five times in the Women's Amateur. She entered for the last time in 1949 at the age of sixty-five. She lost 3 and 2 to Mrs. Albert Hayes in the first round. Margaret received the Bob Jones Award in 1958. This award is given by the United States Golf Association to the person who, by a single act or over the years, emulates Jones's sportsmanship, respect for the game and its rules, generosity of spirit, sense of fair play, self-control, and perhaps even sacrifice. Among the other women to have received this award are Mildred Didrickson Zaharias (1957), Patty Berg (1963), Glenna Collett Vare (1965), JoAnne Gunderson Carner (1981), Maureen Garrett (1983), and Peggy Kirk Bell (1989).

# October 18

## 1935: Johnny Revolta Eliminates Walter Hagen, 1-Up, Goes On to Win PGA Championship

Johnny Revolta eliminated medalist Walter Hagen in the first round of the PGA Championship, held at the Twin Hills Country Club in Oklahoma City. Hagen was down three holes by the seventh hole of the 18-hole opener, but closed to one down at the thirteenth. He missed a 4-foot putt on the fourteenth to even the match, then watched Revolta get up and down from greenside bunkers on the next two holes. The match was even going into the eighteenth, which Revolta bogeyed. However, Hagen missed his par putt and was eliminated from the tournament. Revolta met Tommy Armour in the 36-hole final on a bitter-cold day. Revolta went out in 33 to build a 3-up lead and was never overtaken as he closed out the match, 5 and 4. Revolta played the whole tournament without three-putting. He had thirteen one-putt greens.

Johnny Revolta, who was Wisconsin Caddie Champion in 1925 at the age of fourteen, turned professional in 1929 and joined the tournament circuit in 1933. He won the Western Open in 1935 and the Texas Open in 1944. He led the Tour in earnings in 1935 with $9,543 and won a total of eighteen tournaments in his career. He played on the 1935 and 1937 Ryder Cup teams. Revolta's tournament success was interrupted by World War II, when the Tour was severely cut back. He served as professional at the Evanston Golf Club in Illinois from 1937 until 1966.

# October 19

## 1912: Birthday of Vic Ghezzi, Winner of 1941 PGA Championship

Vic Ghezzi, originally from Rumson, New Jersey, played on the PGA Tour from 1935 through 1958 and was elected to the PGA Hall of Fame in 1965. Ghezzi won the Los Angeles Open, Canadian Open, and Maryland Open in 1935, but it took until 1941 for him to win his first and only major, the PGA Championship, held at the Cherry Hills Club in Denver. Ghezzi had won five match-play contests to reach the final against Byron Nelson, and three of those matches were won 1-up over August Nordone, Jack Grout (later Jack Nicklaus's teacher), and Lloyd Mangrum. Nelson defeated Ben Hogan, 2-up, in the quarterfinals, and Gene Sarazen, 2 and 1, in the semifinals before meeting Ghezzi for the championship.

Ghezzi won his PGA Championship on the second extra hole as Nelson missed a three-foot putt for par but Ghezzi made his slightly shorter putt. Ghezzi won $1,000 for his efforts. Nelson also finished second in the Masters and the Western Open that year.

Ghezzi was drafted into the U.S. Army during World War II. He and fellow notable professionals Herman Keiser, Clayton Heafner, Horton Smith, and Lloyd Mangrum were sent overseas. Mangrum, the only well-known American professional golfer to see real combat, was wounded in the Battle of the Bulge and received the Purple Heart.

Vic Ghezzi was selected to the Ryder Cup team in 1939 and 1941, but the matches were never held because of World War II. His last significant tournament win was in 1947, when he won the Greensboro Open. Vic Ghezzi died in Miami in 1976.

# October 20

## 1972: Don Massengale Shoots 66 in Second Round, Goes On to Win PGA Club Professional Championship

Don Massengale, a thirty-six-year-old professional from White Plains, New York, shot a 66 in the second round and put together rounds of 72, 66, 74, and 68 for 280 to win the fifth PGA Club Professional Championship at the Pinehurst Country Club. Three courses were used for the event, the 7,051-yard, par-72 No. 2 course (one round and the final day); No. 4: 6,784 yards, par 72; and No. 1: 6,129 yards, par 70. A total field of 358 entered and 94 finished. Defending champion Sam Snead of the Greenbrier in West Virginia finished third. Notable professionals such as Tommy Bolt, Mike Souchak, Ernie Vossler, Ed Kroll, Davis Love Jr., Skee Riegel, Bob Rosburg, Jim Ferree, Freddie Haas, Jerry Barber, Charlie Sifford, and Dow Finsterwald have competed in this event. Current Senior Tour players Jim Albus, Tom Wargo, Gibby Gilbert, and others have played in the PGA Club Professional. Larry Gilbert of Lexington, Kentucky, who won the event in 1981, 1982, and 1991, has won the most Championships.

# October 21

## 1974: Sandra Palmer Wins Cubic Corporation Classic, Won U.S. Women's Open in 1975

Sandra Palmer was born in Fort Worth, Texas, in 1941, won the Texas State Amateur in 1963, and won the West Texas Women's Championship three times (1960, 1962, 1963). She graduated from North Texas State, then joined the LPGA Tour in 1964. She won her first regular Tour event in 1971 by holing a wedge from a trap for an eagle on the final hole of the nationally televised Sealy Classic. Her first major victory came in 1972, when she won the Titleholders.

Palmer's best year was 1975, when she won two majors, the U.S. Women's Open and the Colgate–Dinah Shore. She led the LPGA Tour in earnings ($76,374) and was selected LPGA Player of the Year. She won the Open on the 6,165-yard, par-72 Atlantic City Country Club course when she shot 78, 74, 71, and 72 for 295 to defeat Sandra Post, JoAnne Carner, and Nancy Lopez (then an amateur) by four shots. The 5-feet-1-inch Miss Palmer has won twenty-one LPGA tournaments (her last was the 1986 Mayflower Classic) and over $1.3 million on the Tour. Her win in the 1974 Cubic Corporation Classic was her eleventh Tour victory.

# October 22

## 1978: Donna Caponi Wins Houston Exchange Clubs Classic, Third Tournament Win of the Year

Donna Caponi shot a 54-hole score of 207 to win the Houston Exchange Clubs Classic and the $7,500 first prize. Caponi also won the Sara Coventry and Ping Classic Team Championship (with Kathy Whitworth) in 1978. Caponi was born in Detroit in 1945 and turned professional in 1965. She went on to win over $1.3 million and twenty-four tournaments before retiring in 1989. Her most significant wins were consecutive one-shot victories in the U.S. Women's Open in 1969 and 1970. In 1969, she shot a final-round 69 to total 294 at the 6,308-yard, par-72 Scenic Hills Country Club in Pensacola. The following year she shot a final-round 77 but held on to win with a 72-hole total of 287 at the 6,210-yard, par-71 Muskogee Country Club in Oklahoma. Caponi has won twenty-four LPGA Tour events, including five majors: the U.S. Women's Open (1969, 1970), Peter Jackson Classic (now the du Maurier, 1976) and the LPGA Championship (1979, 1981).

# October 23

## 1993: Nick Faldo Defeats David Frost, 2 and 1, Advances to Final of Toyota World Match Play

Nick Faldo defeated David Frost 2 and 1 and advanced to the singles final of the Toyota World Match Play Championship at the Wentworth Club West Course, a 6,957-yard, par-72 venue, in Surrey, England. Faldo faced Corey Pavin in the final and lost, 1-up. Other golfers to compete in the event were Steve Elkington, John Daly, Seve Ballesteros, Peter Baker, Colin Montgomerie, and Yoshinori Mizumaki. Pavin won 160,000 British pounds sterling for his efforts. Pavin, considered one of the best wedge players in the game, and an excellent putter, used his short game to become the first American to win this event in ten years. His low, running wood shots also proved very effective at Wentworth. When it came down to it on the final hole, Faldo blinked first as he hit his second shot on the finishing par-5 into a rhododendron bush for an unplayable lie. He eventually took a 6 as Pavin made a critical putt to par the hole and win by one.

Nick Faldo was born in Hertfordshire, England, in 1957. He won the Masters Tournament in 1989 and 1990, and the British Open in 1987, 1990, and 1992. A nine-time member of the European Ryder Cup team, Faldo has won over $11 million since turning professional in 1976 and was ranked third in the world Sony rankings behind Nick Price and Greg Norman in 1994.

# October 24

## 1993: Davis Love III Wins Las Vegas Invitational, Shoots 29-Under-Par Total of 331

Davis Love won his only Tour event of 1993 by shooting a five-round total of 331 to win the $252,000 Las Vegas Invitational. The event was played on a rotation of three courses, the 7,243-yard TPC at Summerlin, the 7,111-yard Desert Inn Country Club, and the 7,164-yard Las Vegas Country Club, all par-72 layouts in Las Vegas. Love joined the Tour in 1986 after attending the University of North Carolina. He had won eight tournaments and over $4 million through 1994. Love played on the 1993 Ryder Cup team and was 4-0-1 on the victorious U.S. President's Cup team in 1994. He won $474,219 on the PGA Tour in 1994, earning himself thirty-third place. Davis's father, who competed in the 1964 Masters, was a golf professional and an excellent teacher.

# October 25

## 1904: Birthday of Denny Shute, Winner of British Open and PGA Championships

Denny Shute won the 1936 and 1937 PGA Championships and the 1933 British Open. He finished tied for first in the 1939 U.S. Open, then lost to Byron Nelson, the eventual winner, and Craig Wood in a three-way play-off at the Philadelphia Country Club. Shute defeated Craig Wood in a 36-hole play-off, 149 to 154, to win his only British Open title, at St. Andrews. Shute, a native of Cleveland, Ohio, won fifteen PGA Tour events in his career and was a member of three Ryder Cup teams (1931, 1933, 1937). He three-putted on the final hole at the Southport Course in the 1933 Ryder Cup to lose the final crucial singles match 1-up to Sydney Easterbrook, contributing to the first loss of the United States in that event (6 and 5). A few weeks later he came back to win the British Open. Ironically, Easterbrook carded a 7 on the fourteenth hole of the final round and finished one stroke behind Shute and Craig Wood, who tied at 292 in regulation play.

# October 26

## 1986: Ben Crenshaw Wins Vantage Championship, Second Win of the Year

Ben Crenshaw won his first PGA Tour event in 1975 when he captured the San Antonio Texas Open, the first tournament he entered as a professional, and won his twelfth event when he took the Vantage Championship to earn $180,000. Through 1994, Ben had eighteen Tour wins and over $6 million in the bank. His biggest win was his 1984 Masters victory, his only major. As an amateur, Crenshaw won just about every tournament that mattered, and many felt he was the most gifted amateur since Nicklaus. He has not reached the superstar level, but he is an excellent golfer, keen golf historian, developing golf architect, and one of the best putters on the Tour. He has played on three Ryder Cup teams (1981, 1983, 1987).

# October 27

## 1956: Birthday of Patty Sheehan, Winner of Two U.S. Women's Opens and Member of LPGA Hall of Fame

Patty Sheehan was born in Middlebury, Vermont, then moved west and won the Nevada State Amateur (1975, 1976, 1977, 1978) and the California Amateur (1978, 1979). She attended San Jose State and won the AIAW National Championship in 1980. She then played on the 1980 Curtis Cup team before turning professional in 1980. Her first Tour victory came in the Mazda Japan Classic in 1981. Since then she has won over $4 million on the LPGA Tour and over thirty tournaments, including the 1992 and 1994 U.S. Women's Open. She was named LPGA Player of the Year in 1983, won the Vare Trophy in 1984 (71.40 strokes per round average), and was inducted into the LPGA Hall of Fame in 1993, the thirteenth golfer to be so honored.

After losing an eleven-shot lead to blow the 1990 Open, she came back in 1992 to win the Open in an 18-hole play-off against Juli Inkster at Oakmont, after shooting a 4-under-par 280 in regulation. In 1994 she outdueled Tammie Green to win by one stroke on the final hole of the Indianwood Golf and Country Club in Lake Orion, Michigan. Her 7-under-par 277 tied Liselotte Neumann's 1988 U.S. Open record. Sheehan's caddie, Carl Laib, was with her when she won her first Open, and he also caddied for Betsy King when she beat Sheehan to win the Open in 1990 at the Atlanta Athletic Club. He was also with King in 1989 when she won her first Open.

Patty Sheehan has won five major LPGA events, including the LPGA Championship (1983, 1984, 1993) and the U.S. Women's Open (1992, 1994). She has been a member of all the U.S. Solheim Cup teams (1990, 1992, 1994).

# October 28

### 1993: Jim Gallagher Shoots Course Record 8-Under-Par 63 at Olympic, Goes On to Win $540,000 First Prize in Tour Championship

Jim Gallagher Jr. shot a course-record 63 to take a lead of five strokes in the first round of the $3 million Tour Championship held at the Olympic Club Lake Course, a 7,005-yard, par-71 venue in San Francisco. Gallagher then shot rounds of 73, 72, and 69 to total 277 and win by one stroke over David Frost, John Huston, Greg Norman, and Scott Simpson. Gallagher collected $540,000 for his efforts, the largest first-place check on the Tour.

Gallagher, the son of a PGA professional, started to play golf at the age of two. His wife played on the LSU golf team and was a member of the LPGA Tour. After graduating from the University of Tennessee, he joined the Tour in 1984 and has earned over $3.2 million, including $1,078,870 in 1993, his best year thus far. Gallagher played on the 1993 Ryder Cup team, winning a critical singles match, 3 and 2, over Seve Ballesteros. He played on the first U.S. President's Cup team in 1994 and posted a 3-1-1 record in a winning cause.

# October 29

## 1967: Jack Nicklaus Wins Sahara, Leads Tour in Winnings in 1967

At the beginning of the 1967 Tour year, Jack Nicklaus, twenty-seven, had won six majors and was the leading golfer in the world. In the 1967 U.S. Open, he set a new tournament record by shooting 275 at Baltusrol to pick up his seventh major. In addition to the Sahara and the Open, he won the Bing Crosby, Western Open, and Westchester Classic. Nicklaus won a total of $188,998 to lead the Tour in earnings, as he had in 1964 and 1965 and as he would in 1971, 1972, 1973, 1975, and 1976. Nicklaus would register over $5.3 million in career Tour earnings, win seventy tournaments, play on six Ryder Cup teams, captain two, and be named PGA Player of the Year five times. Since joining the Senior Tour in 1990 he has won six tournaments and over $1.2 million through 1994. In 1986, he became the oldest player to win the Masters, when at age forty-six he won his record sixth title.

# October 30

## 1983: Mark McCumber Shoots 266, Wins Pensacola Open

Mark McCumber, a thirty-two-year-old native of Jacksonville, Florida, shot a 266 to win the Pensacola Open and $45,000. Earlier in the year McCumber won the Western Open. McCumber turned professional in 1974 and won his first tournament, the Doral-Eastern Open, in 1979, his second year on the Tour. His richest win was a 1994 victory in the Tour Championship, when he won $540,000 at the Olympic Club in a play-off with Fuzzy Zoeller. McCumber had his best year on the PGA Tour in 1994, when he finished third in earnings ($1,208,209) and fifth in stroke average (69.56). McCumber was a member of the 1989 Ryder Cup team, and he is also a member of the American Society of Golf Course Architects. McCumber has designed Osprey Cove in Georgia, Queens Harbour Yacht and Country Club in Florida, Ohtake Golf Club in Japan, and others in the Southeast and abroad.

# October 31

## 1993: George Archer Wins Ping Kaanapali Classic in Three-Way Play-off, His Second Senior Tour Win in a Month

George Archer shot a final-round 63 to tie Dave Stockton and Lee Trevino at 199 for 54 holes. He then won the play-off with a birdie on the first extra hole on the 6,590-yard, par-71 North Course at the Kaanapali Resort in Hawaii. Archer won $82,500 to go along with the $90,000 he won earlier in the month by winning the Raley's Senior Gold Rush Tournament at the Rancho Murieta Country Club in California. Archer won four tournaments in 1993 to finish second in earnings with $963,124. Since joining the Senior Tour in 1989, he has earned well over $4.3 million.

The 6-feet-5-inch Archer was born in San Francisco in 1939 and joined the PGA Tour in 1964. He won twelve Tour tournaments, including the Masters in 1969. His final total of 67, 73, 69, and 72 for 281 was one shot better than Tom Weiskopf, George Knudson, and Billy Casper. Archer, who won over $1.8 million on the Tour, is an outstanding putter. In 1994 he averaged 69.96 strokes per round, sixth on the Senior Tour. He was tenth in earnings ($717,578).

# November 1

## 1935: Birthday of Gary Player, First Non-American to Win the Masters

Born in Johannesburg, South Africa, the son of a coal miner, Gary Player is the role model for anyone who admires true grit on the golf course. A relatively small man of 5 feet 7 inches and 150 pounds, Player dedicated himself to a rigorous regime of physical exercise and a regulated diet. He also overcame early flaws in his grip and his swing to build a reliable repetitive stroke that could withstand tournament pressure.

A turning point in Player's career was his victory in the Dunlop Masters at Sunningdale, England, in 1956, which gave him the confidence to compete on the international circuit. He won the first of his thirteen South African Open titles the same year. Player won his first major in 1959 when he captured the British Open at Muirfield. In 1961 Player won the first of his three Masters victories in a duel with Arnold Palmer and Charles R. Coe. Player, who had a stroke average of 69.2 per round in forty-nine official rounds prior to entering the tournament, fired 69, 68, and 69 the first three rounds to take a four-stroke lead, but almost lost the tournament when he shot 40 on the first nine holes in the final round. Player hung on to win by one stroke over Coe and Palmer with a total of 69, 68, 69, and 74 for 280. He was the first non-American to win the Masters.

By the time Player finished his career on the regular Tour, he had won nine majors including the U.S. Open (1965), British Open (1959, 1968, 1974), Masters (1961, 1974, 1978), and PGA Championship (1962, 1972). He has won well over 125 tournaments worldwide including seven Australian Opens and five Suntory World Match Play titles. Player is one of only four golfers—the others are Jack Nicklaus, Gene Sarazen, and Ben Hogan—to win the four major professional championships.

*Opposite:* Nancy Lopez

303

At the peak of his career, Player was considered one of the Big Three along with Palmer and Nicklaus. All three were managed by Mark McCormack, the sports agent who revolutionized the business of golf, and all three amassed great fortunes on and off the course. Player joined the Senior Tour in 1985 and continues to thrive.

# November 2

### 1941: Birthday of Dave Stockton, Leader on World Senior Money List in 1993

Dave Stockton, a direct descendant of Richard Stockton, who signed the Declaration of Independence for New Jersey, and the son of a golf professional, earned a golf scholarship to the University of California and graduated in 1964 with a degree in business management. He joined the PGA Tour in 1964 and won eleven tournaments through 1976, including the PGA Championship in 1970 and again in 1976.

Stockton's first PGA Championship was earned on the 6,962-yard, par-70 Southern Hills Country Club in Tulsa, Oklahoma, when he scored 279 to defeat Bob Murphy and Arnold Palmer by two strokes. His second PGA victory came when he holed a critical 10-foot putt on the seventy-second hole at the 7,054-yard, par-70 Congressional Country Club in Bethesda, Maryland, to outlast Raymond Floyd and Don January by one stroke. Over the years Stockton blended his business and golf skills to become "King of the Corporate Outings," where he earned more off the Tour from corporate events than he did from playing golf. Through the 1980s he averaged more than ninety outings per year. His playing career was revived when he joined the Senior Tour in 1991 and was named the Senior Tour Rookie of the Year in 1992, his first complete season, when he won $656,458. Stockton led the World Senior Money List in 1993 and finished second, behind Ray Floyd, with more than $1.4 million.

Dave Stockton was a member of the Ryder Cup team in 1971 and 1977. He was the captain of the 1991 Ryder Cup team, which eked out a 14½–13½ win over a formidable European team, which included Seve Ballesteros, Nick Faldo, Jose Maria Olazabal, Ian

Woosnam, Colin Montgomerie, and Bernhard Langer, all winners of major tournaments. Langer had the misfortune of missing a 6-foot par putt on the eighteenth hole, which would have tied the match. It was the first time the U.S. team had won the Ryder Cup since 1983. Stockton led the senior tour in earnings, with over $1.4 million in 1994.

# November 3

### 1949: Macdonald Smith Dead at Age 59, Member of PGA Hall of Fame

Macdonald Smith was born in Carnoustie, Scotland, in 1890. He came from a golfing family that included his brothers Alex and Willie, both U.S. Open champions. Macdonald had a smooth, dependable golf swing and was considered one of the best golfers of his era. However, titles in the U.S. Open and the British Open eluded him. He finished in a three-way tie with his brother Alex and Johnny McDermott in the 1910 Open at the Philadelphia Cricket Club, but came in third in the play-off with a 77 as Alex took the title with a 71 and McDermott was second with a 75. In total, he came within three strokes of the winner of the U.S. or British Opens nine times. His toughest loss in the British was at Prestwick in 1925 when he skied to an 82 on the last round to lose the Open by three strokes after shooting rounds of 76, 69, and 76.

Macdonald Smith won the Western Open, then a major tournament, in 1912, 1925, and 1933. The first Western Open, held in 1899 at the Glenview Golf Club in Chicago, was won by his brother Willie. Macdonald's brother Alex won the event in 1903 and 1905. Walter Hagen won the Western a record five times. Macdonald Smith also won the Canadian Open in 1926. In 1913, Harry Vardon pronounced Macdonald Smith the best golfer he had seen in America. No one knows what toll the accumulating losses took on Smith's ability to win the major events that make or break a golfer's reputation. Smith was still respected enough by his peers to be selected to the PGA Golf Hall of Fame in 1954.

# November 4

## 1873: Royal Montreal, the Oldest Golf Club in North America, Established

The Montreal Golf Club was established in Quebec province in 1873, requiring $60 as an entrance fee and $25 as a subscription fee. In 1884, Queen Victoria granted it permission to prefix the word *royal* to its name. The first twenty-three years of the club's existence were spent on Fletchers Field on the eastern slopes of Mount Royal, now in the heart of Montreal. In 1881 the club brought from England the first professional to move to North America, W. F. Davis of Hoylake. He was given his passage and his wages were approximately $5 per week. He also received all that he could from making and repairing clubs and balls. He also received fees for lessons and was responsible for golf-course maintenance, especially the greens.

By 1896 the membership opted to move the club to Dorval on Lake St. Louis, ten miles from the center of Montreal, where it remained for over sixty years. Two 18-hole layouts of 6,453 yards and 6,527 yards were designed by Willie Park Jr. of Musselburgh, Scotland. The pressure of urban growth forced the club to move to its present 650-acre location on the Ile Bizard in the 1950s. Dick Wilson was selected to design and build forty-five holes of golf, finishing in May 1959. The layout consists of the 6,738-yard Blue Course, the 6,708-yard Red Course, and a nine-hole layout, called the Dixie Nine, measuring 3,111 yards. Wilson commented on his enterprise: "There is a sweep and dimension to this layout which can only be described as exciting. That vista of the Lake of Two Mountains is the perfect backdrop to these courses. . . . I have designed these courses for the present and the future. With the improvement in players' abilities and training with better equipment, older courses will become old-fashioned and inadequate in the next fifteen years. The Red and Blue Courses will remain modern and can be even more challenging for the next fifty years."

The Canadian Open was played here in 1975, and Jack Nicklaus dueled Tom Weiskopf down the stretch on the Blue Course, which has four tough finishing holes. Nicklaus hooked his tee shot into the water at the dogleg of the 450-yard, par-4 finishing hole and fell into a 72-hole tie with Weiskopf at 294, six strokes under par. The tiebreaker was played on the 420-yard, par-4 fifteenth, a dogleg right with the approach over water to a green bunkered in front. Both golfers hit their second shots, 7-irons, to within a few feet of the pin. Nicklaus missed his 8-footer, but Weiskopf made his 2-footer to win the Canadian Open, which was first held in 1904.

The event was moved to Glen Abbey, a Nicklaus-designed course, outside of Toronto in 1977. The Open was held at Royal Montreal in 1980, but Glen Abbey, headquarters of the Royal Canadian Golf Association, is the venue. The Canadian Open is one of the few significant tournaments Jack Nicklaus has never won.

# November 5

### 1927: Walter Hagen Wins His Record Fourth Straight PGA Championship, Takes Match Play Final, 1-Up

Walter Hagen shot the low qualifying score, 141 for thirty-six holes, then won five consecutive 36-hole match-play contests to win his record fourth consecutive PGA Championship at the Cedar Crest Country Club in Dallas. Hagen defeated Jack Farrell, 3 and 2; Tony Manero, 11 and 10; Tommy Armour, 4 and 3; Al Espinosa, 1-up (37 holes); and Joe Turnesa, 1-up, to win the match. Hagen was down two holes after the first round of the final, but squared the match at the twenty-ninth hole, went 1-up at the thirty-first, and held off Turnesa, who missed several short putts, to win.

As a youth in Rochester, New York, Walter Hagen was torn between becoming a professional golfer or a baseball pitcher. He finally decided on golf, beginning as a caddie at the Country Club of Rochester, where he worked up to assistant professional and entered the 1914 U.S. Open at Midlothian after finishing tied for fourth the preceding year at the Country Club. Hagen set the course record with a 68 on the 6,355-yard layout, one of the longest and most difficult in the country, and followed with rounds of 74, 75, and 73 to win by one stroke over Chick Evans. A flashy dresser and a flamboyant competitor, especially when it mattered down the stretch, Hagen quickly became the most charismatic golfer of his age. An excellent putter and deadly from 165 yards into the green, Hagen knew how to play to the galleries and build a following. He was erratic off the tee and with fairway woods and long irons, but he was brilliant at recovery shots, which he practiced often, making him exciting to watch and unnerving to play against.

Herbert Warren Wind, in *The Story of American Golf,* characterized Hagen's mental attitude that enabled him to master his game:

> Hagen was seldom able to play eighteen holes without hitting at least one or two weirdly loose shots. Nine hundred and ninety-nine golfers out of a thousand would have been ruined by this affliction, would have worn themselves out worrying about when that wild shot was coming, and fretted themselves helpless when it eventually raised its ugly arc. Hagen didn't let these errors upset him. . . . He accepted the fact that three times or so a round he would hit a very poor shot—and what was so calamitous about that? No golfer could expect to hit every shot perfectly. As a result, Walter was able to forget about a bad shot almost instantly. . . . Equally unique and invaluable was his penchant for remaining relaxed at all times.

Hagen won two U.S. Opens (1914, 1919), four British Opens (1922, 1924, 1928, 1929) and four PGA Championships (1924, 1925, 1926, 1927). He was the captain of the first six Ryder Cup teams (1927, 1929, 1931, 1933, 1935, 1937). Hagen not only had style, but he also had substance. He was a competitive force for more than twenty years and helped put American golf on the international map. The only person to win more PGA Championships was Jack Nicklaus, who won five.

# November 6

## 1979: Charles "Chick" Evans Dies at Age 89, Won the U.S. Amateur and U.S. Open in 1916

Charles "Chick" Evans is one of those unique athletes who has a broad influence on the game beyond the narrow confines of its playing fields. Born in Indianapolis, Indiana, Evans showed great early promise as a golfer, winning the first of his six Chicago City Amateur Championships at the age of seventeen. A lifetime amateur who played competitively for sixty years, Evans won the 1916 U.S. Open at Minikahda in Minneapolis, with a record score of 286. He then won the Amateur, 4 and 3, in the match-play final, at the Merion Cricket Club East Course in Ardmore. Only Bobby Jones has won an Open and an Amateur in the same year since then. That was accomplished in 1930, the year of Jones's Grand Slam. Evans also won eight Western Amateurs (1909, 1912, 1914, 1915, 1920, 1921, 1922, 1923), the French Amateur Open (1911), the Western Open (1910), and the North and South Amateur (1911). He won the U.S. Amateur again in 1920, 7 and 6, over Francis Ouimet.

Evans won the national Open and the national Amateur with seven hickory-shafted clubs. His record of 286 in the Open stood for twenty years until Tony Manero shot 282 at Baltusrol in 1936. The record withstood the advent of steel-shafted clubs, matched sets of woods and irons, and a golf ball of uniform size and weight. Also, in 1916, the Open was an endurance test of seventy-two holes of golf played over two days. In 1925 the format was changed to two days of 18-hole rounds and a final day with thirty-six holes. In 1965, following the 1964 Open at Congressional when Ken Venturi almost collapsed from heat-stroke on his way to victory, the Open format was changed to four 18-hole days.

# November 7

## 1993: Fred Couples Wins Kapalua International by Four Strokes, Second Tournament Victory of Year

Fred Couples shot a 274 at the Lincoln-Mercury Kapalua International, which was held at the Kapalua Resort in Maui, Hawaii, on the 7,263-yard, par-73 Plantation Club and the 6,600-yard, par-71 Bay Course layouts. Couples put together rounds of 69, 68, 67, and 70 to win by four shots over Blaine McCallister. Couples collected $180,000, then won $130,000 the following week when he teamed up with Davis Love III to win the Heineken World Cup of Golf at Lake Nona in Florida. Couples picked up another $260,000 in the Skins Game at the Bighorn Golf Club in Palm Desert, California, to win a total of $570,000 in the month of November.

Couples, who joined the Tour in 1981 after attending the University of Houston, had his best year in 1992, when he led the Tour in earnings with $1,344,188, won the Masters, and was named Player of the Year. He played on the Ryder Cup team in 1989, 1991, and 1993 and was the hero of the first President's Cup competition in 1994 when he closed out Nick Price on the eighteenth in singles with a dramatic 9-iron hit 147 yards to within inches of the cup for a birdie and the championship for the American team. Couples finished twenty-fourth in PGA Tour earnings in 1994 ($625,654) and ranked seventh in the Sony rankings.

# November 8

## 1992: Chi Chi Rodriguez Wins Ko Olina Senior
## Invitational, Winner of 1989 Bob Jones Award

Chi Chi Rodriguez won the Ko Olina Senior Invitational with a 54-hole score of 206 to win by six shots on the 6,673-yard, par-72 Ko Olina layout. Rodriguez's victory was his twenty-first win since joining the Senior Tour in 1985. Chi Chi has earned over $5 million on the Senior Tour and a considerable amount of cash from other events such as the Senior Skins Game.

One of the most popular players on the Senior Tour, Chi Chi has contributed greatly to Junior golf and other causes. For his efforts he was awarded the USGA's highest honor in 1989, the Bob Jones Award. This award is made annually by the United States Golf Association in recognition of "distinguished sportsmanship." The citation says that "sportsmanship" can be difficult to define, but the USGA has in mind "the demonstration of personal qualities esteemed in sport: fair play, self-control, and perhaps self-denial; generosity of spirit towards the game as a whole, and the manner of playing or behaving so as to show respect for the game and the people in it."

# November 9

## 1895: Mrs. Charles S. Brown Wins the First U.S. Women's Amateur Championship

Mrs. Charles S. Brown won the first U.S. Women's Amateur with an 18-hole score of 69-63 for 132 at the Meadow Brook Club in Hempstead, New York. Nine holes were played before lunch and nine after lunch, then the silver pitcher donated by Messrs. R. D. Winthrop and W. H. Sands was presented to Mrs. Brown. Thirteen golfers entered the tournament. In 1896, Miss Beatrix Hoyt, a sixteen-year-old golf phenomenon from Shinnecock Hills, won the qualifying medal with an 18-hole score of 95 and then won the match-play championship. In 1905, Margaret Curtis and Georgianna Bishop both shot 87 to become the first medalists to break 90 in the event. In 1924, Glenna Collett became the first medalist to break 80 when she shot a 79 at the Rhode Island Country Club. Glenna Collett won the event a record six times (1922, 1925, 1928, 1929, 1930, 1935).

The silver pitcher won by Mrs. Brown was donated to the USGA's Golf House after her death. The present permanent trophy was donated in 1896 by Robert Cox, of Edinburgh, Scotland, a member of the British Parliament. The Cox Cup, a two-foot silver vase of Etruscan design, is the only USGA trophy donated by a person from another country. The U.S. Women's Amateur has been a match-play event since 1896. The record for lowest 18-hole medalist score, 70, is held by Deborah Massey (1974) and Beth Daniel (1976). Margaret Curtis and Glenna Collett Vare share the record for most times medalist (six). The largest field in the U.S. Women's Amateur was 441 golfers (1992). The smallest was thirteen in 1895.

# November 10

## 1957: Charlie Sifford Wins Long Beach Open, Breaks Golf's Color Barrier

Charlie Sifford shot a 54-hole total of 203 to win the Long Beach Open and $1,200 in prize money. Charlie, an African American, won this event before the PGA deleted its "Caucasians only" clause from its membership in 1961. The clause had been in effect since 1916, prohibiting black golfers and other minorities from playing on the Tour. The PGA Tour media guide does not credit Sifford with this win as an "official" Tour event, but he is credited with winning the 1967 Greater Hartford Open, the first PGA Tour event won by an African American. Charlie Sifford regularly played Tour stops in California and Arizona during the mid-1950s. He dropped out when the Tour swung through the South, then picked it up after the Masters when the circuit moved north. Charlie was the Jackie Robinson of golf, but there was no Branch Rickey in the PGA to help him.

# November 11

## 1951: Birthday of Frank Urban "Fuzzy" Zoeller, Winner of 1979 Masters and 1984 U.S. Open

Fuzzy Zoeller was born in New Albany, Indiana, attended Edison Junior College in Ft. Myers, Florida, and the University of Houston. He won the 1972 Florida State Junior College Championship, then took the Indiana State Amateur in 1973. He turned professional in 1973 and won his first PGA Tour events in 1979, when he won the Wickes San Diego Open and the Masters. He was six shots down to Ed Sneed after three rounds in that tournament, but wound up in a tie with Sneed and Tom Watson at the end of regulation. Zoeller birdied the second play-off hole to win his green jacket.

Fuzzy's second major win came in 1984 at the U.S. Open at the Winged Foot Golf Club in Mamaroneck, New York. Zoeller led by one stroke going into the final round, but the match came down to a tie between him and Greg Norman as Norman teed off on the eighteenth, one hole ahead of Fuzzy. Norman pushed his second shot to the right of the 448-yard, par-4 finishing hole. After a free drop from the grandstand area, he flew his approach across the green to its far edge, approximately forty-five feet from the hole. It was from this general vicinity that Bobby Jones had rolled in a curling 12-foot putt to tie Al Espinosa and later win the Open in a play-off in 1929. Norman proceeded to putt the ball along a left-to-right line; the ball rolled downhill the last ten feet, directly into the cup. Norman had made a miracle recovery shot to keep his chances alive. Zoeller, still on the eighteenth fairway, pulled out a white towel and waved it in surrender, thinking Norman had birdied. Soon alerted that he needed only a par to tie, Zoeller carded his 4. Both golfers had shot 276, 4 under par, the only subpar scores at Winged Foot.

Zoeller got off to an early lead in the 18-hole play-off the following day and coasted to a 67 to 75 win.

Fuzzy Zoeller, one of the most popular players on the Tour, has ten victories and over $4.5 million in the bank. A bad back has slowed him up in recent years, his last victory having been in the Anheuser-Busch Golf Classic in 1986. He was a member of the Ryder Cup team in 1979, 1983, and 1985. Fuzzy finished fifth in earnings in 1994 ($1,016,804) and ranked twelfth on the Sony Worldwide list headed by Nick Price.

# November 12

## 1978: Nancy Lopez Wins Colgate Far East Open, Her Ninth Tournament Victory of the Year

Nancy Lopez shot a 54-hole total of 216 to win the Colgate Far East Open, her ninth tournament victory of the year. Lopez had previously won the Bent Tree Ladies Classic, Sunstar Classic, Greater Baltimore Classic, Coca-Cola Classic, Golden Lights Championship, LPGA Championship, Bankers Trust Classic, and Colgate-European Open to win a total of $189,813, placing her at the top of the LPGA earnings list at the age of twenty-one. Lopez was the 1977 LPGA Tour Rookie of the Year and was named Player of the Year in 1978. She won the Vare Trophy in 1978, 1979, and 1985, was again named Player of the Year in 1979, 1985, and 1988, and again led the tour in earnings in 1979 and 1985. She was inducted into the LPGA Hall of Fame in 1987. She has won forty-seven tournaments and over $4 million on the LPGA Tour.

# November 13

### 1988: Miller Barber Wins Fairfield Barnett Senior
### Classic, His 22nd Career Senior Victory

Miller Barber won his twenty-second tournament since joining the Senior Tour in 1981 by shooting a 54-hole total of 197 to win the Fairfield Barnett Senior Classic. When Barber joined the Tour, he was the leading money winner with $83,136 in 1981. In 1994, Dave Stockton was the earnings leader with $1,402,519. By the end of 1994, Barber was the all-time leader in Senior Tour wins (tied with Lee Trevino) with twenty-four and had earned $3,393,652, placing him eleventh all-time.

Miller Barber, a native of Shreveport, Louisiana, joined the regular Tour in 1959 after graduating from the University of Arkansas in 1954. He won eleven Tour events and over $1.6 million and became the tenth Tour player to pass the $1 million mark in earnings when he did it in February 1976. Barber played on the 1969 and 1971 Ryder Cup teams. He won the first World Open, at Pinehurst in 1973, and a record $100,000 first prize.

# November 14

## 1993: United States Wins 26 to 6 in Dupont Cup, Japan vs. U.S. Seniors Match

Dave Stockton, Mike Hill, George Archer, Gibby Gilbert, Al Geiberger, Jim Ferree, Bob Murphy, and Jim Colbert teamed up to win the Dupont Cup, an annual event, for the United States for the fifth straight year, 26 to 6. The U.S. team won three of the four alternate-shot matches during the first round to take a 6–2 lead, then won 7 of 8 points in the second round four-ball event to go up 13–3 going into the singles matches. The event was played at the 6,727-yard, par-72 Kitaura Golf Club near Tokyo, Japan. Each U.S. team member received a $45,000 winners' share, and each Japanese team member received $18,750. George Archer, Gibby Gilbert, and Al Geiberger won all of their matches.

# November 15

## 1967: First World Senior Amateur Team Championship Begins, United States Wins Tournament by 17 Strokes

On a suggestion by the USGA, the World Amateur Golf Council inaugurated a World Senior Amateur Team Championship for golfers fifty-five years of age and older. Eleven countries participated in the competition for the Shun Nomura Trophy presented by Friends of Golf in Japan through the Japan Golf Association. Each team was allowed four players; each day the three best individual scores made up the team's score. The sum of the four daily totals determined the winner.

The first event was held at the 6,415-yard, par-72 Pinehurst No. 2 course in North Carolina. The U.S. team included George C. Beechler, David Goldman, Robert B. Kiersky, and Raymond Palmer. J. Ellis Knowles, six times champion of the United States Seniors Golf Association, was nonplaying captain. The U.S. team totaled 903 strokes, 17 less than the second-place Canadian team. The event was held in 1969 for the second and last time at the Old Course at the Royal and Ancient Golf Club in St. Andrews, Scotland. The United States won that tournament and Canada finished second again, 21 strokes off the pace.

# November 16

## 1894: Birthday of Bobby Cruickshank, Leading Money Winner in 1927

Bobby Cruickshank was born in Scotland but turned professional and moved to the United States after World War I, during which he was a prisoner of war. Even though he won seventeen PGA tournaments, he is possibly best remembered for the play-off that he had with Bobby Jones in the 1923 U.S. Open at the Inwood Country Club in New York. Cruickshank birdied the final regulation hole to shoot 73 and tie Jones at 296. Jones won the 18-hole play-off on the par-4 last hole, 76 to 78, with an approach shot hit over a lagoon to within feet of the pin. Jones, an amateur, received a medal for his win. Cruickshank earned $500.

Bobby Cruickshank won the North and South Open, then a significant professional event held at Pinehurst, in 1926, 1927, and 1944. He was elected to the PGA Hall of Fame in 1967.

# November 17

## 1973: Lloyd Mangrum, Winner of 1946 U.S. Open, Dies

Lloyd Mangrum was born August 1, 1914, in Trenton, Texas, and proved a deadly player from twenty yards into the pin. A cool, tough competitor, Mangrum served in World War II after joining the professional circuit in the 1930s and was wounded at the Battle of the Bulge and received the Purple Heart. Before returning home from the war, he won the U.S. Army Golf Championship in Paris and the British G.I. Championship at St. Andrews. He won the first postwar U.S. Open, which was not played 1942–45, at the Canterbury Golf Club in Cleveland. Regulation play ended in a three-way tie among Mangrum, Byron Nelson, and Vic Ghezzi. All three golfers tied at 72 in the first 18-hole play-off round, but Mangrum won by a single stroke in the rain-soaked second 18-hole play-off, 72 to Nelson's and Ghezzi's 73s.

Mangrum was a member of the 1947, 1949, 1951, and 1953 (captain) Ryder Cup teams. He was picked for the 1939 Ryder Cup team, but the matches were never played because of the war. Mangrum won the Vardon Trophy in both 1951 and 1953. He led the Tour in earnings in 1951 with $26,688.83 in winnings. Lloyd Mangrum won thirty-six PGA Tour events in a career that lasted until 1956. He ranks tenth on the all-time PGA tournament winning list behind Gene Sarazen. Mangrum was elected to the PGA Hall of Fame in 1964.

# November 18

## 1901: Birthday of Craig Wood, Winner of Masters and U.S. Open in 1941

Craig Wood, an outstanding professional from Lake Placid, New York, had the reputation of being a perpetual runner-up. In the first Masters held in 1934, Wood was victimized by Horton Smith, who dropped a 12-foot putt on the seventeenth hole in the final round, then parred out for the win. In the first Masters, today's back nine was played as the front nine. Wood lost to Gene Sarazen in a play-off in the 1935 Masters after Sarazen holed his famous double eagle at the 485-yard fifteenth, then finished his round in par to tie at 282. Wood had played the last eight holes in 4 under par but could not sustain his momentum in the 36-hole play-off, which he lost by five strokes, 144–149. Again Wood lost out in the 1939 U.S. Open, held at the Philadelphia Country Club in West Conshohocken, Pennsylvania, when he ended the seventy-two holes of regulation in a three-way tie at 284 with Byron Nelson and Denny Shute. Wood and Nelson tied at 68 in the 18-hole play-off as Shute dropped out with a 76. Wood led Nelson by one stroke going into the last hole, a par 5, but parred after hooking his brassie second shot and injuring a spectator. Nelson birdied the hole to force a second play-off. Nelson then fired a 70 in the two-way 18-hole play-off to win by three strokes.

Wood shook the runner-up jinx in 1941 when he won both the Masters and then the U.S. Open, which was held at the Colonial Country Club in Fort Worth, Texas. In the Masters, he started with a strong 66 to gain a commanding five-stroke lead, then shot 71, 71, and 72 for a 280 to edge Byron Nelson by three strokes. Wood wore a heavy corset belt in the Open to overcome chronic back problems. The Open was held for the first time south of the Mason-Dixon Line, and Texas favored their native sons Guldahl, Nelson, Demaret, Hogan, Cooper, and the Mangrum brothers.

The 7,000-yard, par-70 Colonial Course was a tough test with narrow fairways bordered by swamps, ravines, and groves of pecan trees. Tough Bermuda grass and deluges of rain made the course even more difficult. Only one player, Denny Shute, a Northerner playing out of Chicago, bettered par with a 69. Wood was four strokes back at 73. After thirty-six holes Shute and Wood were tied for the lead at 144. The next day in the 36-hole final rounds, Wood shot a pair of 70s in 95-degree heat to win by three strokes over Shute. Ben Hogan finished first among the Texans with a 289.

Wood won the 1942 Canadian Open and played on the 1931, 1933, and 1935 Ryder Cup teams. He finished as runner-up in all the major tournaments: U.S. Open (1939), Masters (1934, 1935), PGA (1934), and the British Open (1933).

# November 19

### 1993: Steve Elkington and Raymond Floyd Lead Off With 62, Go On to Win Franklin Funds Shark Shoot-out

Steve Elkington and Raymond Floyd started out with a better-ball 62, then fired rounds of 64 and 62 for a total of 188 and a one-stroke victory over four teams at the Franklin Funds Shark Shoot-out. The event was played on the 7,025-yard, par-72 Sherwood Country Club in Sherman Oaks, California. Each player won $150,000. Raymond Floyd sank the winning putt, a 6-footer for birdie, on the final hole. The tournament's best round was turned in by host Greg Norman and Nick Price, a 17-under-par 55 in the final round. This tournament has an unusual format: better ball in the first round, alternate shot in the second, and scramble in the third. Five of the ten teams in the event went to the last hole with a chance to win with a birdie, but only Floyd and Elkington could do it. In 1994 Fred Couples and Brad Faxon combined for a 68, 54, and 58 for a total of 190 to win the event by two shots.

# November 20

## 1929: Birthday of Don January, Winner of 1967 PGA Championship

Don January was a member of the NCAA championship North Texas State golf teams of 1950, 1951, and 1952 before joining the PGA Tour in 1956 after a stint in the U.S. Air Force. The highlight of his career came in 1967 when he won the PGA Championship at the 7,436-yard, par-72 Columbine Country Club in Denver, Colorado. January and Don Massengale tied at 281 after seventy-two holes of regulation play. January won the 18-hole play-off with a 3-under-par 69 to Massengale's 71. This was the second time the PGA Championship has been decided in a stroke-play play-off since it changed from match play in 1958. The other play-off, held in 1961, was won by Jerry Barber, who tied Don January at the end of regulation play.

Don January won the Vardon Trophy in 1976 for his low stroke average of 70.56 on the PGA Tour. He was a member of the Ryder Cup team in 1965 and 1977 and joined the Senior Tour in 1980. He won $1,140,925 on the regular PGA Tour and had ten victories. He has earned more than $2.6 million on the Senior Tour, including twenty-two victories.

# November 21

## 1993: Ernie Els Wins the Dunlop Phoenix Tournament, Finishes 20th in 1993 Sony Worldwide Rankings

Ernie Els, twenty-four, from Johannesburg, South Africa, showed more of his future promise as he shot 68, 69, 65, and 69 for 271 on the 6,993-yard, par-72 Phoenix Country Club in Miyazaki, Japan, to win the Dunlop Phoenix Tournament by four strokes over five other golfers. Els finished twentieth in the Sony rankings in 1993 and won $971,706 in all events, to place him twenty-fourth in worldwide earnings.

Els tied for seventh in the U.S. Open in 1993 and won a three-way 18-hole play-off against Loren Roberts and Colin Montgomerie to win the 1994 Open at Oakmont. Els, Montgomerie, and Roberts tied at 279 in regulation, then Els and Roberts tied at 74 in the play-off round while Montgomerie dropped out with a 78. Els won the tournament when Roberts bogeyed the second extra play-off hole. The fifth non-American to win the Open since World War I, Els commented on his golf progress in the post-play-off interview: "I wasn't any good at all until I was thirteen and won a pretty good Junior tournament, and then we came over here to San Diego and won the thirteen-to-fourteen-year-old age group in the Junior World Championship."

Els burst on the South African golf scene when he opened the 1992 season by winning the South African Open, the South African PGA, and the South African Masters. Els then finished fifth at the 1992 British Open at Muirfield after opening with a 66. He is the second South African after Gary Player to win a U.S. Open. Ernie Els earned $684,440 on the PGA Tour in 1994 and finished sixth in the Sony rankings. In 1994 Els played in thirty-five events on five continents and won approximately $2.9 million, tops in the world.

# November 22

## 1911: Birthday of Ralph Guldahl, Winner of Consecutive U.S. Opens in 1937 and 1938

Ralph Guldahl, a native of Dallas, Texas, won fourteen events from 1932 through 1941 including successive victories in the U.S. Open (1937, 1938), a 1939 Masters win, and three straight Western Open victories (1936, 1937, 1938). A member of the 1937 Ryder Cup team, Guldahl was noted for the peaks and valleys of his career. After finishing second in the U.S. Open in 1933, Guldahl's game began to fall apart, and by 1935, when his total tournament winnings were $54, he came near to quitting the Tour altogether. After working odd jobs as an assistant carpenter at Hollywood movie studios, he was persuaded to continue after making some adjustments to his swing and putting stroke. An observer described his style as follows: "Though he made a full pivot of his shoulders, he moved the lower half of his body very little, keeping his feet firmly planted on the ground. Such a seemingly awkward style was made possible by his sledgehammer action with the right hand, which he allowed to slide down the grip as he completed the backswing. . . . Once settled, he drew back the clubhead with explosive speed and struck the ball with what looked like an uppercut; but his concentration was tremendous and he never putted until he outstared the hole."

One of five golfers to win two U.S. Open Championships in succession (along with Willie Anderson, John McDermott, Bobby Jones, and Curtis Strange), Guldahl fired a final-round 69 at Oakland Hills to win the 1937 Open by two strokes over Sam Snead. He started out the final round tied with Snead, holed a 50-foot birdie putt on the eighth, then birdied the ninth with a 25-footer. Guldahl had reached the turn at 33, but then bogeyed holes ten and eleven. Earlier in his career Guldahl missed a 4-foot putt on the eighteenth to tie Johnny Goodman in the 1933 Open after gaining nine strokes on Goodman the final day. In the 1937 Masters he put two balls in the water on the back nine and was overtaken by Byron Nelson's final-nine 32 to lose the tournament by two strokes.

Guldahl did not let the pressure overwhelm him in the 1937 Open as he birdied the twelfth and thirteenth and parred out for a score of 69 and 72-hole total of 281, a new U.S. Open record. Snead, who would never win an Open in a long and illustrious career, shot a final-round 71. In the 1938 Open, Guldahl gained an astounding ten strokes on Dick Metz in the final round to win the Open, at Cherry Hills in Denver, by six strokes. This was the largest Open margin since 1921, when Jim Barnes won by nine strokes.

# November 23

## 1894: Arthur Conan Doyle Introduces Golf to Rudyard Kipling in Vermont

Arthur Conan Doyle, the author and creator of Sherlock Holmes, visited writer Rudyard Kipling at his estate near Brattleboro, Vermont, and introduced his host to golf, demonstrating the game to an intrigued local citizenry.

# November 24

## 1946: Lew Worsham Wins Atlanta Invitational, Won
## 1947 U.S. Open

Lew Worsham was born in Alta, Virginia, in 1917 and came up through the caddie ranks before turning professional at the age of eighteen. Lew won his only tournament during the 1946 Tour season when he shot 279 to win $2,200 in the Atlanta Invitational. Most tournaments on the 1946 professional circuit were being won by Byron Nelson, Ben Hogan, and Sam Snead, who accounted for twenty-two wins in the forty-two events played. Worsham won his only major in 1947 when he defeated Sam Snead in an 18-hole play-off at the St. Louis Country Club in the U.S. Open.

Snead and Worsham tied at 282 on the 6,532-yard, par-71 layout. In the play-off both golfers were even going into the final hole, a par-4. Both golfers hit tee shots of approximately 260 yards, and their approach shots were within twenty-five feet of the pin. Both putted to within a few feet of the cup, but just as Snead was about to stroke his second putt, Worsham asked for a measurement. Snead was away, thirty and one-half inches from the cup, and Worsham was an inch and a half closer. Snead hurried his downhill putt and missed by two inches. Worsham holed his for the championship.

Snead had birdied the seventy-second hole, sinking an 18-foot-putt to force a play-off with Worsham, who had already finished. Worsham had been down two strokes with three holes to play in the play-off, but came back to capture the major that Snead would never win.

# November 25

## 1923: Birthday of Art Wall, Winner of 1959 Masters

Art Wall Jr., a veteran from Honesdale, Pennsylvania, turned professional in 1949, won the 1959 Masters, the 1978 U.S. National Senior Open, and was a member of the 1957, 1959, and 1961 Ryder Cup teams.

Wall started the final round of the 1959 Masters six shots behind Stan Leonard and Arnold Palmer. Wall capitalized on Palmer's 6 on the par-3 twelfth, a short water hole at "Amen Corner." Wall shot an improbable 66, his only sub-70 round in the Masters up until that point, while Palmer struggled to finish with a 74. Art Wall's total of 284 gave him the Masters title by one stroke over Cary Middlecoff, two over Palmer, and three over Dick Mayer, who finished with a fine 68, and Stan Leonard. Wall had birdied five of the last six holes for one of the best final-round finishes in Masters history.

In 1969, Wall was named PGA Player of the Year and finished the leading money winner.

# November 26

## 1993: Tony Johnstone Fires 68 in Second Round, Goes On to Win Zimbabwe Open

Tony Johnstone, a native of Zimbabwe, shot a second-round score of 68 and went on to win the Zimbabwe Open at the 7,000-yard, par-72 Chapman Golf Club in Harare, Zimbabwe. Johnston's 15-under-par total of 273 included rounds of 71, 68, 66, and 68. Earlier in the year, Johnstone won the South African Masters, another mainstay of the African Tour. Johnstone closed out the year by winning the South African Open by seven strokes over Ernie Els at the Durban Country Club, a 6,643-yard, par-72 venue in Durban, South Africa. Johnstone's 21-under-par 64, 69, 69, and 65 for 267 bettered the tournament record by five strokes. Els was within one stroke of Johnstone going into the par-5 fourteenth on the final round, but Johnstone hit a 230-yard 2-iron to within three feet of the hole on his second shot and eagled to go two strokes ahead. Johnstone birdied the final hole to pick up the nineteenth victory of his career while Els faded with a triple bogey. Zimbabwe golfers had a good year on the African Tour in 1993: Johnstone won three events, Nick Price won the ICL International and Sun City Million Dollar Challenge, and Mark McNulty won the FNB Players Championship and Lexington PGA Championship.

# November 27

## 1965: Birthday of Danielle Ammaccapane, Winner of
## 1985 U.S. Public Links

Danielle Ammaccapane was born in Babylon, New York. She won the U.S. Women's Amateur Public Links Championship in 1985 when she defeated Kristie Kolacny 6 and 5 at the Flanders Valley Golf Club in Flanders, New Jersey. Danielle was the medalist in that event with a 36-hole total of 145. Miss Ammaccapane attended Arizona State University and won the NCAA individual championship in 1985. She turned professional in 1987 and won her first LPGA Tour event when she won the Standard Register Ping and $82,500 in first-prize money in 1991. She has won over $1.6 million on the Tour. Her best year to date was 1992, when she won the Standard Register Ping, Centel Classic, and Lady Keystone Open.

# November 28

## 1921: Birthday of Peggy Kirk Bell, Outstanding Leader in American Women's Golf

Margaret Anne (Peggy) Kirk was born in Findlay, Ohio, and has had a long career in golf, as both amateur and professional, and as teacher and resort owner. An outstanding all-around athlete, she graduated from Rollins College in Florida with a degree in physical education. She won numerous tournaments including the North and South, Eastern Women's Titleholders, International Four-Ball (with Babe Zaharias), and played on the 1948 Curtis Cup team. Mrs. Bell turned professional in 1950 and became a charter member of the LPGA, but soon left the tour. She married Warren E. (Bullet) Bell, a former pro basketball player, in 1953, and then, with Julius Boros and the Cosgrove family, bought a run-down Donald Ross course in Southern Pines, North Carolina. In 1955 the Bells bought out their partners and built what is now Pine Needles Lodge and Country Club.

Mr. Bell passed away, but Peggy Bell continues as an outstanding golf instructor and activist in golf circles. In 1961 she won the LPGA Teacher of the Year Award, given to the woman professional who has most exemplified her profession during the year. In 1990, she received the Bob Jones Award, given by the USGA for distinguished sportsmanship in golf.

# November 29

## 1992: Payne Stewart Wins $220,000 in Skins Game

An example of the tremendous entertainment value that golf has on television is the Skins Game, conceived of and developed by Don Ohlmeyer, a sports-programming executive who recently departed from NBC to start his own communications company, and Barry Frank, a senior corporate vice president at the International Management Group who represents many of the Tour's stars, most notably Arnold Palmer, one of its first clients. The first Skins Game was broadcast in 1983, featuring Jack Nicklaus, Tom Watson, Gary Player, and Arnold Palmer. That year the television ratings for the contest were slightly below the U.S. Open and equal to the British Open.

The format of the 1992 Skins Game, which included Payne Stewart, Fred Couples, Greg Norman, and Tom Kite, was $20,000 per hole for holes one to six, $30,000 each for holes seven to twelve, and $40,000 each for the last six holes. Halved holes are carried over. The event was held at the Bighorn Golf Club, a 6,848-yard layout in Palm Desert, California. Payne Stewart netted 6 skins to win $220,000, Fred Couples with 8 skins won $210,000, Norman won 4 skins and $110,000, and Kite was shut out. The event had a 4.4 television rating, or 4,605,000 homes, better than the PGA Championship or the British Open.

Through 1993 Payne Stewart was the all-time Skins money winner with $760,000 earned in three events. Through 1993, the other golfers who have participated in the event are Fuzzy Zoeller, Jack Nicklaus, Curtis Strange, Fred Couples, Lee Trevino, Raymond Floyd, Tom Watson, Arnold Palmer, Greg Norman, Gary Player, John Daly, Nick Faldo, and Tom Kite.

The Senior Skins, featuring Lee Trevino, Jack Nicklaus, Arnold Palmer, and Chi Chi Rodriguez, outdrew the regular Skins game in 1992 by pulling a 5.3 rating or 4,990,000 homes. Through 1993, Arnold Palmer was the all-time Senior Skins leader with $749,000 in earnings. Raymond Floyd won his second Senior Skins game in a row in January 1995.

Floyd dropped a dramatic 8-foot putt to win $290,000 on the par-4, 406-yard seventeenth. Jack Nicklaus, Lee Trevino, and Arnold Palmer were in Floyd's foursome. Raymond took home $420,000, Jack $120,000, and Lee and Arnie were shut out.

# November 30

### 1969: Arnold Palmer Wins First Heritage Classic

Arnold Palmer fired a 283 to win the first Heritage Classic, held at the Pete Dye (with Jack Nicklaus) designed 6,657-yard, par-71 Harbour Town Golf Links, newly opened in 1969. Palmer earned $20,000 for his efforts, then captured the Danny Thomas–Diplomat Classic, then a Tour event, the following week. Palmer never won the Heritage again, but Johnny Miller, Hubert Green, Hale Irwin, Tom Watson, Fuzzy Zoeller, and Payne Stewart have won it twice, and Davis Love III is the only three-time winner. When Love won it for the third time in 1992, he earned $180,000 when he fired a 269, one above Payne Stewart's tournament record 268.

The Heritage Classic became the Sea Pines Heritage Classic in 1971 and was renamed the MCI Heritage Classic in 1987.

# December 1

## 1983: Isao Aoki Shoots 72 in Second Round of Japan Series, Goes On to Win Tournament by One Stroke

Isao Aoki shot a 72 on the second round at the 7,065-yard, par-73 Yomiuri Country Club in Osaka, then finished with 66 and 74 at the Yomiuri Country Club in Tokyo, a 7,017-yard, par-72 layout, to win the Japan Series by one stroke 281–282 over runner-up Mashiro Kuramoto. The Japan Series brings together the best home-based performers of the current year on the Japan Tour. Aoki had previously won this event twice.

The forty-one-year-old Aoki had a banner year in 1983. He won four tournaments in Japan, one in Europe, and one in the United States to finish fourth on the World Money List with $439,935. Only Tommy Nakajima (8) and Greg Norman (7) won more tournaments than Aoki. Aoki's win in the Hawaiian Open in February was the first time a Japanese golfer has won on the PGA Tour. Aoki trailed Jack Renner by one shot going into the last hole, a 539-yard, par-5 dogleg left at the Waialae Country Club in Honolulu. Aoki hit his third shot, a 138-yard wedge, to the front of the green and it rolled into the hole for an eagle and the tournament win.

*Opposite:* Old Tom Morris

# December 2

## 1929: Birthday of Dan Jenkins, Irreverent Chronicler of Golf and Other Human Follies

Dan Jenkins was born in Fort Worth, Texas, and graduated from Paschal High, the same high school attended by Ginger Rogers and Ben Hogan. Jenkins had been the medalist in the Fort Worth Junior Championship when he was fourteen and fifteen, then played on the Texas Christian University golf team, which he captained in 1953. Jenkins was hired to cover golf by Blackie Sherrod, the sports editor of the *Fort Worth Press,* before Jenkins was out of high school. In 1962, he joined the staff of *Sports Illustrated,* where he was the back-up golf writer and head football writer. He later became the head golf writer and has written many sports articles and books since then, now as a contributor to a variety of publications.

Jenkins's irreverent, down-home style set him apart from his sports-writing peers. His novel *Semi-Tough* is a football classic. His best golf book is *The Dogged Victims of Inexorable Fate,* published in 1970. The title comes from a succinct statement about golf, written by Bobby Jones: "On the golf course, a man may be the dogged victim of inexorable fate, be struck down by an appalling stroke of tragedy, become the hero of unbelievable melodrama, or the clown in a disc-splitting comedy—any of these within a few hours, and all without having to bury a corpse or repair a tangled personality."

Jenkins has his own way of describing the game, especially a betting game on the local "Goat Hills" Course back in Fort Worth:

> With only eight players this day the game was fairly simple to bookkeep. It worked like this, you played each of the other seven individually on the front nine, the back, and the eighteen. And you and your partner played all other two-man combinations, or nine other twosomes, the same way. Any man or team who got one down automatically pressed, which meant starting a new bet right there. And everything was doubled, tripled,

quadrupled—whatever it took—to get you even on the ninth and eighteenth holes if you were. It was certainly nice to birdie the ninth and eighteenth holes sometimes.

—from *The Dogged Victims of Inexorable Fate*

# December 3

## 1972: Mike Brady Dead, Lost U.S. Open Play-off in 1911

Michael Joseph Brady was born in Brighton, Massachusetts, in 1887 and became a longtime contender but never quite a champion in many national golf events. Until 1926, when he had been playing in the U.S. Open for twenty years, he never scored better than 74 in the final round of the event. In 1911, carrying only six clubs, he tied with Johnny McDermott and George Simpson, losing the play-off with an 82. In 1912, he held a four-stroke lead after three rounds but closed with an 80 to tie for third place. In 1919, he led by five shots after three rounds and again finished with 80. Walter Hagen tied him with a 75 and won the play-off by one stroke. Hagen had exercised gamesmanship by summoning Brady from the clubhouse to watch his 8-foot putt to win the tournament on the seventy-second hole. Brady obliged, Hagen missed, but Brady lost the play-off anyway. Brady served as golf professional at Commonwealth, Wollaston, Oakley, Oakland Hills, and spent many years at Winged Foot.

Brady was an excellent golfer and one of the best early American professionals. He won eleven tournaments in 1917 including the North and South. In 1922, he won the Western Open by ten strokes. Brady was inducted into the PGA Hall of Fame in 1960.

# December 4

### 1993: Curtis Strange Takes Lead With 69 on Third Round, Goes On to Win Greg Norman's Holden Classic

Curtis Strange shot a third-round 69 then closed with a 70 to total 274 (68, 67, 69, 70) and win Greg Norman's Holden Classic at the Lakes Golf Club, a 6,856-yard, par-73 course, in Sydney, Australia. Strange, who has seen some lean years since his back-to-back U.S. Open wins in 1988 and 1989, picked up Australian $126,000 for his efforts. At the end of 1993, Strange was ranked seventy-fourth worldwide on the Sony ranking of professional golfers and sixty-second on the World Money List with a healthy $536,881. In 1985, 1987, and 1988, Curtis lead the PGA Tour in earnings.

Strange, a native of Norfolk, Virginia, joined the PGA Tour in 1977 after attending Wake Forest University, where he won the 1974 NCAA individual title and was named College Player of the Year. His first PGA tournament win was in 1979 at the Pensacola Open. Curtis's first significant breakthrough came in 1985 when he won three tournaments, including the Canadian Open, and won $542,321 and the Arnold Palmer Award for most earnings. He was named PGA Player of the Year in 1988 when he won his first major, the U.S. Open, at the Country Club in Brookline, Massachusetts, in a play-off against Nick Faldo. The Country Club was the scene of the U.S. Open's most significant play-off when a local lad, the twenty-year-old Francis Ouimet, bested Ted Ray and Harry Vardon in 1913.

Approximately twenty-five thousand spectators turned out to see the play-off in 1988. Strange made the turn, one stroke ahead of Faldo, mainly because of his recovery shots and putting stroke. Strange won the Open at the thirteenth, a par-4, where he hit a 6-iron approach shot to within twenty feet, then birdied, while Faldo bogeyed. Curtis nailed two 2-irons and then two-putted to par the last hole to win by four strokes 71–75.

In the post-play-off press conference, Curtis Strange dedicated his win to his late father, a golf professional: "He started me out years ago. When I was nine, I would arrive at work with him in the morning and go home with him late at night. I did it for four or five years. I learned the basics of a golf swing from him, and it's still with me. . . . I just wish he could have been here. . . . This is the greatest thing I have ever done; this is the greatest feeling I have ever had."

Strange won the Open again, by a stroke, at the Oak Hill Country Club in Rochester. Tom Kite led after three rounds with a 67, 69, and 69, but ballooned to a 78 to finish five strokes back.

To date, Curtis Strange has won over $6 million on the Tour and has won seventeen Tour tournaments. He played on the Ryder Cup team in 1983, 1985, 1987, and 1989.

# December 5

### 1949: Birthday of Lanny Wadkins, Winner of 1977 PGA Championship in a Play-off

Born in Richmond, Virginia, Jerry "Lanny" Wadkins had an excellent amateur career, having won the Southern Amateur Championship at age seventeen and joining the 1969 Walker Cup at age eighteen. He won the U.S. Amateur in 1970, defeating Tom Kite by one shot at the 6,496-yard, par-70 Waverly Country Club in Portland, Oregon. Wadkins turned professional in 1971 after attending Wake Forest University, where he was an all-American golfer. Wadkins, now forty-five years old, has won twenty-one PGA Tour events including the 1977 PGA Championship, his only major.

A fierce competitor, Lanny Wadkins won the 1977 PGA in a play-off with Gene Littler at the 6,804-yard, par-72 Pebble Beach Golf Links in California. Wadkins began the final round six shots behind Littler and was still five shots behind with nine holes to play despite two front-nine eagles. But Littler bogeyed five of the first six holes on the back nine, and Watkins tied the match with a birdie on the par-5 eighteenth, setting the stage for the first sudden-death play-off in a major championship. Wadkins made a 6-foot par putt on the third extra hole of the tournament to win the $45,000 first prize.

# December 6

## 1953: Bob Toski Birdies Final Hole to Win the Havana Open by a Stroke

Bob Toski was considered one of the longest hitters in the game, pound for pound. At 116 pounds, Toski got the most out of his natural gifts. In 1953, Toski, on the Tour five years, had fallen in love with Lynn Stewart but did not have enough financial security to wed. He arrived at the Havana Country Club in Cuba with less than $500 to his name. With his newfound incentive to win, Toski played himself into a tie for the tournament lead as he approached the seventy-second tee. Tied with him were Walter Burkemo, who later won the PGA Championship; Al Besselink, a talented veteran; Peter Cooper, a regular on the Caribbean circuit and a feared competitor in that arena; and Freddie Haas, the man who ended Byron Nelson's record string of eleven victories in 1945.

The eighteenth hole at the Havana Country Club is a 380-yard, par-4 that doglegs left around the clubhouse. To the left is out of bounds, and tall palm trees guard the fairway on the right. Toski pushed his tee shot into the seventeenth fairway and was partially blocked by a long row of royal palms. Toski needed a cut shot to have any chance at all. Aiming his 4-iron shot at the gallery to the left, he threaded it through the palm trees and sliced it almost forty yards, landing it in front of the green and rolling it up to within a few feet of the hole. Toski made his birdie putt, won the $2,000 first prize, and became a married man. He and his wife, Lynn, have four children and he plays on the Senior Tour. He is an excellent golf instructor and author of *The Touch System for Better Golf* (1971), *Golf for a Lifetime* with Jerry Tarde (1981) and *How to Become a Complete Golfer* with Jim Flick (1984).

# December 7

## 1980: Arnold Palmer Wins His First PGA Seniors' Championship

Arnold Palmer, who was a central figure in enhancing golf's popularity in the 1950s and 1960s in the United States, revitalized the PGA Seniors' Championship by winning a sudden-death play-off in his first appearance in the event. Palmer, who never won the PGA Championship on the regular Tour, although he finished tied for second in 1964 and again in 1968, tied Paul Harney at 289 at the 6,800-yard, par-72 Turnberry Isle Country Club in North Miami, Florida. Palmer then birdied the first hole of the play-off to win the $20,000 first prize. Palmer won the tournament again in 1984 with a 6-under-par 282 at the PGA National in Palm Beach Gardens, now the permanent home of the tournament.

Arnold Palmer turned professional in 1954 and joined the PGA Tour in 1955. He won sixty regular Tour events, placing him fourth on the all-time list behind Sam Snead (81), Jack Nicklaus (70), and Ben Hogan (63). He was the leading money winner in 1958, 1960, 1962, and 1963. Palmer earned over $1.9 million on the regular Tour and has won ten PGA Senior Tour events, including the U.S. Senior Open in 1981. Arnie has earned over $1.4 million on the Senior Tour and much more through his golf-course-design, construction, development, and other business interests. He was inducted into the World Golf Hall of Fame in 1974 and the PGA Hall of Fame in 1980.

Palmer is the coauthor or author of several books, including *Portrait of a Professional Golfer* (1964), *The Arnold Palmer Method* (1968), and *Play Great Golf* (1987).

# December 8

## 1925: Birthday of Harvie Ward, Winner of U.S. Amateur and British Amateur

Harvie Ward was born in Tarboro, North Carolina, and became one of America's best amateur golfers. Ward won the North and South Amateur in 1948 and the NCAA individual title in 1949. He won the British Amateur in 1952 at Prestwick, the U.S. Amateur in 1955 and 1956, and the Canadian Amateur in 1954. He was a member of the Walker Cup team in 1953, 1955, and 1959 and was a member of the U.S. America's Cup team in 1952, 1954, 1956, and 1958. He was low amateur twice in the U.S. Open and three times in the Masters.

Before Ward could defend his 1956 U.S. Amateur title, he was briefly suspended by the USGA for allegedly having been paid by his employer for playing in amateur events. Although reinstated a year later, Ward lost some of his zest and flair for competitive golf as a result of this incident. At the top of his game, he was noted for his smooth, classic swing and his ability to compete successfully in critical situations.

# December 9

## 1984: Tour Rookie Corey Pavin Wins New Zealand Open by Four Strokes

Corey Pavin shot rounds of 68, 67, 65, and 69 for 269 to win the Broadbank, New Zealand Open at the 6,492-yard, par-72 Paraparaumu Beach Golf Club in Paraparaumu, New Zealand. Pavin had joined the Tour in 1984 and was named Rookie of the Year as he won the Houston Coca-Cola Open and collected $260,536 in total Tour earnings to rank eighteenth. He ranked twenty-fifth on the World Money List with $305,476 in winnings. Pavin bested better-known players such as Bob Charles, Peter Senior, Ian Baker-Finch, and Frank Nobilo to win the event. Bob Charles, New Zealand's greatest golfer, holds the record with four New Zealand Open wins.

Pavin, a fierce competitor, ranked tenth in the 1994 Sony rankings and earned $906,305 on the PGA Tour. He finished in the top ten nine times and won the Nissan L.A. Open with a 67, 64, 72, and 68 to total 271 at the Riviera Country Club. Pavin averaged 69.63 strokes per round, seventh on the Tour. He ranked first in sand saves.

# December 10

## 1966: Jack Nicklaus and Arnold Palmer Win the PGA National Team Championship

Arnold Palmer and Jack Nicklaus birdied thirty-four of the seventy-two holes to win the PGA National Team Championship with better-ball rounds of 63, 66, 63, and 64 for 256 to win the $25,000-per-player top prize. The event was held at the PGA National Golf Club in Palm Beach Gardens, Florida, on the East Course (par 72, 6,896 yards) and the West Course (par 72, 6,548 yards). The colorful team of Doug Sanders and Al Besselink put the heat on the favored Nicklaus and Palmer, as Besselink birdied the last four holes on the front nine of the last round to go two strokes ahead. Nicklaus then birdied the tenth, twelfth, thirteenth, and fifteenth to put his team up by one shot. Then Palmer sank a 20-foot putt on the sixteenth for his first birdie of the day. He birdied the last two holes, and the Nicklaus/Palmer tandem had a three-shot victory.

# December 11

## 1983: Fred Couples and Jan Stephenson Win J C
## Penny Mixed Team Classic by Five Strokes

Fred Couples and Jan Stephenson combined for a score of 66, 67, 62, and 69 for 264 to each win $50,000 in the J C Penny Mixed Team Classic at the 7,015-yard, par-72 Bardmoor Country Club in Largo, Florida. Lon Hinkle and Jane Geddes finished second as they were overwhelmed by the 24-under-par 264 performance of Couples and Stephenson. The women players seem to be the critical factor in this event, which requires the partners to play each other's drives, then alternate shots. Each woman must be strong enough either to reach the green off her partner's drive or to drive long enough so that he can hit the green. Stephenson and Couples got rolling on the back nine of the third round as Stephenson birdied the tenth and the eleventh, then Couples birdied the twelfth. Stephenson birdied the thirteenth, and they birdied out on the last three holes for a 33-29 total of 62 and a six-shot lead.

The J C Penny Mixed Team Classic is supposed to be a year-ending "fun event" for leading players from the PGA and LPGA Tours. Stephenson threw down the gauntlet at the outset, however, when she said, "Having a good time is winning the tournament."

# December 12

### 1916: Birthday of Charles A. Boswell, 13-Time Champion of the United States Blind Golfers' Association

Charles A. Boswell was born in Birmingham, Alabama, and was a three-year football player at the University of Alabama before entering the U.S. Army in 1941. His service ended in 1944 when he was blinded in battle in Germany as a member of the Eighty-fourth Infantry. While recuperating from his wounds, he learned how to play golf at Valley Forge General Hospital. He retired from the Army in 1946 with a rank of major. Boswell won the first tournament of the United States Blind Golfers' Association in 1950 and twelve more after that. He was honored with the Ben Hogan Award by the Golf Writers Association of America in 1965 and has received many other honors including the President's Distinguished Service Award from the Committee on the Employment of the Handicapped.

Approximately twenty-five to thirty golfers qualify for the National Blind Golfers Tournament held every year at the Lake Buena Vista Course at Disney World. Each golfer is assisted by a guide who provides yardages and aligns the club head for the golfer, who must do the rest of the work. In order to qualify for the national tournament a golfer must have an ability to shoot 125 or better. Pat Browne, an 18-handicapper, has won the last eighteen national tournaments.

# December 13

## 1987: Orville Moody Wins the GTE Kaanapali Classic

Orville Moody shot 65-67 for 132 to win the rain-shortened Kaanapali Classic held on the 6,750-yard, par-72 North Course of the Kaanapali Golf Club on Maui in Hawaii. Moody's first-round 65 in heavy winds tied a course record before rain washed out the second round. Moody won $45,000 then picked up another $22,500 the following week when he and his partner, Jan Stephenson, finished in a tie for third in the Mazda Champion's event won by Miller Barber and Nancy Lopez at the Tryall Golf and Beach Club in Jamaica.

Orville Moody, the son of a golf-course superintendent, was born in Chickasha, Oklahoma, in 1933. Moody won the Oklahoma State Scholastic Golf Championship and was offered an athletic scholarship to the University of Oklahoma, but left college shortly after enrolling in 1953 and enlisted in the U.S. Army. During his fourteen-year service career he won three Korean Opens and was All-Service Champion in 1962. He left the Army and qualified for the PGA Tour in 1967, then surprised the golf world and perhaps himself by winning the 1969 U.S. Open at the Champions' Club in Houston. The "Sarge" shot a 71, 70, 68, and 72 for 281 to edge Deane Beman, Al Geiberger, and Bob Rosberg by a stroke. Orville Moody overcame the yips (putting nerves) that even his cross-handed grip had difficulty controlling. He said to his wife, who was in the gallery on the seventeenth, "Honey, I just can't line up a putt. I'm stroking it all right, but I just can't line it up." She didn't comment.

Orville finished like a champion that day. He crushed a drive on the eighteenth, a par-4, then hit an 8-iron to within fourteen feet of the pin, replaced his divot while the gallery streamed by to the green, then two-putted for the win.

The Sarge had just won the U.S. Open, $30,000, and a future in professional golf. Orville won $389,915 on the PGA Tour before joining the Senior Tour in 1984. He has thrived on the Senior Tour, winning eleven tournaments through 1994 and earning in excess of $3 million. Moody won the U.S. Senior Open in 1989. Not bad for someone who had never taken a lesson in his life and did not believe in regular practice when he won his Open title.

# December 14

### 1902: Birthday of Billy Burke, Winner of 1931 U.S. Open

Billy Burke, an American from Connecticut, is often remembered as the man who "had to play two U.S. Opens to win one." Burke and George Von Elm tied for first at 292 after seventy-two holes of regulation play at the Inverness Club in 1931. Von Elm, in regular play, birdied the last hole to force a play-off, then a 36-hole affair. Again Von Elm birdied the last hole to tie, forcing another 36-hole contest. Burke won the second play-off by a single stroke, 148 to 149, to win his only major championship. He was a member of the 1931 and 1933 Ryder Cup teams. Burke was voted into the PGA Hall of Fame in 1966.

# December 15

### 1985: Raymond Floyd and Hall Sutton Win Chrysler
### Team Invitational in Five-Way Sudden-Death Play-off

Raymond Floyd and Hal Sutton won the Chrysler Team Invitational at the Boca West Resort and Club in Florida after shooting a 28-under-par, better-ball 63, 65, 68, and 64 for 260 to tie four other teams in regulation play. The ten-man play-off, the largest in PGA Tour history, included the Floyd/Sutton, Purtzer/Colbert, Bolling/Fabel, Hoch/Hallberg, and Fought/McGowan teams. The first play-off hole was the 200-yard par-3 fifteenth. Sutton's tee shot was approximately fifteen feet above the hole and Floyd's two and a half feet below it. Sutton rolled in his birdie putt to win the hole and $55,000 each for himself and his partner.

# December 16

### 1974: Helen Hicks, Early American Professional Golfer,
### Dies

Before turning professional in 1934, at the age of twenty-three, Helen Hicks was an internationally known amateur who had defeated Glenna Collett Vare in the U.S. Women's Amateur final, 2 and 1, in 1931. She won the Women's Metropolitan in 1931 and 1933 before signing as a professional with the Wilson Sporting Goods Company. Miss Hicks, born in Cedarhurst, New York, in 1911, was a member of the first Curtis Cup team in 1932.

# December 17

### 1988: Dave Hill and Colleen Walker Shoot 62 in
### Second Round, Go On to Win Mazda Champions

Dave Hill and Colleen Walker combined for 62 in the second round and went on to win the Mazda Champions and $250,000 each at the Hyatt–Dorado Beach East Course in Puerto Rico. The men's tee distances were 6,740 yards and the women's 6,265 yards. Walker and Hill totaled 186 on rounds of 60, 62, and 64 to edge Chi Chi Rodriguez and Jan Stephenson by four shots. The Hyatt–Dorado Beach replaced the Tryall Course in Jamaica as the tournament site because Tryall suffered fall hurricane damage.

Walker led her team during the second round when she nearly holed her approach at the first hole, then scored three other birdies and an eagle at the par-5 tenth. Hill had six birdies on the final round. The tournament's best score came from Kathy Postlewait and Arnold Palmer on the final day. Palmer had nine birdies as the team carded a 59 to go with its opening rounds of 67 and 69 to finish sixth in the twelve-team event.

# December 18

## 1993: Shank, Pet Chow, Attacks Mochrie

Dottie Mochrie was attacked by her pet chow, Shank, reports Steve Ellis in *Golf Week*. Mochrie woke her sleeping chow, who thought she was an intruder. The dog then bit the LPGA star in the leg, requiring fifteen stitches. This was not Shank's first mulligan. He had bitten Mochrie's mother a year earlier, sending her to the emergency room for one hour with a puncture wound.

Shank was unable to deter Mochrie, who won the Chrysler-Plymouth Tournament of Champions and $472,728, to finish fourth in earnings on the LPGA Tour in 1994. Dottie, who attended Furman University, where she twice was Female Athlete of the Year, was a three-time all-American in golf. She has won eight LPGA events and over $2.6 million since joining the Tour in late 1987.

# December 19

### 1993: Larry Mize Wins Johnnie Walker World
### Championship by Ten Strokes

Larry Mize shot rounds of 67, 66, 68, and 65 to win $550,000 against some of the best golfers in the world at the Johnnie Walker World Championship, held on the 6,760-yard, par-71 Tryall Golf Club layout at Montego Bay, Jamaica. Mize's total of 266 was ten strokes better than that of runner-up Fred Couples.

Mize also won the Northern Telecom Open and Buick Open on the PGA Tour in 1993. He is best remembered for winning the 1987 Masters against Greg Norman when he dropped a long chip shot on the second play-off hole to sink the "Great White Shark." Ironically, Norman elected to drop out of the 1993 Johnnie Walker event and take his family to his native Australia for a holiday. Mize was selected as his replacement in the field of twenty-eight golfers. Faldo, the defending champion, was the pretournament favorite at 13–2 odds; Mize wasn't even quoted as a long shot. Mize's win enabled him to move up in 1993 to twenty-first in the Sony rankings and twelfth on the World Money List with $1,320,945 in earnings. Mize earned $386,029 on the Tour in 1994 and has won over $4.4 million since turning professional in 1980. He was a member of the 1987 Ryder Cup team.

# December 20

## 1811: The Savannah Golf Club Ball

There is considerable debate as to where American golf began. An early indication of nascent interest in golf in America was the Savannah (Georgia) Golf Club Ball held in 1811. Eighteenth-century records indicate that Scottish tobacco merchants played golf in the Williamsburg, Virginia, area, and records show that William Deas Master brought eight dozen golf clubs and three gross of golf balls into Charleston, South Carolina, in 1743. By 1786 the first American golf club is said to have been established in Savannah. Credit has usually been given to the St. Andrews Club, established by the "Apple Tree Gang," four friends who in 1888 started the first club of lengthy continuance in the United States.

# December 21

### 1986: Bob Charles and Amy Alcott Win Mazda
### Champions in Three-Way Play-off

The Mazda Champions is a special year-ending event teaming the leading players of the season on the LPGA and Senior PGA Tours. The tournament, played at the Tryall Golf and Beach Club in Jamaica, included twelve players from each of the two circuits. In the first round, the teams of Bruce Crampton and Pat Bradley and Miller Barber and Judy Dickinson were tied at 63. On the second day of the 54-hole event, Billy Casper and Jan Stephenson produced a 62 for a 36-hole total of 127 and a one-shot lead. Bob Charles and Amy Alcott then rallied for a 64 on the final round and a 54-hole total of 193. The teams of Casper/Stephenson and Ferree/Okamoto also posted totals of 193 to force a sudden-death play-off. Amy Alcott dropped a 10-foot birdie putt on the first extra hole to clinch the victory and earn each player from the winning team $250,000. This was the second year that this tournament was held. Don January and Alice Miller won the inaugural event, then a 36-hole contest, on the second play-off hole against Pat Bradley and Lee Elder.

# December 22

## 1894: The United States Golf Association Is Formed, Five Charter Clubs

The United States Golf Association was formed and included five charter members: Shinnecock Hills, the Country Club, St. Andrews Golf Club, Newport (R.I.) Golf Club, and the Chicago Golf Club. The original name of the association was the Amateur Golf Association of the United States. The name was later changed to the United States Golf Association because it dealt with both amateur and professional golf. One of the most important functions of the USGA is to develop and coordinate the rules of golf with the Royal and Ancient. Among its other important functions are to stage national and international tournaments, improve turf conditions and upgrade the quality of golf courses, and preserve and communicate the history and traditions of the game. The first president of the USGA was Theodore Havemeyer, a wealthy sugar merchant from the Newport Golf Club. The first USGA-sponsored tournament, the U.S. Amateur, was held at the Newport Golf Club in October 1895.

Today the United States Golf Association has more than eight thousand member clubs and courses. Based in Far Hills, New Jersey, the organization conducts thirteen national championships: the U.S. Open, U.S. Women's Open, U.S. Senior Open, U.S. Girls' Junior, U.S. Junior Amateur, U.S. Amateur Public Links, U.S. Women's Amateur Public Links, U.S. Amateur, U.S. Women's Amateur, U.S. Mid-Amateur, U.S. Women's Mid-Amateur, U.S. Senior Amateur, and U.S. Senior Women's Amateur. In cooperation with the Royal and Ancient Golf Club of St. Andrews, Scotland, the USGA conducts the Walker Cup when held in the United States. The USGA, in cooperation with the British Ladies Golf Union, conducts the Curtis Cup Match, also a biennial event between teams of amateur golfers. The USGA also conducts the World Amateur Team Championship and the Women's World Amateur Team Championship in cooperation with the World Amateur Golf Council.

# December 23

## 1909: Birthday of Herman Barron, 1963 PGA Senior Championship Winner

Herman Barron was born in Port Chester, New York, and was a longtime contender on the professional golf circuit. He won the Pinehurst Four-Ball (1931, 1933) with Tom Creavy, the Philadelphia Open (1934), Metropolitan PGA (1934, 1940), Western Open (1942), the All-American and *Philadelphia Inquirer* tournaments in 1946, and just fell short in the 1946 U.S. Open when he closed with a 69, one stroke behind Lloyd Mangrum, Byron Nelson, and Vic Ghezzi. Barron played on the 1947 Ryder Cup team and won the 1963 PGA Senior Championship with a then-record score of 272.

# December 26

### 1993: Rodriguez, Floyd, and Nicklaus Win Wendy's
### Three-Tour Challenge

Chi Chi Rodriguez, Raymond Floyd, and Jack Nicklaus teamed up to represent the PGA Senior Tour and won the Wendy's Three-Tour Challenge and $100,000 each with a 10-under-par combined score of 206 for thirty-six holes. Greg Norman, Paul Azinger, and Lee Janzen, representing the PGA Tour, finished second at 211 and collected $66,666 each. The LPGA team, represented by Nancy Lopez, Patty Sheehan, and Lauri Merten, finished twelve strokes back at 218 and earned $50,000 each. The event was held at the Colleton River Plantation in Hilton Head, South Carolina.

# December 27

### 1933: Birthday of Dave Marr, Winner of the 1965 PGA Championship

Dave Marr, a native of Houston, Texas, joined the PGA Tour in 1960 after turning professional in 1953 after attending both Rice and the University of Houston. His peak years on the PGA Tour were from 1964 through 1968, which included a PGA Championship at Laurel Valley in Ligonier, Pennsylvania, in 1965 and a second-place finish in the Masters, with Jack Nicklaus, in 1964. Marr played on the victorious 1965 Ryder Cup team and was nonplaying captain of the winning 1981 effort. The 18½ to 9½ U.S. win at the Walton Heath Golf Club in Surrey, England, was the last time the United States dominated the Europeans in Ryder Cup competition.

Marr's victory in the PGA at the 7,090-yard, par-71 Laurel Valley Golf Club was his only major title in a Tour career running from 1960 through 1977. He defeated Jack Nicklaus and Billy Casper by two strokes by firing a 70, 69, 70, and 71 for 280. On the last hole of the tournament, a par-4, he hooked his drive into a trap, then hit a recovery shot short of a lake in front of the green. He then hit a clutch 9-iron to within three feet of the cup and made his par to earn the $25,000 first prize.

# December 28

### 1946: Birthday of Hubert Green, Winner of 1977 U.S. Open and 1985 PGA Championship

Sixteen of Hubert Green's nineteen PGA Tour victories came in the 1970s when he joined the Tour after attending Florida State University. He won the 1977 U.S. Open, despite a rumored death threat called into the Oklahoma City office of the FBI, at Southern Hills in Tulsa, Oklahoma. Lou Graham was in the clubhouse with a 279, having played the back nine in just 31 strokes. Green was notified of the death threat as he was leaving the fourteenth tee and was given the option to withdraw, to ask for play to be suspended, or to continue. He elected to continue and completed a par-70 round for a 72-hole total of 278. The death threat was never traced. Upon hearing about it, Green joked that it must have come from an old girlfriend.

Green's game faded in the 1980s, when he won only three tournaments. His last Tour win was his second major title, the 1985 PGA Championship, held at the 7,089-yard, par-71 Cherry Hills Country Club in Englewood, Colorado. Green was able to outduel Lee Trevino with a 72-hole score of 67, 69, 70, and 72 for 278 to win by two strokes.

Hubert Green was the 1971 Rookie of the Year on the PGA Tour and was a member of the 1977, 1979, and 1985 Ryder Cup teams.

# December 29

### 1925: Birthday of Pete Dye, Designer of Bewitching and Beguiling Golf Courses

Pete Dye, one of the most imaginative and flamboyant golf-course designers of the twentieth century, was born in Urbana, Ohio, and was a fine amateur golfer. He attended Rollins College, where he captained the golf team and met Alice O'Neal, an excellent amateur golfer from Indianapolis who became his wife and partner in golf-course design. Dye was runner-up in the Indiana Amateur in 1954 and 1955, then won it in 1958 while working full-time with Alice in the insurance sales business. Pete was extremely successful as an insurance salesman, but wanted to design golf courses for a living. He had served on the green committee at the Country Club of Indianapolis, and he had studied some of the best golf courses in the United States, especially Pinehurst No. 2, which he had played many times while stationed in the Army at nearby Fort Bragg in North Carolina.

Pete and Alice laid out their first golf course in 1959, then did a series of low-budget courses in the Midwest. A trip to Scotland in 1963, where they played some of the great old golf courses such as St. Andrews, led Dye to incorporate features of links-style layouts into his designs. These features included small greens, pot bunkers, undulating fairways, deep native rough, and railroad-tie bulkheads. Dye at first thought St. Andrews was a "cow pasture" when he played there in the British Amateur in 1963, but soon grew to love and respect the course after he played it a few more times.

After the Dyes' pilgrimage to Scotland, Pete designed a noteworthy list of courses such as Crooked Stick in Indiana (1964); Casa de Campo (Teeth of the Dog), Dominican Republic (1971); Golf Club, Ohio (1967); Amelia Island Plantation, Florida (27 holes, 1973); Carmel Valley Ranch, California (1980); Kingsmill (River Course), Virginia (1974); TPC Sawgrass (Stadium Course), Florida (1981); Blackwolf Run, Wisconsin (36 holes, 1988–90); and the Honors Course, Tennessee (1983). These courses have all been rated among the best in the world at various times.

# December 30

## 1969: Birthday of Michelle McGann, Winner of 1987 USGA Junior Girls Championship

Michelle McGann, noted for her length off the tee and the exquisite variety of her golf hats on the LPGA Tour, was born in West Palm Beach, Florida, and later attended Rosarian Academy, where she was a member of the National Honor Society. The 5-feet-11-inch McGann started playing golf at the age of seven and won the Florida State Junior Championship three times.

The year 1987 was a big one for Michelle. She captured the USGA Junior Girls Championship, winning 7 and 5 in the match-play final at the Orchards Golf Club in South Hadley, Massachusetts. McGann was named American Junior Golf Association Rolex Junior Player of the Year and was ranked the number one Junior girl in 1987 by both *Golf* magazine and *Golf Digest*. Michelle joined the LPGA Tour in 1988, at the age of eighteen, and has steadily improved, reducing her strokes per round average every year (71.63 in 1993) and increasing her earnings ($315,921 in 1993). By the end of 1993 she was twenty-eighth on the Women's World Money List, and by late 1994 she ranked thirteenth in LPGA Tour earnings. McGann won $269,936 on the LPGA Tour in 1994 but has yet to win her first event.

# December 31

## 1966: Jack Nicklaus Leads 1966 World Money and Stroke Average Lists

In 1966, Jack Nicklaus led the World Money List compiled by Mark McCormack's International Management Group to reflect not only U.S. PGA Tour earnings but earnings from international tournaments such as the British, South Africa, and Australian Opens, and special events such as the PGA National Team Championship and World Series of Golf. Nicklaus won $168,088.59, followed by Arnold Palmer ($165,128.24), Billy Casper ($156,872.92), Gene Littler ($131,917.63), and Doug Sanders ($121,451.24). The only non-Americans in the top worldwide money winners were Bruce Devlin of Australia, sixth with $90,058.37, and Gary Player of South Africa, twenty-ninth with $47,507.30. Nicklaus led in stroke average with 70.65 per round, closely followed by Palmer with 70.65.

By 1993, the distribution of wealth had changed considerably in golf as the sport became truly international. Nick Price of Zimbabwe led with $2,825,691 in earnings, followed by Greg Norman ($2,285,280), Bernhard Langer ($2,059,384), Fred Couples ($1,854,313), and Paul Azinger ($1,714,574). Thirteen Americans were in the top thirty money winners, which included golfers from twelve different countries. The 1993 Sony ranking, a complex rating system based on a three-year rolling average weighted to favor more recent results and taking into account such factors as number of tournaments played, major championships, and so forth, rated Nick Faldo the world's best player (20.65 points), followed by Norman (18.79), Langer (17.19), Price (15.89), and Couples (14.93). In 1994, the rankings were led by Price, Norman, Faldo, Langer, and Olazabal. Ernie Els topped the World Money List with $2,862,854.

# Index

Fazio, George, 83, 97
Fehr, Rick, 208, 230
Ferree, Jim, 290
Ferrier, Jim, 97
Finger, Joe, 83
Finsterwald, Dow, 200
Fishwick, Diana, 136
Fleck, Jack, 168
Floyd, Raymond, 66, 71, 107, 150, 322, 349, 359
Ford, Doug, 40, 94
Ford, Gerald, 145
Forrester, Jack, 271
Fort Myers Golf and Country Club, 18
Fotheringham, George, 284
Foulis, James, 198
Fownes, William C., Jr., 239
Fox, Charlie, 145
Fream, Donald, 74
French, Emmett, 271
Fresh Meadows Country Club, 155, 253
Frost, David, 68
Furgol, Ed, 37

## G

Gagliardi, Joseph, 225
Gallacher, Bernard, 255
Gallagher, Jim, 226, 230, 298
*Gallery of Women Golfers*, 72
Gamez, Robert, 78
Garagiola, Joe, 145
Gardner, Robert, 189, 239, 246
Gardner, Stewart, 281
Garner, James, 145
Garrido, Antonio, 255
Geiberger, Al, 46
Ghezzi, Vic, 243, 289

Gilder, Bob, 286
Glen Abbey Golf Club, Ontario, 22, 248
Glenn, Rhonda, 84, 258
Glutting, Charlotte, 287
Goalby, Bob, 71
Goetze, Vicky, 228, 230, 234
Golddust Twins, 52
Golden, John, 267
Golf ball, 3
*Golf Monthly*, 13
Golf Writers Association, 73
*Golf's Golden Grind*, 139
Gonzales, Fernando, 225
Goodman, Johnny, 159
Gordon, Richard, 199
Gourley, Molly, 136
Graham, David, 138
Graham, Lou, 8
Grand Cypress, Florida, 22
Green, Hubert, 255, 361
Green, Tammie, 249
Gregory, Ann, 256
Grey Oaks, 126
Griffen, George, 267
Griffin, Ellen, 19
Grout, Jack, 22
*Guide to Good Golf*, 259
Guilford, Jesse, 189, 239
Guldahl, Ralph, 92, 96, 98, 325
Gunn, Watts, 189, 246

## H

Haas, Fred, Jr., 28, 29
Haas, Jay, 286
Hagen, Walter, 17, 30, 77, 153, 186, 191, 259, 267, 271, 288, 307
Hagge, Marlene, 19

Hamlin, Shelly, 182
Hammond, Donnie, 68
Hanson, Beverly, 73, 277
Harbert, Chick, 49, 140
Harmon, Claude, 98
Harney, Paul, 25
Harper, Chandler, 68, 176
Harriman, H. M., 187
Harris, Robert, 239
Harrison, Ernest Joe "Dutch," 40
Hartley, Rex, 130
Haskell, Coburn, 3
Hawkins, Fred, 94
Hayes, Mark, 255
Haynie, Sandra, 200
Heard, Jerry, 75
Hebert, Jay, 203
Hebert, Lionel, 78, 284
Held, Edmund R., 33
Hemphill, Kathryn, 19, 287
Hershey Country Club, Pennsylvania, 262
Hicks, Helen, 42, 136, 349
Hill, Dave, 107, 350
Hill, Mike, 110, 132
Hill, Opal, 19
Hillcrest Golf Club, Sun City West, Arizona, 107
Hilton, Harold H., 13
Hirase, Mayumi, 90
Hobday, Simon, 245
Hoch, Scott, 244
Hogan, Ben, 4, 9, 11, 15, 30, 61, 77, 92, 96, 107, 140, 160, 168, 235, 243
Holderners, Sir Ernest, 130
Hollins, Marian, 136
Honorable Company of Edinburgh Golfers, 64

Honors Course, Tennessee, 362
Hooman, C. V. L., 240
Hope, Bob, 41, 145
*How I Play Golf*, 59
*How I Played the Game*, 92, 113
Hoyt, Beatrix, 121
Humer, William, 246
Hunter, Robert, 137
Hurd, Dorothy Campbell, 247
Hutchinson, Jock, 14, 18, 271

**I**

*Illustrated History of Women's Golf*, 113
Indian Wells Country Club, 41
Indianwood Golf and Country Club, Lake Orion, Michigan, 249
Inglewood Country Club, Kenmore, Washington, 245
Ingram, Sarah Lebrun, 254
Inkster, Juli, 121
Inman, John, 230
Inverness Country Club, Toledo, Ohio, 7, 11, 124, 141, 186, 223
Inwood Country Club, Far Rockaway, New York, 271
Irwin, Hale, 38, 141, 255

**J**

Jacklin, Tony, 255, 286
Jacobsen, Peter, 135
James, Mark, 255
Jameson, Betty, 19, 42, 181, 183

January, Don, 25, 71, 105, 202, 323
Jemsek, Marla, 254
Jenkins, Dan, 336
Joes, Bobby, 195
Johnnie Walker World Championship, 352
Johnston, Harrison, 130
Johnstone, Tony, 329
Jones, Bobby, 14, 21, 59, 81, 83, 96, 130, 137, 154, 178, 189, 192, 237, 239, 246, 257, 279
Junior Amateur Championship, 10

**K**

Kalles, Harold, 75
Kapalua International, 310
Kauffmann, Carl F., 33
Kayak Point Golf Club, Washington State, 74
Keeler, O. B., 59
Keiser, Herman, 98
Keller Golf Club, St. Paul, Minnesota, 49
Kelly, Peter, 225
Kerrigan, Tom, 284
Kertes, Stan, 230
Kesselring, Jerry, 225
Kimball, Judy, 277
Kimura, Toshimi, 90
King, Betsy, 90, 93
King, Michael, 255
King James II, 64
King's Course, Gleneagles, Scotland, 120
Kingsmill (River Course), Virginia, 362
Kipling, Rudyard, 326

Kirby, Ron, 216
Kirk, Peggy, 19
Kite, Tom, 12, 41, 101, 215, 255
Knepper, Rudolph, 239
Knight, A.W., 151
Koch, Gary, 10
Kroll, Ted, 50

**L**

La Foy, John, 83
Lacey, Charles, 253
Lacoste, Catherine, 182
Ladies' Professional Golf Association, 19, 42
Lady Margaret Scott, 162
Laffoon, Ky, 15
Lakewood Country Club, 45
Langer, Bernhard, 99, 153, 208, 286
Lardner, Ring, 263
Las Colinas Country Club, 182
Lawrence, Mary, 51
Leitch, Cecil, 162
Lema, Tony, 107
Lemmon, Jack, 145
Leonard, Stan, 206
Lietzke, Bruce, 111
Lightning storms, 75
Lind, Dean, 10, 224
Litten, Karl, 216
Little, Lawson, 158, 173
Little Rock Country Club, 40
Littler, Gene, 9, 115
Lockhart, Robert, 126
Lopez, Nancy, 43, 209, 217, 315
Love, Davis, Jr., 290

Olazabal, Jose Maria, 5, 60, 154
Oldfield, Ed, 93
Oliver, Ed "Porky," 97, 235
Olympia Fields Country Club, 109
O'Neal, Alice, 268
Oosterhuis, Peter, 255
Orcutt, Maureen, 19, 136, 268, 287
Ottawa Park Course, Toledo, Ohio, 33
Ouimet, Francis, 85, 130, 189, 237, 239

**P**

Page, Estelle Lawson, 287
Palmer, Arnold, 21, 25, 30, 54, 70, 74, 78, 83, 94, 101, 103, 107, 333, 341, 344
Palmer, Sandra, 291
Park, Doris, 136
Parks, Sam, 157
Pavin, Corey, 68, 260, 343
Pebble Beach Golf Links, 5, 22, 24, 30, 170
Peck, Michael, 244
Peete, Calvin, 87, 286
Pelham Golf Club, Pelham Manor, New York, 267
Penick, Harvey, 12
Phoenix Country Club, 15, 26
Picard, Henry, 45, 95, 98
*Picture Analysis of Golf Strokes*, 259
Pinehurst Country Club, Pinehurst, North Carolina, 77
Piping Rock Club, 274

Pittsburgh Field Club, Aspinwall, Pennsylvania, 146
Plainfield Country Club, New Jersey, 244
Platt, J. Wood, 264
Player, Gary, 26, 63, 71, 79, 103, 201, 216, 303
Poppy Hills, 5
Porthcawl, Wales, 145
Portland Golf Club, Portland, Oregon, 235
Post, Sandra, 291
Prestancia Golf Course, Sarasota, Florida, 55
Prestwick, 13
Price, Charles, 59
Price, Nick, 16, 99, 208, 226, 248, 251, 293
Prince of Wales, 254
Prosper Jules Alphonse Berckmans, 81
Pung, Jackie, 16, 207, 240

**Q**

Quast, Anne, 233

**R**

Rancho Bernardo, 268
Rancho Park Municipal Golf Course, 6
Rancho Santa Fe Country Club Course, 24
Randolph, Sam, 236
Randolph Municipal Golf Course, Tucson, 9
Rankin, Judy, 128
Rawlins, Horace, 274
Rawls, Betsy, 19, 43, 181, 207

Ray, Ted, 85, 223
Raynor, Seth, 274
Reid, Mike, 30
Revolta, Johnny, 288
Riley, Polly, 19, 232
Rio Pinar Country Club, Orlando, Florida, 78
River North Country Club, 108
River Oaks Country Club, 54
Riviera Country Club, 4, 11
Robert, Clifford, 82
Rodriguez, Juan "Chi Chi," 44, 103, 127, 311, 359
Romack, Barbara, 229, 258
Rosburg, Bob, 212, 290
Rosenthal, Elaine, 279
Ross, Donald, 77
Royal and Ancient Golf Club of St. Andrews, 3, 36, 64
Royal Liverpool Golf Club, 13
Royal Melbourne, 137
Royal St. George's, 39, 76
Rudolph, Mason, 10
Rummells, Dave, 50
Russell, Alex, 137

**S**

Saint Andrews, 114
San Diego Country Club, 50
Sander, Anne Quast, 232
Sanders, Doug, 91, 212
Sarazen, Gene, 14, 15, 17, 95, 98, 140, 158, 174, 186, 267
Sauers, Gene, 226
Savannah Golf Club Ball, 353
Sawgrass (Stadium Course), Florida, 362
Scholefield, Cindy, 254

Vare, Glenna Collett, 42, 121, 136, 229, 241
Veeck, Bill, 219
Venturi, Ken, 5, 10, 29, 73, 94, 167, 224, 225
Verplank, Scott, 230
Vintage Club, Indian Wells, California, 74
Voight, George J., 130
Von Elm, George, 130, 186, 189, 237, 257, 262
Vossler, Mike, 290

## W

Wadkins, Lanny, 26, 255, 339
Wailea Golf Club Blue Course, Kihei, Maui, Hawaii, 57
Waites, Brian, 286
Walker, Colleen, 350
Walker, George Herbert, 239
Wall, Art, 206, 328
Walsh, Richard J., 33
Walt Disney World Resort, Orlando, Florida, 28, 34

Walton Health Club, 36
Wampler, Fred, 34
War Department, 56
Ward, Harvie, 225, 342
Wargo, Tom, 104
Watrous, Al, 14, 153
Watson, Tom, 22, 24, 39, 60, 170
Way, Paul, 286
Weiskopf, Tom, 20, 38, 55, 104
Wentworth Golf Club, 136
Weslock, Nick, 225
Westchester Country Club, 50
Westward Ho! Club, England, 76
Wethered, Joyce, 43, 136
Wethered, Roger, 130, 240
White, Ronald, 6
Whitworth, Kathy, 43, 84, 106, 131, 149, 172, 201, 265
Williams, Eddie, 18
Williams, Ted, 73
Willing, V. F., 130
Wilson, Enid, 72, 136, 162
Wilson, Jim, 6
Wilson, Nick, 65

Wind, Herbert W., 131, 140, 215, 250
Winged Foot West Golf Course, 141, 178
Women's Professional Golf Association, 19, 42
Wood, Craig, 7, 26, 39, 81, 95, 98, 146, 161, 321
Wood, Willie, 230
Woods, Eldrick "Tiger," 10, 238
Woosman, Ian, 5, 60, 153
Worsham, Lew, 219, 327
Wright, Mickey, 16, 43, 70, 80, 84, 125, 131, 149, 181, 201, 231, 258

## Y

Yale University Golf Club, 274

## Z

Zaharias, Mildred Didrikson "Babe," 19, 43, 73, 80, 83, 113, 175, 181, 183, 266
Zoeller, Frank Urban "Fuzzy," 250, 255, 314